SURFACE AND DESTROY

SURFACE
AND
DESTROY

THE SUBMARINE GUN WAR
IN THE PACIFIC

Michael Sturma

THE UNIVERSITY PRESS OF KENTUCKY

Editorial and Sales Offices: The University Press of Kentucky
663 South Limestone Street, Lexington, Kentucky 40508-4008
www.kentuckypress.com

15 14 13 12 11   5 4 3 2 1

Maps by Jeff Levy, University of Kentucky Cartography Lab

Library of Congress Cataloging-in-Publication Data

Sturma, Michael, 1950–
  Surface and destroy : the submarine gun war in the Pacific / Michael Sturma.
      p.   cm.
  Includes bibliographical references and index.
  ISBN 978-0-8131-2996-9 (hardcover : alk. paper) —
  ISBN 978-0-8131-2999-0 (ebook)
  1. World War, 1939–1945—Naval operations—Submarine. 2. World War,
1939–1945—Naval operations, American. 3. World War, 1939–1945—
Campaigns—Pacific Ocean. I. Title.
  D780.S78 2011
  940.54'51—dc22
                        2010047402

This book is printed on acid-free recycled paper meeting
the requirements of the American National Standard
for Permanence in Paper for Printed Library Materials.

Manufactured in the United States of America.

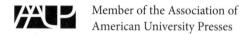

Member of the Association of
American University Presses

To Susan and Barbara

Contents

Acknowledgments   ix

Introduction   1

Part I. Unrestricted Warfare

1. Pearl Harbor   11
2. Trouble with Trawlers   25
3. *Wahoo*   41
4. Atrocities   50

Part II. Battle Stations Surfaced

5. Sampans and Schooners   63
6. Pickets and the Picayune   73
7. Straits of Malacca   89
8. Boarding Parties   101
9. Mopping Up   113

Part III. Face-to-Face

10. Survivors   131
11. Japanese Prisoners   146
12. Submarines and Bombers   159

Conclusion   170

Appendix: Submarine Gun Attacks in the Pacific,
1942–1945   179

Notes   183

Bibliography   219

Index   237

Illustrations follow page 150

Acknowledgments

As they had during my previous research on World War II submarines, Charles Hinman and Nancy Richards of the USS *Bowfin* Submarine Museum at Pearl Harbor made me feel a welcome visitor. I owe special thanks to Charles for his assistance with many of the photos in this volume, and for contributing information from his Web site, On Eternal Patrol.

Molly Orme patiently helped me at the Australian Archives in Melbourne, and John R. Waggener assisted with research materials from the American Heritage Center at the University of Wyoming in Laramie. I have benefited from the advice of Nathaniel S. Patch at the National Archives and Records Authority, College Park, Maryland, and of Roy Grossnick, head of the Operational Archives Branch at the Naval Historical Center, Washington, DC. Tim Frank assisted with research at the National Archives and Records Authority, and Robert G. Price helped garner material at the Submarine Force Museum in Groton, Connecticut.

I gratefully acknowledge the support of a Vice Admiral Edwin B. Hooper Research Grant by the Naval Historical Center, an Australian Army History Grant, and the Research Excellence Grant Scheme administered by the International History Group at Murdoch University in Perth.

This is an opportunity to publicly express my appreciation to colleagues at Murdoch University: Andrew Webster, Jim Trotter, Alex Jensen, and John Dunhill. Ian Chambers generously afforded IT support. I owe special thanks to Michael Durey for his years of support, both as an academic and as a friend.

I have also been extremely fortunate to have the unstinting support of family, including Joan and Rell Roberts; my sisters, Susan Witt and Barbara Eblen; their respective husbands, Wes and Mike; and their now-adult children, Thomas, Lauren, Heather, and Nicci. As always, with love, I thank my wife, Ying, for helping me negotiate the intricacies of information technology as well as many other challenges and opportunities that have come along.

Introduction

For a submarine crew there was no maneuver more exhilarating, or more fear-inducing, than a surface gun action. Relying on surprise and speed, the submarine would suddenly punch through to the surface, while half-drenched sailors scrambled through the hatches to reach their guns and ammunition lockers. A crack team aimed to get off the first shots within twenty seconds of surfacing. Men who were usually kept cramped beneath the sea were at last unleashed to encounter the enemy face-to-face.

For Ignatius "Pete" Galantin the human face of the enemy materialized when the USS *Sculpin* battle surfaced to attack a sampan in 1943. The submarine quickly riddled the small wooden craft with bullets, leaving a heavy tang of gunpowder hanging in the air that enveloped even those below decks. When the *Sculpin* moved in closer to the sampan the crewmen witnessed the effects of their automatic weapons—they were close enough now to see the purple eruptions of bullets in bodies and the blood-stained water sloshing in the bilges. "How different, how personal was war when the target was flesh and blood instead of steel," Galantin observed.[1]

His experience was far from exceptional. George Grider recalled a similar incident when he ordered the USS *Flasher* to gun attack a sampan. After the craft burst into flames and it appeared that the occupants had jumped overboard, the *Flasher* pulled alongside to lob in hand grenades. A man who had been hiding behind the gunwales leaped up and went overboard, but not before staring directly at Grider "with an expression of piercing accusation." At least for that moment, Grider recalled, the war had become "intolerably personal."[2]

Such images contrast with the popular view of the submarine war in the Pacific as a series of stealthy torpedo attacks. The pervasive idea of submarines waging battle from beneath the surface is conjured by book titles such as *Silent Victory, Undersea Victory, Battle Below, Battle Submerged,* and *War beneath the Sea.* During the course of the war American submarines fired about 11,000 torpedoes. They sank not only 200 Japanese men-of-war but also more than 1,000 merchant ships.[3] These Allied attacks have been well documented and constitute the main criteria for submarine success in the Pacific. It is a view, however, that is incomplete.

There was another side of the submarine war most often ignored or dismissed. These were surface gun attacks, often on relatively small craft such as patrol boats, schooners, sampans, fishing trawlers, and junks. The Joint Army-Navy Assessment Committee (JANAC), established to record the losses inflicted on Japanese shipping, deliberately excluded vessels of under 500 tons from its investigations.[4] As Japanese merchant ships became scarcer, however, America's growing flotilla of submarines increasingly turned its attention and firepower on smaller vessels of dubious military value. Calvin Moon, who served on the USS *Razorback,* recalls that by 1945 "[w]hat was left were small things that we usually polished off with a gun."[5] C. Kenneth Ruiz, who served on the USS *Pollack,* similarly observes that by late in the war "the Silent Service was reduced to cutting Japan's sampan fleet to ribbons."[6]

Often the stories of these attacks run counter to the "good war" narratives that tend to dominate interpretations of the Allied experience during World War II. As Geoffrey Till reminds us in writing about the battle of the Atlantic, though, historians should never forget that the war at sea was "not some kind of giant board game, but cruel hard war in all its horrors."[7] The brutality of "total war" became starkest on the surface.

This is not to question the heroism so evident in the submarine war, but to offer a more nuanced account. While surface actions encapsulate the horror of war, they also reveal a transcendent humanity. If close-up encounters magnified the cruelty of war, they also extended the potential for mercy. Given that submarines typically operated with a high degree of autonomy, we can find examples at both extremes. As emphasized in the pages that follow, many submariners acted on their conscience rather than following the logic of "unrestricted warfare."

Using submarines as submersible gunboats was nothing new. German U-boats had employed their deck guns extensively against Allied shipping in coastal waters and in the Mediterranean during the First World War. They continued the practice during World War II; during one week in November 1942, for example, the German ace Wolfgang Lüth sank four ships using the *U-181*'s deck guns.[8] Eventually, Allied antisubmarine measures made such attacks far too dangerous to continue in the Atlantic theater. In the Pacific, on the other hand, Allied surface attacks became more common as Japanese antisubmarine forces dissipated during the course of the war.

Within the American submarine service, the efficacy of surface gun attacks became a bone of contention. A Control Force Conference in 1931 chaired by Rear Admiral Thomas C. Hart recommended against arming submarines with deck guns. On the other hand, Admiral Charles Lockwood, who became commander of Submarines Pacific in February 1943, had long advocated mounting large guns on submarines as offensive weapons. The experienced men who comprised the Submarine Officers' Conference before the outbreak of war shared Lockwood's view and recommended that new submarines be equipped with five-inch guns. Others in the navy, however, argued that having such a powerful arsenal might encourage submarine commanders to take untenable risks on the surface.[9]

Most U.S. submarines entered World War II with relatively small-caliber three-inch guns. With torpedoes as the primary weapon, the navy anticipated that deck guns would be deployed against unarmed or lightly armed vessels, or for finishing off targets already damaged.[10] Not untypically, squadron commander John "Babe" Brown warned that "gun fights must be carried out only after careful consideration of the value of the target and the risk involved."[11] Charles Lockwood confessed his horror after the USS *Gato* used its deck guns to fight off an attacking Japanese float plane. Current doctrine insisted that aircraft or combatant ships should be engaged with gunfire only if a submarine were unable to dive.[12]

At times, dire necessity did indeed force submarines to fight it out on the surface. In April 1943 the already fatally damaged USS *Grenadier* tried to stave off attacking Japanese aircraft with its two 20 mm and two .30-caliber machine guns. The *Grenadier* crew managed to damage one of the planes before scuttling the submarine. On its third war patrol the USS *Salmon,* commanded by Harley Kent "Kenny" Nauman, was forced to the surface by a depth charge attack. The submarine fought a running gun battle with two enemy escorts and managed to escape. The USS *Sculpin* proved less fortunate. After suffering a relentless depth charge attack in November 1943, skipper Fred Connaway decided that surfacing was the submarine's last hope. In the ensuing gunfight, the destroyer *Yamagumo* made short work of the submarine, killing Connaway along with most of the others on deck. The remaining crew scuttled the *Sculpin,* and many crew members were taken prisoner by the Japanese.[13]

The notorious shortcomings of American torpedoes in the war's opening years encouraged some submariners to turn to their deck guns more often than they might have otherwise. An article published in the April 1942 issue of *Scientific American* proclaimed U.S. torpedoes to be "the most intricate and perfect engine of destruction which scientific military design has yet produced."[14] In reality, not only did the torpedoes run deeper than set, but they were riddled with faults that only gradually revealed themselves. The so-called magnetic exploder, designed to detonate under the keel of enemy ships, proved unreliable. Particularly irksome were torpedoes that exploded prematurely, revealing the attacking submarine's position to the enemy. In what one historian terms "an extraordinary tale of incompetence," it took nearly two years of war before America's torpedoes performed consistently.[15]

After two failed torpedo attacks on a freighter the night of 30 April 1942, the USS *Greenling* unsuccessfully attempted to stop the vessel with its three-inch gun. The engagement ended with the *Greenling* being struck by return fire, fortunately a glancing blow that ricocheted off the hull. Faced with multiple torpedo mishaps in

December 1942, the USS *Thresher* used its deck gun to attack a Japanese transport, the *Hachian Maru,* in the Java Sea. Using binoculars lashed to the gun as a makeshift telescopic sight, the *Thresher* crew disabled the transport with gunfire and tried to finish the ship off with a torpedo. The torpedo proved to be a dud, but it still managed to punch a hole in the transport's hull below the waterline. Indeed, there were documented instances of Japanese ships entering ports with unexploded American torpedoes sticking out of them.[16]

Similarly bedeviled by torpedoes that exploded prematurely or ran erratically on its sixth war patrol, the USS *Pompano* missed the chance to sink two tankers. When they encountered a sampan the *Pompano*'s crewmen vented their frustration by pulverizing the craft with their deck guns.[17] Many submarine commanders, though, regarded guns as a weapon of last resort, if not a positive hindrance. At the beginning of the war, Creed Burlingame thought deck guns "a bit silly."[18] Like anything protruding from the hull, a large gun could create drag and slow a submarine's performance underwater. Richard O'Kane, as the commissioning skipper of the USS *Tang,* requested that the deck gun be mounted aft of the bridge, anticipating it would be used only if the submarine were desperately fleeing the enemy. Another, anonymous skipper is quoted saying, "I don't care whether the gun's forward or aft, but put it on wheels. . . . we'll push it over the side."[19]

On a heaving sea, a submarine made for a poor gun platform, and any surface action greatly increased its vulnerability. As with galleys centuries earlier, a surfaced submarine's lack of firepower and protection for its crew made it no match for a heavily armed warship. A lurking aircraft outside the range of the periscope or a misidentified target could spell disaster. One well-placed or lucky hit by the enemy could make it impossible to dive, leaving the submarine a sitting duck. At the beginning of the war, Rear Admiral Thomas Withers, commander of Submarines Pacific, personally cautioned skippers before they departed on patrol to avoid gun actions.[20] Nevertheless, as the war continued submarines increasingly operated on the surface for torpedo as well as gun attacks.

Before the war American submarines trained almost entirely

on submerged daylight tactics, probably encouraged by knowledge that four-fifths of the submarines destroyed during World War I were caught on the surface. On the other hand, German U-boats had already demonstrated the efficacy of night surface tactics during war games in the early 1930s.[21] A handful of U.S. skippers, such as Freddy Warder on the *Seawolf* and Dick Voge on the *Sealion,* were left to experiment with night surface tactics on their own initiative. Carrying out one of the first night surface attacks in May 1942, the USS *Drum* sank the 9,000-ton seaplane tender *Mizuho,* the largest enemy ship sunk by an American submarine to that date.[22]

The speed and maneuverability of submarines on the surface, especially when used with newly developed radar, proved a winning combination. U.S. submarines entered the war with a fairly primitive SD radar that, when working, provided an early warning of approaching aircraft. By the end of 1942 more sophisticated surface-search SJ radar became available, allowing submarines to accurately track the course and speed of targets in darkness or in conditions of poor visibility.[23]

The addition of a target-bearing transmitter (TBT) facilitated surface attacks by allowing the accurate determination of an enemy ship's bearing from the submarine bridge. The Mare Island Naval Shipyard began installing TBTs a short time before the attack on Pearl Harbor, but most submarines entered the war without them. Once equipped with a TBT and with information easily transmitted from the bridge to the fire control system, the feasibility of night surface attacks greatly increased. Improved camouflage also allowed submarines to work their way closer to targets without detection.[24]

Lawson P. Ramage, skipper of the USS *Parche,* spectacularly demonstrated the efficacy of night surface tactics against a convoy on the night of 31 July 1944. Maneuvering the *Parche* almost as though it were a PT boat, Ramage launched ten torpedoes and sank four ships in less than an hour. Although one of Ramage's superiors described the action as "foolhardy," the skipper received the first Congressional Medal of Honor of the war awarded to a still-living submariner.[25] Some skippers reasoned that, although it was dangerous, at least fighting on the surface precluded the possibility of being depth charged.

The success of night surface torpedo attacks further stimulated the installation of more effective deck guns. If for no other reason, they could be used to fend off enemy escorts while making a torpedo attack. After an enemy escort pursued the USS *Puffer* off Surabaya in May 1944, for example, the patrol report commented, "A four inch gun aft would have pulled us out of this spot very nicely."[26] The patrol report recommended installing large guns fore and aft if they could be obtained.

Although the standard-issue three-inch gun could fire a sixteen-pound projectile up to five miles, many submariners demeaned them as "popguns." Submarines had mounts capable of supporting heavier guns, however, and this facilitated the transition to larger weapons.[27] As a result of lobbying by Charles Lockwood, new-construction submarines from the *Tambor*-class onward included foundations for a five-inch gun. Lockwood personally supervised the installation of the first five-inch gun on the USS *Gar* in November 1942.[28] For the time being, though, the most widely used heavy gun became the four-inch/50-caliber weapon originally used on the submarine force's aging S-boats. By late 1943 the guns were being installed on all new submarines and were replacing the three-inch guns during shipyard refits.[29]

As early as 1942 the Bureau of Ordnance began development of a five-inch/25-caliber gun specifically for submarine use. The five-inch/38-caliber gun employed on aircraft carriers and destroyers had already built a reputation as the best long-range antiaircraft gun in the navy. Hundreds of modifications, though, were needed before these would be adopted by submarines in 1944. The gun's shorter barrel, 125 inches long, allowed for greater accuracy when fired from a submarine's heaving deck. Its "wet" gun construction of noncorrosive materials with an alloy liner meant that muzzle and breech covers could be dispensed with. Taking hand-loaded shells weighing sixty-five pounds each, the gun had a range of ten miles. In early 1944 the USS *Spadefish*, undergoing refit at Mare Island, became the first submarine installed with the gun.[30] By the end of the war many submarines were carrying two five-inch/25-caliber guns as well as multiple 40 mm, 20 mm, and .50-caliber weapons. When dry-docked in July 1945, for example, the *Spadefish* had an additional five-inch/25-caliber gun installed forward of the conning tower to match the one aft. The 20 mm bridge guns were also replaced by larger 40 mm guns. Half a dozen submarines were also equipped with basic computer fire control systems, although none of these would be put into action before the war ended.[31]

Changing armament reflected the changing nature of the Pacific war. With most of Japan's larger ships destroyed, Allied submarines increasingly directed their attention to smaller craft. But if Japanese shipping could be attacked at less risk, the morality of doing so became more questionable. Many submarine officers expressed ambivalence about mounting gun attacks on small craft of questionable value to the enemy. Some refused to make such attacks altogether, while others worked to minimize casualties.

In effect, by the latter stages of the war many submariners were reverting to traditional prewar protocols that many believed submarines had made obsolete. It became common for boarding parties from submarines to check the cargoes and evacuate the crews of suspect ships before destroying them. The way in which submariners reacted to their victims defined different outlooks on unrestricted warfare and exemplified how personal standards of morality could mediate even "total war."

Shifting the focus from torpedo attacks to surface gun actions raises new questions about the nature of submarine warfare. In particular, this approach brings submariners' attitudes and relationships with the enemy and civilians into sharper relief. Surface actions were more likely to bring submarines in contact with survivors and potential prisoners whose individual stories rarely find their way into narratives of war. This cross-cultural dialog, however truncated, adds a different perspective on the war in the Pacific.

PART I

UNRESTRICTED WARFARE

1

Pearl Harbor

The first American submarine gun actions of the war took place during the Japanese attack on Pearl Harbor. The USS *Tautog* and the USS *Narwhal,* two of only five submarines in port at the time, shared credit with a destroyer for shooting down a low-flying Japanese torpedo plane. The submarines, tethered to the base finger piers for refit, managed to muster gun crews as the Japanese planes swept in. On the *Tautog,* after the three-inch gun seized up, enlisted men manned a .50-caliber machine gun and were credited with single-handedly bringing down another plane as it buzzed overhead.[1]

The devastation of Pearl Harbor shaped the future course of the submarine war and the attitudes of the men who fought it. The Japanese attack changed everything: policy, strategy, and psychology. Within six hours the chief of Naval Operations, Admiral Harold Stark, ordered a policy of "unrestricted submarine and air warfare." As later explained by Admiral Chester Nimitz, Japan's attack on U.S. bases and ships without warning or a declaration of war justified such an order; it was thus not rationalized by international law but instituted as a form of reprisal. Given America's former insistence on freedom of the seas and the safety of noncombatants, unrestricted submarine warfare, at least one writer claims, was the most momentous foreign policy reversal in U.S. history.[2]

While customary rules for the conduct of war had existed for centuries, the codification of international humanitarian law began in 1864 with the first Geneva Convention dealing with wounded soldiers. Attempts to regulate naval warfare came later. Although the Hague Convention of 1899 did not directly refer to submarines, it specified that warships should not resort to sinking merchant vessels unless they were first searched for contraband and the crews safely evacuated. The Declaration of London in 1909 similarly required warships to ensure the safety of merchant crews and passengers before sinking ships. These rules in turn could be traced back centuries to the "prize laws" that required privateers and commerce raiders to visit and search vessels before either seizing or destroying them.[3]

Despite the obvious problems such conventions posed for submarines, efforts were initially made to apply them during World War I. In the first German U-boat attack of the war, before sinking the British steamer *Glitra* off Norway on 20 October 1914, the *U-17* ensured that the crew members were in lifeboats and even towed them near shore.[4] To the growing horror of Americans, however, such restraint quickly fell by the wayside. On 4 February 1915 the Germans declared a war zone around the British Isles, including the English Channel and western portion of the North Sea, in which any merchant ship might be destroyed without warning.[5] The sinking of the liner *Lusitania* by a U-boat on 7 May 1915 was a major catalyst in spurring America to enter the war. Once Germany proclaimed a policy of unlimited submarine warfare, on 1 February 1917, American participation in the Great War became inevitable.

After the First World War there appeared to be a determination that unrestricted submarine warfare would not rear its ugly head again. The British listed eighteen German submariners as war criminals.[6] The Washington Conference of 1922 resolved that merchant vessels could be attacked only if they resisted search, and were not to be destroyed unless the safety of those on board was ensured. The same conventions for submarine warfare were stipulated by the Treaty of London in 1930 and reiterated in the London Protocol of 1936. At a General Disarmament Conference in 1932 a number of delegates had argued that submarines were too small to rescue survivors and were too vulnerable on the surface to resist recalcitrant merchant ships. Winston Churchill described the belief that a submarine code of conduct, if maintained during war, would be "the acme of gullibility."[7] But if the restraints imposed on submarines seemed unrealistic for wartime operations, the major powers nevertheless agreed to them.[8]

Attempting to avoid the international censure that had resulted from the sinking of the *Lusitania* during World War I, at the outbreak of World War II Germany issued its U-boat skippers elaborate rules of engagement. Yet on the first day of the war between Germany and Britain, 3 September 1939, the policy came undone. Lieutenant Fritz-Julius Lemp, commander of the *U-30*, gave the order to torpedo the British passenger liner *Athenia* as it sailed in the North Atlantic some 250 miles from the Irish coast, bound for Canada. The 13,581-ton ship went down with the loss of 118 crewmen and passengers, many of them women and children, including twenty-two American citizens.

Numerous explanations have been offered for Lemp's rashness: that he assumed the ship to be an armed merchant ship or auxiliary cruiser or troop transport. According to one account, Lemp failed to properly check the target because he was "over-excited" by the declaration of war. In Germany there was talk of court-martialing the twenty-six-year-old Lemp, but in the end the Nazi propaganda machine circulated a story that Churchill had ordered the *Athenia*'s sinking in order to draw America into the war.[9]

German U-boat skippers were warned to exercise more restraint. When the *U-47* spotted the British ship *Bosnia* off the coast of Spain on 5 September, the submarine first fired a shot across the freighter's bow. The U-boat shelled the 2,400-ton *Bosnia* only after it refused to stop. Before the vessel sank, the *U-47*'s captain, Gunther Prien, made sure that the *Bosnia*'s crew members got into their boats and arranged for their pickup by a Norwegian steamer. Similarly, in its first wartime action the *U-36*, commanded by Wilhelm Frolich, carefully looked after the crew of the British steamer *Truro*. Frolich allowed the men of the crew to lower their lifeboats, towed them within sight of other ships, and even sent an SOS on their behalf. Before sinking the *Blair Logie* on 11 September, a thoroughly chastised Fritz-Julius Lemp allowed the freighter's crewmen into their lifeboats, then supplied them with schnapps and cigarettes.[10]

Such courtesies, however, proved short-lived. The British Admiralty, assuming the worst after the sinking of the *Athenia,* instructed merchant ships to ram hostile U-boats. Britain also began arming its merchantmen, supplying 1,000 with guns within the first three months of the war and arming some 3,400 vessels by the end of 1940. This in itself afforded a pretext for U-boats to attack them without warning. The adoption of convoys further eroded the possibility of submarines observing prize rules. In October 1939 the Germans authorized U-boats to sink enemy merchant ships without warning, and the following month announced that they could not guarantee the safety of neutral ships off the British Isles or French coast. Even so, at the beginning of 1940 U-boats were still instructed to choose their targets carefully. The Nazis hoped that mines might be blamed for any neutral shipping sunk.[11]

In the meantime, the British edged their own way toward unrestricted submarine warfare. Initially, submarines had been expected to follow detailed rules set out in *The Prize Manual.* The book was not issued to submariners by the Admiralty until late 1939, and in some ways it was even more restrictive than international law. After Germany's invasion of Norway, however, Royal Navy submarines in the vicinity of and approaches to Norway were no longer bound to ensure the safety of crews before sinking merchant ships. In September 1940 the British further unleashed their submarines, allowing unrestrained attacks on all enemy merchant shipping.[12]

The most significant aspect of unrestricted warfare is often assumed to be the attack on merchant shipping without warning, but arguably more significant was the abrogation of any responsibility for survivors. Ships had attacked one another from time immemorial, but aiding those in the water formed part of the traditional law of the sea. The London Protocol of 1936 compelled warships or submarines attacking merchant ships to take into account the safety of passengers and crew according to the prevailing sea conditions and proximity to land or other ships.[13] In actual war situations, however, such expectations were often unrealistic, especially as it became common for merchant ships to be escorted by warships and air cover. In orders issued in late 1939, Admiral Dönitz instructed his U-boat commanders to suspend any rescue efforts, telling them, "We must be hard in this war."[14]

For the Germans a further turning point came on 12 September 1942, when the *U-156* sank the 19,700-ton British passenger liner *Laconia* 600 miles south of the Azores. The ship, en route from Cape Town to Britain, carried about 2,700 people, including 1,800 Italian prisoners of war from the Libyan campaign, their Polish guards, and British families returning from Kenya. Once the *U-156* surfaced in the vicinity of the sinking, the captain, Werner Hartenstein, was shocked to hear cries for help in Italian. He ordered rescue operations, at one stage crowding the submarine with 200 survivors, including 21 British. Stirred partly by barracuda and shark attacks on the survivors, Hartenstein called for other U-boats to assist, and the *U-506* and *U-507* joined his efforts on 15 September. He also sent out a message in English calling on any ships in the vicinity to help. The following morning, despite having four lifeboats in tow and displaying a large Red Cross flag, the *U-156* came under attack by an American B-24 Liberator from Ascension Island.

Although the *U-156* escaped, Admiral Dönitz, incensed by the aircraft attack, issued radio orders to his U-boats on the night of 17 September, instructing, "No attempt of any kind must be made at rescuing members of ship wreck" and "Rescue runs counter to the rudimentary demands of Warfare for the destruction of enemy ships and crews."[15] The words later returned to haunt Dönitz, but they in fact simply articulated a policy already followed by most submarines, whether Axis or Allied.

In the wake of the attack on Pearl Harbor, the Americans sidestepped the attenuated German-British *danse macabre,* declaring a policy of unrestricted submarine warfare from the outset. The strategy was born out of both spite and necessity. The attack on Pearl Harbor killed 2,403 Americans and left another 1,178 wounded, while the Japanese destruction of the battleship row gave submarines a new significance. Despite the Japanese destruction of twenty-one ships and 188 aircraft, the submarine base at Pearl Harbor escaped without substantial damage. Admiral Chester Nimitz, the new commander in chief of the Pacific Fleet, had a background in submarines; he made the submarine base his temporary headquarters and declared the submarine USS *Grayling* his flagship. With twenty-two submarines based at Pearl, and another twenty-nine in the Philippines, submarines offered America the most immediate way of taking the fight to the enemy.[16]

America's aircraft carriers, at sea during the attack, had similarly escaped being destroyed at Pearl Harbor. The one-off Doolittle raid of 18 April 1942, in which sixteen modified B-25s were launched from the carrier *Hornet,* demonstrated the ability to reach Japan with U.S. aircraft. Although a great shot in the arm for American morale, however, the forty 500-pound bombs dropped inflicted relatively little serious damage to the enemy.[17] Submarines remained the one U.S. asset capable of causing real concern to the Japanese in their own waters.

Like Britain, Japan's status as an island nation with an overseas empire made it especially vulnerable to submarine attacks. Many island outposts were completely dependent on supply by sea, while the home islands required a steady flow of raw materials—oil, metals, and rubber—to support the war. Among the upper echelon of the U.S. Navy, the likelihood of a war on shipping had been discussed for over a year before the attack on Pearl Harbor. In November 1940 Admiral Stark informed Admiral Thomas C. Hart, commander in chief of the Asiatic Fleet, that in the event of war, America would pursue Japan's "economic starvation."[18]

The fact remained, however, that unrestricted submarine warfare had received no approval from the civilian chain of command and contravened America's treaty obligations. There had been no serious preparation for attacking merchant ships in prewar training; only one out of thirty-six exercises conducted during 1940–1941 by the submarines of the Pacific Fleet had simulated an attack on a convoy of cargo ships.[19] During the interwar period most naval officers assumed that in the event of war, submarines would be used for reconnaissance and attacking enemy battle fleets. As described by one submarine skipper, prewar planning was "unimaginative and lazy"; another skipper observes, "Neither by training nor indoctrination were the submarines prepared to wage unrestricted warfare."[20] Anticipation of a war on commercial shipping could have shaped the development of submarine weapon systems. Believing that submarine attacks would be on armored battleships, the navy fitted its Mark XIV torpedoes with magnetic exploders designed to detonate beneath the exposed underbelly of their targets. As previously noted, both the torpedoes and the exploders proved full of defects; a less complicated torpedo could have been developed if a war against merchant ships was planned.[21]

For the Japanese submarine service, Pearl Harbor might have resulted in a change of policy no less revolutionary than that of the United States. Like the Americans, the Japanese built up their submarine fleet on the assumption that it would be directed against warships. Although Japan assisted Allied antisubmarine efforts during the First World War, future attacks on merchant shipping were never seriously contemplated. Exercises in the 1930s and early 1940s highlighted the problems of attacking surface warships, but the Japanese discounted their own postaction reports and generally ignored a suggestion by Vice Admiral Inoue Shigeyoushi that submarines might focus on attacking commercial shipping.[22]

The Japanese contingent at Pearl Harbor included twenty-seven oceangoing I-class submarines as well as five Type-A midgets, considered at the time a "secret weapon." The two-man midget submarines, armed with two 1,000-pound torpedoes each, were supposed to slip into the harbor and attack ships at anchor, while their larger counterparts picked off any warships attempting to enter or leave. Even before the first planes arrived, one of the midgets was sunk at the harbor entrance, and although the Japanese initially believed another midget sank a battleship, it, too, was destroyed without inflicting damage on the fleet. Yet another midget ran aground, yielding the Americans their first Japanese prisoner of war.[23]

The larger I-class submarines fared little better than the midgets. Patrolling off Oahu the night before the attack, the crew of the *I-24* could see the blazing lights of Waikiki beach, but none of the Japanese submarines sighted a U.S. warship, and one fell victim to planes from the USS *Enterprise*. Given this lack of success, the Japanese submarine command suggested that its efforts might be more profitably directed against merchant shipping than capital ships. The Combined Fleet remained unimpressed, believing submarines' primary mission should be to operate with the fleet toward a decisive confrontation with the enemy.[24]

Some Japanese successes attacking capital ships in the eastern Solomon Islands during 1942 probably hardened this resolve. Submarines torpedoed the U.S. fleet carriers *Saratoga* and *Wasp,* sinking the latter and putting the former out of commission for over two months. The battleship *North Carolina* became another submarine casualty, requiring two months of repairs at Pearl Harbor. During the course of the war, however, Japanese submarines sank only about twenty warships, one-tenth the number of enemy warships destroyed by U.S. submarines. In spite of the urging of Germany's Naval Ministry to attack freighters in the Pacific, the Japanese insisted that such ships could be easily replaced and that submarines should be conserved for assaults on the U.S. Fleet.[25]

As it transpired, Japanese submarine resources were often squandered in desperate transport operations as quick successes left the Japanese supply lines dangerously overextended. In their first land offensive of the Pacific war, the Americans invaded the island of Guadalcanal on 7 August 1942, triggering a bitter and protracted campaign. Mochitsura Hashimoto, commander of the *RO-31,* recalled being surprised in 1942 when a military truck arrived loaded with sacks of rice for experimental purposes. Officials wanted to test the feasibility of ejecting rice from torpedo tubes in order to supply the Japanese garrison on Guadalcanal but, after several days of experiments, the *RO-31* succeeded only in spreading a lot of rice over Tokyo Bay. Eventually, some twenty submarines were largely stripped of their offensive weapons in order to carry provisions to the army and, against the wishes of their commanders, dispatched almost daily to supply Guadalcanal until the island was abandoned in February 1943.[26]

Many of these submarines were lost to Allied antisubmarine forces, and more disappeared later in the year when used to evacuate Japanese troops from Kiska in the Aleutians. The Japanese further frittered away steel and other scarce resources developing prototypes ranging from midgets to massive cargo-carrying submarines. Such matériel and labor could have been better employed in producing more long-range craft to disrupt Allied supply lines.[27]

Even so, the tendency of Japanese submarines to neglect Allied shipping is often overstated. Admiral Isoruku Yamamoto, the mastermind behind the Pearl Harbor attack, ordered a "Commerce Destruction Unit," including submarines, to disrupt Allied supply lines. Although the Americans were as yet unaware of it, the Japanese had already put their own unrestricted submarine warfare into effect the same day they attacked Pearl Harbor. The *I-26* became the first submarine to claim a U.S. merchant ship, using deck guns and torpedoes to sink the *Cynthia Olson* with all hands 1,000 miles northwest of Honolulu on 7 December. Only four days after the Pearl Harbor attack, a Japanese submarine used its deck guns to sink the Matson liner *Lahaina*, and the following week two more steamships were sunk traversing the waters between Hawaii and America's West Coast. Before the end of 1941 two tankers, the *Emidio* and *Montebello*, were also sunk.[28]

The Japanese carried out a similar campaign in the Far East. On 4 January 1942 a Japanese submarine sank the British merchantman *Kwantung* southeast of Java. Between January and March 1942, Japanese submarines claimed another 41 ships in the East Indies and Indian Ocean, compared to only 26 confirmed ships sunk by American submarines during the same period. During the course of the war, Japanese submarines sank 184 Allied merchant ships, approaching a total of 1 million tons. While the number represented only about one-sixth the merchant ships sunk by American submarines, it was far from negligible, especially when it is remembered that Japanese submarines operated without the huge advantage given to the Allies by signals intelligence.[29]

Japanese success was partly limited by a policy that stipulated firing only single torpedoes at merchant ships. This reduced the likelihood of sinking ships and encouraged submarine commanders to either attack or finish off their prey with deck guns. On 3 March 1942 the *I-3* shelled the steamer *Narbada* off the west coast of Australia, and similarly tried to shell the SS *Tongariro* a few hours later. More gun attacks in Australian waters followed when the *I-29* shelled a Soviet merchant ship off Newcastle and the *I-32* shelled the passenger ship *Katoomba* off South Australia. On 9 June 1942 the *I-24* conducted a five-hour running gun battle with the SS *Orestes* north of Sydney. Such attacks affected morale, prompting the Australian Naval Board to suspend merchant shipping from eastern and southern ports in June 1942, but were relatively ineffectual in sinking ships.[30]

Patrolling the waters off Sydney from January 1943, the *I-21* sank six ships in the space of a month, making its commander, Kanji Matsumura, one of the most successful skippers of the Second World War.[31] Japanese campaigns against merchant shipping, though, remained sporadic. By November 1943 there had not been a Japanese submarine attack in Australian waters for five months, although Australian crews remained cowed, refusing to leave port without naval escorts. As late as October 1944 the *I-12,* dispatched to hunt in the waters between Hawaii and California, sank the U.S. merchant ship *John A. Johnson*. The resulting dislocation of Allied shipping demonstrated just how crippling submarine attacks could be on morale, but it proved to be a symbolic gesture rather than an ongoing threat. The last Allied vessel torpedoed in the Indian Ocean, the American Liberty ship *Peter Silvester,* fell victim in February 1945 not to a Japanese submarine but to a German U-boat.[32]

Japanese strategists have been harshly criticized for not conducting a sustained assault on merchant shipping, but they had envisioned the war as being a short one. Ultimately, the Japanese were correct in assuming that they did not have enough submarines to negate Allied supply lines through a German-style tonnage war. American antisubmarine warfare also proved much more effective than its Japanese counterpart. The destroyer USS *England* managed to destroy six Japanese submarines in a dozen days off Bougainville in May 1944. Although Japan's torpedoes were superior, their long-range I-class submarines were unwieldy, relatively slow to dive, and noisy when submerged. By the end of the war the Imperial Japanese Navy had lost 131 submarines, compared to 52 lost by the Americans.

With the German Reich on its last legs, in April 1945 Vice Admiral Katsuo Abe begged for remaining U-boats to be sent to Japan, only to be rebuffed.[33]

For the Americans, on the other hand, the attack on Pearl Harbor provided not only the pretext and rationale for attacking merchant shipping, but the individual will to carry it out, generating a visceral hatred of the Japanese that persisted to the end of the war and beyond. After viewing the destruction at Pearl, Admiral "Bull" Halsey uttered his famous oath: "Before we're through with 'em, the Japanese language will be spoken only in hell."[34] When Billy Grieves, a torpedoman on the USS *Thresher,* arrived at Pearl Harbor a day after the attack, heavy gray smoke still blocked out the sun and black oil covered the harbor. In Grieves's words, he and his crewmates experienced "an incinerating rage" and an urge to "exact terrible retribution."[35] Quentin Seiler, having arrived at Pearl Harbor on the submarine USS *Grenadier* shortly after the attack, no less vehemently expressed "an unadulterated hatred for the people who had perpetrated this vile deed."[36] Lawson P. Ramage, assigned duty censoring the mail of submarine crews soon after the attack, confessed shock at what he read: "I've never seen such language and such virulent hate and . . . these were letters from the mothers to their sons."[37]

For many who may have had reservations about attacking noncombatant ships and leaving their crews to face death in the water, the memory of Pearl Harbor tended to extinguish compassion. Some of those who would later go to sea in submarines experienced the horrors of 7 December firsthand. Bill Trimmer had been on the battleship USS *Pennsylvania,* losing sixty-two crewmates as well as being wounded himself. In the wake of the attack he watched body parts dredged from the water, and he took those memories with him when serving on the submarines *S-37* and the USS *Redfish.*[38]

But even for those who didn't witness the carnage firsthand, the residual evidence of the attack on Pearl Harbor continued to evoke a powerful emotional response. When torpedoman John Ronald Smith arrived at Pearl, he recalled, "[T]he superstructures of sunken ships sticking out of the water were grotesque reminders of what had happened here—and why I had joined the Navy."[39] Edward Beach Jr., who arrived at Pearl Harbor in early 1942 on the submarine *Trigger,* recalled when his father, a former commandant of the Mare Island Navy Yard, had arranged the launching of the 35,000-ton battleship *California.* The *California* was hit by two torpedoes and a bomb during the attack; Beach professed that the sight of its damaged hulk "brought home the true facts of the war we were in."[40]

Remembering when the USS *Jack* first entered Pearl Harbor on 21 May 1943 and confronted the lingering evidence of sunken battleships, James Calvert professed, "[T]hat morning I felt a deep, burning desire to show these people they could not do that to the United States without paying a dreadful price."[41] Barney Sieglaff, commander of the USS *Tautog,* claimed: "After the carnage at Pearl Harbor—a sneak attack—who could have moral qualms about killing Japanese? Every ship they had, combat or merchant, was engaged in the war effort one way or the other."[42] When the USS *Gudgeon* sank a 4,000-ton freighter in March 1942, crewman Jack Camp confided to his diary that he felt a bit sorry for those lost with the ship. He added, though, that "after Pearl Harbor there's nothing too good for the whole lot of the Japs."[43]

Such sentiments changed little during the course of the war. At the end of the *Bluegill's* first war patrol in mid-1944, the crew displayed its battle flag with a banner proclaiming "Kill the Bastards."[44] Witnessing the enemy's destruction often seemed to elicit an undisguised joy. When the *Flying Fish* torpedoed a freighter in the Sea of Japan, torpedoman Dale Russell recalls "a brief period of cheering, mixed with comments of joy and bravado, none of compassion."[45] Having torpedoed two freighters off Saipan in February 1944, the *Tang's* skipper, Richard O'Kane, described the ensuing explosions as "wonderful, throwing Japs and other debris above the belching smoke."[46] One of the *Tang's* torpedomen, Don Sharp, stood lookout duty when the submarine sank another ship, on 4 July 1944. He watched the ship slide slowly under the water as the Japanese crew jumped from the bow. In a diary he noted that it "was a sight I've been wanting to see ever since I've been in subs—to see a ship go down."[47]

Of course many submariners never did *see* a ship go down. Stuck at their stations within the recesses of the hull, they experienced battle mainly through the reports of their officers, the sounds of explosions, or the breaking-up noises of a sinking target. Because it was necessary to be prepared to make an emergency dive on short notice, relatively few men were allowed topside. More often than not attacks were followed by a deep dive in an endeavor to avoid retaliatory depth charge attacks. Only occasionally did the submarine surface to observe the aftermath of a torpedo attack, allowing some of the crew members on deck a closer look at their dying prey. Even more rarely, the skipper might let the enlisted men line up for a quick glimpse through the periscope. Not untypical was the complaint voiced by Carl Vozniak, an electrician's mate from Philadelphia on the USS *Finback:* "I was always belowdecks and had never had a chance to see the war."[48]

In contrast, surface gun actions allowed more men of the crew to experience the exhilaration and terror of combat firsthand. A large-bore deck gun required a gun captain, pointer, trainer, spotter, loaders, and a hot-shell man to catch ejected shells. The smaller-caliber weapons also required loaders in addition to the men firing them, and many of the remaining crew members formed a conga line of ammunition passers from the lockers belowdecks.

Compared to a torpedo attack, gun actions were more democratic. Those personnel not usually involved with weaponry, such as the stewards and cooks, could directly participate in the action. On the USS *Crevalle,* for example, one of the stewards served as the first loader for the four-inch deck gun, while the other acted as the fuse setter. On the USS *Spadefish* the baker, Tom Riley, filled the role of shell loader on one of the .30-caliber machine guns after requesting a place on the battle surface team.[49]

In a sense, surface gun attacks were not only more democratic but potentially more heroic. Whereas an underwater battlefield depended largely on the elements of stealth, mathematical computation, and complex machinery, a gun attack depended less on technological precision and more on individual initiative and courage. As one crew member from the USS *Bowfin* explained, submerged attacks were "all numbers" but a surface firefight "got more personal with the war."[50] From the often-close proximity of a gun attack, the enemy no longer seemed an abstraction or appeared as an insectlike creature viewed from a great distance. On the surface, submariners often expressed greater ambivalence about the enemy—and ambiguity in defining who the enemy was.

2

Trouble with Trawlers

The survivors of the attack on Pearl Harbor included Thomas Patrick McGrath, a crew member of the battleship USS *California*, which was sunk by two torpedoes. During the attack, an enraged McGrath had fired a pistol at Japanese dive-bombers from the *California*'s signal bridge. McGrath later declared, "I want to go out on the first ship that's going out after those bastards."[1] Even though he had no submarine training, McGrath joined the crew of the USS *Pompano* when it sailed on its first war patrol on 18 December 1941.

At the time of the attack on Pearl Harbor, the *Pompano*, along with the *Pollack* and the *Plunger*, was returning from Mare Island after undergoing refit. The submarines were about 125 miles northeast of Pearl when they received word of the attack. On the *Pompano*, skipper Lewis Parks immediately began pumping water into the trim tanks, previously purged for more surface speed. Parks's intuition that they might have to dive materialized all too quickly when several Japanese planes, returning to their carriers, appeared, and the *Pompano* struggled to get underwater as the planes strafed it with machine-gun bullets.[2]

The *Pompano*'s initial war patrol, among the first extended submarine patrols of the war from Pearl Harbor, carried out reconnaissance off the Marshall Islands. The patrol proved largely a frustrating round of engine failures and dud torpedoes; the submarine was credited with sinking one Japanese naval auxiliary.[3] On 20 April 1942 the *Pompano* departed for its second war patrol. On the evening of 24 May, cruising on the surface east of Formosa (today Taiwan), the crew picked up a contact. Parks ordered his executive

The Southwest Pacific

officer, Slade Cutter, to man a .50-caliber machine gun mounted aft. The target proved to be a fishing boat, and when the submarine drew within about 300 yards, Parks gave the order to open fire. After the initial burst of bullets, one of the fishing-boat crew held up a lantern to illuminate a Japanese flag, apparently believing the attack to be a case of mistaken identity. He was quickly proved wrong as Parks ordered his men, "Let them have it." A fresh burst of bullets riddled the craft, setting it on fire.

Slade Cutter, once he realized they were firing on a fishing boat, felt uneasy about the attack. When he later said as much to Parks, he found his skipper unrepentant. "Don't worry about that," Parks told him. "They are feeding them [the enemy], and they are fair game."[4] To Parks's mind, unrestricted warfare meant that the enemy could be killed without mercy. Less than two weeks later the *Pompano* sank another trawler, again leaving no survivors.

Despite his unease about attacking fishing boats, Slade Cutter was certainly not among the fainthearted. At the Naval Academy, where he graduated with the class of 1935, he had gained a reputation as a tough competitor—both as a heavyweight boxer and All-American football star. He was over six feet tall and weighed in at some 200 pounds; one sport journalist described his physique as "mastodonic."[5] He would long be remembered for kicking the winning field goal at the 1934 Army-Navy game. Having completed training at the Submarine School in June 1938, he went on to become one of the most highly respected and decorated men in the submarine service. As described by Lew Parks in later years, Cutter also possessed "moral courage."[6]

After serving under Parks on the *Pompano* for three years, Cutter was detached in November 1942 and sent to the new-construction submarine *Seahorse* at the Mare Island Navy Yard near San Francisco. Following a frustrating first patrol on the *Seahorse* as executive officer under Donald McGregor, Cutter assumed command of the submarine on 30 September 1943. Assigned a patrol area in the East China Sea, Cutter determined to improve on the *Seahorse*'s lackluster performance under McGregor.

The *Seahorse* encountered its first Japanese vessel on 29 October 1943, a fishing trawler estimated at 150 tons. Cutter professed a reluctance to attack the trawler, and later claimed he and his officers spent hours debating whether it was worth sinking. Among the most vocal was Cutter's old friend Lieutenant Ralph F. Pleatman, who had served with him on the *Pompano*. Pleatman insisted they had a responsibility to damage the enemy at every opportunity.[7]

At 2:17 in the afternoon the *Seahorse* battle surfaced and hammered the luckless trawler with its deck guns for fifty minutes before turning it into a blazing hulk. As described by the war patrol report, fifty rounds of four-inch high-capacity ammunition set for point detonation were used. Thinner walled than either the common or armor-piercing varieties, the high-capacity shells carried more explosive. They represented the most significant breakthrough of the war in terms of projectiles.[8] Although the trawler evaded the first twenty rounds by making a radical change in course, the patrol report noted, "Pointer group and spotting officer took full advantage of the practice and then settled down nicely with excellent results."[9] The shells wiped out the trawler's superstructure and tore holes four feet in diameter through its wooden hull.

In the meantime the *Seahorse* sprayed the target with another 300 rounds of 20 mm and .50-caliber ammunition that the patrol report described as "used for training only." The U.S. Navy adopted the Swiss-designed Oerlikon 20 mm cannon primarily as an anti-aircraft weapon, but it proved effective against small craft and enemy personnel. On submarines the guns were typically installed on the cigarette decks fore and aft of the conning tower. The gun was the smallest naval weapon to fire exploding shells; "20 mm" referred to its bore size. Easily manned, the gun used drum magazines and had a high rate of fire at 450 rounds per minute. Meanwhile, the .50-caliber machine guns could pump out 600 rounds per minute.[10]

The trawler returned no fire and sank into the sea at 3:37, leaving nine of the crew spotted in the water. The episode left a bad taste in Cutter's mouth, but he sensed that his young crew looked upon the attack as "a game" and was encouraged to become increasingly aggressive.[11] Early the next day the *Seahorse* attacked another trawler, Cutter having first observed about seven young men working a fishing net. After surfacing, the submarine began firing with its four-inch gun from about 800 yards. With the trawler soon sinking by the stern, Ralph Pleatman and four others rowed over to the craft in an inflatable boat to have a look. The trawler crew, mainly teenagers, tried to hide, leading Cutter to describe the incident as "just pitiful."[12] The boarding party confiscated charts and logs, a Japanese flag, and some freshly caught fish, and then left the doomed vessel to its fate.

The *Seahorse* attacked a third trawler the following afternoon. Fearing to get caught on the surface by Japanese aircraft, Cutter waited to surface until after sunset. This time the victim made at least a semblance of resistance; although seemingly unarmed, the trawler turned its bow toward the submarine with the apparent intention of ramming it. The third round from the *Seahorse's* four-inch gun destroyed the trawler's bridge, however, and the craft burned as the submarine continued firing into it.[13]

Having sunk trawlers on three successive days, Slade Cutter professed finding it "just too much" and declined to make any subsequent attacks on small craft. After returning to port, he raised the issue with Robert Henry Rice, his soft-spoken former skipper on the *S-30*. Rice told him that he left trawlers alone. Cutter also spoke with Charles Lockwood, describing the trawler attacks as "just murder." Lockwood reportedly told him, "[L]et your conscience be your guide."[14]

Whether to attack fishing boats remained a persistent dilemma, both moral and tactical, throughout the war. The USS *Pollack* made the first submarine gun attack on a war patrol. After departing Pearl Harbor for its second patrol, on 10 March 1942 the *Pollack* spotted two sampans fishing; the vessels appeared unarmed and without radios. In the early hours of 11 March the submarine closed to attack, opening up with its three-inch gun. One of the sampans began burning after two hits, but the gun flash blinded the pointer and trainer, making it impossible for them to properly aim the big gun. The *Pollack* crew riddled the second sampan's hull with .50-caliber machine-gun bullets until it too started to sink.[15]

As the first submarine gun action on a war patrol, the attack had important implications. There had been speculation that small craft with their lights on might be used to lure submarines into traps sprung by their Japanese counterparts. Indeed, in his endorsement of the *Pollack's* first war patrol, the commander of Submarine Division 43, Norman S. Ives, made this very point. Such notions possibly gained currency from the experience of the First World War, when the British had some limited success using trawlers as decoys to lure German U-boats within range of their own submarines.[16]

The *Pollack's* successful sinking of the sampans without incident ran counter to these ideas. The new commander of Submarine Division 43 from March 1942, George C. "Turkey Neck" Crawford, commented on the basis of the *Pollack*'s second war patrol that sampans did not appear to be "some type of patrol vessel" as previously thought; the *Pollack*'s experience indicated "they are only fishing boats and are no cause for a submarine to dive as has been done in many cases in the past."[17] The endorsement of the patrol report by Thomas Withers Jr. further lauded the advantages of sinking sampans. Withers pointed out that this not only allowed the *Pollack* greater "freedom of movement, but at the same time started the destruction of Japan's vital fishing fleet."[18]

No doubt encouraged by such comments, the *Pollack* made more gun attacks on its next patrol. After departing Pearl Harbor, on 12 May 1942 the submarine spotted a fishing vessel estimated at 600 tons with a Japanese flag painted on its bow. This time the vessel, because of its high masts and radio antenna, was believed to be a lookout. The *Pollack* battle surfaced and pounded the craft with three-inch shells and .50-caliber machine-gun fire until the vessel began sinking by the stern and burning furiously.

A week later the *Pollack* attacked a group of five sampans spotted fishing. Opening fire with the deck guns just after midnight on 20 May, the *Pollack* managed to sink two or three of the vessels before the others doused their lights. A few hours later the submarine sank another sampan off Toi Misaki, a southern cape of Kyushu. In his endorsement of the patrol, division commander Crawford stated that the attacks proved "conclusively that submarines have little to fear from Japanese sampans and large fishing boats. Judicious destruction of these vessels is a diversion for the crew and is costly to a nation which depends to a great extent on her fishing industry."[19]

Not everyone, however, accepted the efficacy of sinking fishing boats; there were others like Slade Cutter who had reservations. The USS *Tang*'s legendary commander, Richard O'Kane, compared attacking fishing boats to swatting mosquitoes.[20] Nevertheless, such attacks became increasingly common. During 1942 U.S. submarines reported 34 attacks on trawlers and sampans (terms often used interchangeably for small craft, along with the deprecating sobriquet *spitkits*). The number attacked increased to 64 in 1943, 113 in 1944, and in 1945, before the end of hostilities, submarines reported 99 attacks on trawlers and sampans.[21] By the end of the war, the majority of large Japanese fishing vessels throughout Southeast Asia had been destroyed.[22]

At least some skippers saw the sinking of small craft as a way of raising their crew's morale when there were no more worthy targets available. Charles Lockwood, a longtime proponent of submarines carrying large deck guns, professed, "There was no better morale builder than a well-planned gun action."[23] According to Lockwood, a gun attack offered "a stimulating change to men who for days on end had spent much of their time submerged."[24] Pete Galantin similarly praised the "great psychological value" of gun attacks: "What a welcome release of emotion, of pent-up hate, of frustration, of boredom—yes, even fear—came with the order, 'Battle Surface!'"[25]

It is a theme that recurs in patrol reports as well as personal memoirs. Prowling south of Formosa in January 1944, the USS *Thresher* encountered a trawler estimated to be 150 tons. In the ensuing attack the *Thresher* fired 45 shells from its five-inch gun, as well as 770 20 mm shells and 1,000 rounds of .50-caliber ammunition from machine guns. The patrol report noted, "Not much damage was done to the Imperial war effort, but the action had a good psychological effect on the crew."[26] Similarly, after sinking a sailing vessel in June 1944, the patrol report of the USS *Tinosa* conceded that it was not "too much of a target but enough to give all hands a lift and something to talk about."[27] A successful sinking, even of a small craft, could help consolidate a submarine skipper's authority and serve as a confidence-building exercise for the crew.

On the other hand, while gun attacks might give submarine crews a "lift," they could also be divisive. When the USS *Sterlet* encountered a small fishing fleet off Okinawa in October 1944, executive officer Paul Schratz tried his best to dissuade the skipper from attacking it. He believed "submarine policy" was to avoid such craft, which carried neither radios nor supplies. Nevertheless, the skipper insisted on attacking the boats, cutting one in half with the 20 mm cannon and machine guns from only fifty yards. Schratz stayed off the bridge during the action, later expressing his disdain in the patrol report by describing the target's size as "half that of the executive officer."[28]

Gun attacks also didn't always go the submarine's way, as the *Silversides* discovered on the morning of 10 May 1942. The USS *Silversides,* constructed at the Mare Island Navy Yard, became the first new submarine commissioned after America entered the war. Its commander, Creed Burlingame, from Louisville, Kentucky, had once served on the battleship *Utah,* which was sunk at Pearl Harbor. When the *Silversides* encountered a Japanese trawler on its first war patrol, Burlingame didn't hesitate to order a gun attack. To Burlingame's mind, Pearl Harbor had wiped out any sympathy for the Japanese and gave him license to shoot up their fishing boats as payback.[29]

The attack, some 600 miles off Japan, demonstrated the dangers that gun crews were exposed to. On a rolling sea, with waves breaking over the deck, at least two of the crew were knocked overboard and had to be fished out of the water. When they were lucky enough to hit the enemy vessel with the three-inch gun, the high explosive shells went straight through its wooden hull without exploding. The navy had issued many submarines with armor-piercing shells designed to penetrate a ship's protective belt and detonate inside the hull. Armor-piercing shells proved relatively ineffectual against wooden vessels, however, since they tended to pass straight through.[30]

When the *Silversides* finally closed in for the kill, the trawler managed to spray the submarine's bridge and deck with machine-gun and rifle fire from a couple of hundred yards. One of the loaders on the three-inch gun had his arm smashed and another, torpedo-man third class Michael Harbin, died instantly. When the men of the gun crew cleared the deck they were, in the words of executive officer Frank G. Selby, "as far gone as I ever hope to see human beings get."[31] Selby had narrowly eluded catastrophe himself, ducking behind the fairwater of the conning tower just as a bullet hit, spraying his face with paint chips.

Mike Harbin, originally from Rosedale, Oklahoma, became the first sailor killed in a U.S. submarine gun action. Buried at sea the same evening, his body was sewn into a canvas sack and shrouded with a flag. Under an overcast sky, with all of the available crew mustered on deck, Burlingame conducted a burial service before Harbin's remains slid over the side into the broiling whitecaps.[32]

On Slade Cutter's former submarine, the *Pompano,* motor machinist first class Herbert A. Calcattera was another early fatality. At about 10:00 A.M. on the morning of 4 September 1942, some 500 miles east of Japan, the *Pompano* battle surfaced to attack an auxiliary patrol boat. Lew Parks later claimed that his replacement as skipper, Willis Manning Thomas, had been ill advised to close on the patrol boat before knowing the range of its weapons.[33] The patrol boat sprayed the *Pompano* with machine-gun fire, hitting Calcattera in the shoulder as he fed ammunition to the three-inch deck gun.

Nicknamed "Chainfall" because of his strength, Calcattera had on one occasion hurled the furniture out of his room at the Royal Hawaiian Hotel during a drunken leave in Waikiki. Although his wound did not initially appear life threatening, the enemy bullet penetrated his lung and he died just before midnight the same day. He was buried at sea the following morning.[34] In the course of the war, at least twenty submariners became fatalities as a result of surface gun actions.[35]

Many others received life-threatening injuries in gun exchanges. When the USS *Snook* spotted a trawler on 29 September 1943 at the end of its third war patrol, Commander Charles O. "Chuck" Triebel ordered a battle surface. The vessel appeared unarmed, and when the *Snook* began the attack at noon, it quickly scored hits with the three-inch gun. As the *Snook* moved within 700 yards, however, it unexpectedly received machine-gun fire. To make matters worse, the *Snook*'s 20 mm gun suddenly jammed and the crew ran out of .30-caliber machine-gun ammunition. With four men wounded, the *Snook* turned away at full speed, leaving the trawler dead in the water with a heavy list.[36]

Getting too close to an enemy vessel before determining its armament appears to have been a common error. On its second war patrol, the USS *Croaker* attacked a small sampan and schooner in night actions. In both cases the gun crews, unable to see the vessels in the darkness, had forsaken using the four-inch deck gun, relying instead on firing tracer rounds from the 40 mm, 20 mm, and machine guns from the relatively close distance of 400 yards. In his endorsement of the patrol, division commander Thomas M. Dykers criticized "gun actions with strange small craft at night when the weight of armament carried is decidedly an unknown factor and particularly when such short ranges are necessary in order to see the target."[37]

Lawson "Red" Ramage also had his crew shot up after the *Parche* surfaced to finish off a tanker 100 miles north of Lombok in 1943. Although the *Parche* managed to torpedo the bow of the tanker, the ship limped off faster than the submarine could follow underwater; there seemed nothing to do but surface and try to destroy the tanker with gunfire. Amid the gun action, the *Parche* received return fire from a small-caliber machine gun. Before Ramage knew it, the deck was running red with blood and he had seven injured crew members, forcing him to head back to base at Fremantle.[38]

Although the enemy often had only small arms, the danger to submarine gun crews and loaders could be considerable; they had little to take cover behind if fired on. When the *Halibut* made a night attack on a couple of sampans, for example, two of the gun loaders were hit by small-caliber fire. One of the sampans, apparently carrying munitions, wounded another *Halibut* crewman with flying metal when it exploded.[39]

As these incidents suggest, not all trawlers and sampans were simply fishing craft. Thomas Hogan, skipper of the USS *Bonefish*, noted, "Japanese sampans, we had learned, may be just sampans and they may be something else."[40] The use of trawlers as antisubmarine vessels dated back to the First World War, when the British employed hundreds of the craft to combat the menace of German U-boats. In the Dardanelles, the British deployed North Sea fishing trawlers, replete with their fishermen crews, as minesweepers and pickets. The French and Italians resorted to purchasing fishing vessels from neutral countries for antisubmarine patrols and convoy duties.[41]

Similarly, during the Second World War all of the belligerents employed an array of small craft. America posted boats, some armed with as little as a pistol, in an effort to deter German U-boats from operating too close to shore. In Australia converted pleasure craft, the so-called Hollywood Fleet, were used to patrol Sydney Harbour. The British pressed scores of trawlers into escort and antisubmarine duties; they proved especially proficient in picking up the survivors of torpedoed merchant vessels.[42] The first U-boat to fall victim to a British trawler was the *U-551* in March 1941, depth charged by the *Visenda*. By June 1941 Britain's antisubmarine forces included some 300 trawlers and yachts.[43]

For their part, German U-boats carried out their own campaign against trawlers, sinking twenty-six by 1 April 1940. The British counted nine trawlers among their "warships" lost in the English Channel during May and June 1940, including two torpedoed by submarines. British submarines also waged war on trawlers and antisubmarine yachts, with the HMS *Safari* making a series of gun attacks in August 1943 against small craft in the Tyrrhenian Sea. At the end of the war in Europe, the Allies systematically destroyed German fishing craft, ostensibly to prevent Germany from rearming.[44]

The sinking of "innocent" trawlers nevertheless could create moral outrage in the Atlantic. On 5 July 1944 the *U-247* sank the 207-ton fishing trawler *Noreen Mary* off the west coast of Scotland, causing the deaths of eight crewmen from a complement of ten. The crew from other trawlers helplessly observed the attack as the U-boat first fired two torpedoes and then shelled the vessel for forty-five minutes. Like most British trawlers, the *Noreen Mary* was armed, carrying a Savage Lewis gun as well as a rifle for exploding mines. German endorsements of the patrol praised the attack as evidence of "great offensive spirit and verve."[45] After the war, however, the attack represented part of the evidence against Admiral Dönitz at the Nuremberg war crime trials.

The Japanese frequently employed trawlers and other small vessels for combat and auxiliary duties. Indeed, during the 1930s the Japanese Navy encouraged the expansion of fishing fleets as a way of circumventing restrictions on shipbuilding imposed by the Washington Naval Conference of 1922. The military envisioned that long-distance fishing boats, equipped with the latest telecommunication and navigation devices, might serve as a naval reserve. With the outbreak of war, many of these craft were confiscated for military purposes.[46]

On its first war patrol, the USS *Guardfish* sank a trawler estimated to be 400 tons in the waters off Honshu on 22 August 1942. The first five salvos from the submarine's three-inch gun scored hits on the trawler's pilothouse, leading skipper Thomas Burton Klakring to describe the attack as "a remarkably creditable performance for a gun crew which had never faced a practice nor been in actual combat previously."[47] After the trawler caught fire, a number of brilliant explosions shot flames 100 feet in the air, leading to speculation that it was a naval auxiliary carrying oil or gasoline.

While on his first patrol in command of the USS *Guardfish* in 1943, Norvell G. Ward spotted scores of fishing boats off the coast of New Ireland carrying supplies to the Japanese garrison at Rabaul. The boats were shepherded by a "mother ship," the *Suzuya Maru*, which the *Guardfish* torpedoed on 13 June. The submarine then surfaced for a gun action against the fishing boats, but an airplane forced it to dive before doing any damage.[48]

Faced with a shortage of destroyers, the Japanese used a variety of craft as escorts for convoys. In August 1944, for example, the USS *Pintado* encountered a sonar-equipped trawler in the Yellow Sea escorting a convoy.[49] Under Japanese regulations in the so-called Southern Areas, military authorities were empowered to confiscate any local vessels over 500 tons and use smaller ships as desired.[50] In some areas, Allied submarines considered even "native" sailboats as potentially disguised patrol boats. In the Java Sea and Karimata Strait en route to the South China Sea, the lookouts of the *Pintado* were kept in a state of high alert among such craft.[51]

During the war private boat builders in Japan who had previously specialized in fishing boats turned out wooden-hulled vessels that could be used as patrol boats, with the optimistic idea of converting them to fishing craft once the war ended.[52] Some of these vessels were formidably armed, as on the morning of 13 August 1944 when the USS *Archerfish* under command of William Harry Wright encountered a 300-ton diesel trawler. The *Archerfish* took note that the craft not only sported a high antenna but carried machine guns and two depth charges on a stern rack. Believing the range of the trawler's guns to be about 3,000 yards, the *Archerfish* surfaced and opened fire from 5,500 yards. The trawler responded by lighting a smoke canister for cover, jettisoning its depth charges, and then charging toward the submarine. The *Archerfish* managed to destroy the trawler's upper works with its four-inch gun while pouring out 1,500 rounds of smaller-caliber bullets. Nevertheless, the trawler continued to return fire, and the *Archerfish* could never move in for the kill.[53] When the USS *Thresher* mounted a gun attack on a small trawler shortly after sunset on 3 October 1944, it similarly had to back off. The *Thresher*'s five-inch shells were answered by shells falling around the submarine; it made a strategic retreat in the gathering darkness.[54]

Part of the pretext for attacking fishing craft was the assumption that they often served as pickets, alerting the enemy to Allied ship and aircraft movements. Even before the war, Japanese fishermen and fishing boats equipped with powerful radios and engines were suspected of carrying out surveillance in the Dutch East Indies and Singapore, and in fact the Japanese Navy directly encouraged fishers in southern waters to collect all kinds of intelligence.[55]

The carrier task force that supported the Doolittle bombing raid on Tokyo in April 1942 encountered sampans 650 miles offshore, forcing the bombers to take off prematurely. An interrogation of Japanese prisoners indicated that the craft were part of an organized picket line, and added credibility to the belief that scores of converted trawlers equipped with radios maintained vigil about 600 miles off the home islands.[56] The trawler attacked by the *Silversides* on 10 May 1942, an action resulting in the death of Mike Harbin, was indeed a picket boat; although damaged by the *Silversides*' attack, the *Ebisu Maru No. 5* was later rescued by the auxiliary cruiser *Akagi Maru*.[57]

On its fifth war patrol in 1943, the USS *Finback* reported encountering a trawler that used supersonic ranging as well as lookouts on its foremasts.[58] Pete Galantin believed that many fishing vessels were equipped with radio transmitters and ready to alert Japanese antisubmarine forces. Partly for this reason, most submarines tended to avoid small craft early in their patrols, mounting any attacks on the way back to base. On his first patrol commanding the USS *Halibut*, Galantin ordered an attack on a sampan one dark night. As the submarine approached the suspect craft, the crew picked up a flurry of radio transmissions as well as some small-arms fire, quickly terminated by the *Halibut*'s deck guns.[59]

Assumptions that small craft were acting as pickets, however, were sometimes made on circumstantial or questionable evidence. When the *Pompano*, on its sixth war patrol, encountered a trawler crowded with lookouts, the skipper was left wondering whether the fishermen were "searching industriously for local fish—or Pompano."[60] Having sunk a fishing boat off Honshu, the crew of the USS *Pogy* believed that the craft must have transmitted a radio message because an aircraft turned up about twenty minutes later.[61] On patrol in March 1944, the USS *Batfish* encountered what appeared to be a line of sampans on the Bungo-Suido–Saipan route. Because the area seemed an unlikely fishing ground, the *Batfish* crew assumed the boats were acting as spotters or even as "bait."[62] At times closer inspection disproved such theories. The same month, March 1944, the USS *Gunnel* spotted a suspect sampan in the Ceram Sea believed to be equipped with a radio. The boat was boarded, but the patrol report recorded finding "No radio, No Nips." Instead, they found only a few scared "natives" huddling under the deck.[63]

Small vessels that tried to evade submarines were generally assumed to be enemies. Patrolling a channel off Formosa on 3 November 1942, the USS *Finback* sighted an oceangoing sampan estimated to be 100 tons. When the craft attempted to evade, the *Finback* closed to point-blank range. The submarine opened fire with its three-inch gun, 20 mm gun, .50-caliber machine gun, two .30-caliber machine guns, a Browning automatic rifle, and four Tommy guns. All of the sampan crew, about a dozen men, was reported killed.[64]

It is clear, nevertheless, that submarines did attack craft that were exactly what they appeared to be—unarmed fishing vessels. In the early morning of 19 September 1944, about twelve miles off the Telaga Islands, the USS *Redfin* spotted a trawler estimated to be about 85 tons. Through the periscope the trawler's crew could be observed throwing bait over the stern. The *Redfin* surfaced and pulverized the fishing boat, later identified as the *Nanko Maru,* with heavy fire. The patrol report noted that the craft "put up absolutely no resistance at all." Once the trawler caught fire, the *Redfin* submerged and watched it burn through the periscope. Although the submarine picked up one prisoner, the rest of the trawler's crew was left trying to lash together some debris into a makeshift float. Rather optimistically, the patrol report noted, "I imagine most of the 15 survivors reached the shore which was only 12 miles away with a good wind blowing them in that direction."[65]

Discretion rather than concern about civilian lives often motivated restraint. In another incident in 1944, the USS *Batfish,* commanded by Wayne R. Merrill, encountered a sampan while patrolling submerged off the southeast coast of Shikoku. Barely avoiding getting tangled in its fishing net, the *Batfish* looked the vessel over carefully. Merrill pronounced the vessel "innocent," since it carried neither a radio nor arms, but even so noted in the patrol report, "Was tempted to eliminate him, but could not feel justified in taking a chance on disclosing our presence."[66]

In the context of "total war," many submariners felt that attacking fishing craft, and hence Japanese food supplies, was entirely justifiable. Japanese fishing largely supplied the military not only with food but sometimes with other products as well, such as shark liver oil, which was used to lubricate Japanese aircraft engines.[67]

On the other hand, the moral ambiguity of attacking small craft is clear when the shoe was on the other foot. On 3 August 1942, the Japanese submarine *I-175* attacked the 223-ton fishing trawler *Dureenbee* some twenty miles off the eastern coast of Australia. The *Dureenbee* crew's reaction resembled that of the Japanese on the trawler assaulted by the *Pompano,* initially assuming the attack to be a case of mistaken identity. The *Dureenbee*'s master, William Reid, reportedly shouted to the Japanese, "Don't fire! We are only a harmless fishing boat."[68]

After disabling the craft with a dozen shells from its 4.7-inch deck gun, the *I-175* circled the trawler three times to spray it with machine-gun fire. The assault killed three men and wounded three more from the *Dureenbee*'s crew of a dozen; surprisingly, the trawler survived to be towed back to Sydney. A contemporary account denounced the Japanese attack on the *Dureenbee* as an instance of "murder and piracy on the high seas," while a recent writer describes it as an instance of "barbarism."[69] The fact remains, however, that such attacks were far more commonly carried out by Allied submarines than by their enemies.

3

Wahoo

The discovery of the USS *Wahoo* wreck in 2006 sent a ripple of excitement through naval history circles. The submarine went missing in October 1943, apparently sunk by a combination of Japanese planes and patrol ships while exiting the Sea of Japan. In July 2006 Russian divers located the wreck under 600 feet of water on the floor of La Perouse Strait. The U.S. Navy confirmed the submarine's identity on 31 October, ending a mystery that had persisted for over sixty years regarding the precise location of the *Wahoo*'s sinking.[1] But while the final resting place of the submarine and its crew now appears resolved, much remains contested.

The *Wahoo*'s skipper, Dudley Walker "Mush" Morton, is arguably America's most famous submarine commander, but also the most controversial. Even the origin of Morton's nickname is disputed; despite consensus that "Mush" was short for "Mushmouth" and that Morton acquired the moniker while attending the Naval Academy, its provenance remains obscure. Some claim the nickname resulted from Morton's southern drawl, given that he grew up near Owensboro, Kentucky, and later lived in Miami, Florida. Many academy plebes came from the South, however, so it would be surprising if he were singled out for this alone. Other writers have suggested the nickname came from his habit of talking with a cigar clenched in his teeth, or even his reputed ability to speak while holding four golf balls in his mouth. But if Morton's own account is to be believed, the name originated from a character in the syndicated comic strip *Moon Mullins*.[2]

Morton's nickname is not an entirely trivial issue, for one might expect it to reveal something of his personality. Theodore Roscoe attributes the nickname to Morton's "knack for yarn-spinning," and a common denominator in stories about Morton is his penchant for boastful showmanship.[3] Even in high school he appeared adept at making himself the center of attention; his senior yearbook remarked on his facility to "crack a joke" and amuse his companions.[4] At least in hindsight, Morton's gift for embellishment proved something of a liability to his reputation.

When Morton took command of the *Wahoo* on 12 December 1942, he was thirty-five years old. Tall, with broad shoulders, he was described by one fellow officer as "built like a bear."[5] He had played football in high school and then at the Naval Academy, from which he graduated in 1930. Just how Morton assumed command of the *Wahoo* is also subject to conflicting accounts. He had previously skippered the USS *Dolphin* (SS-169), but was relieved of command in 1942 after condemning the submarine as unfit for war patrols. At least one division commander thought Morton too erratic to be given command of a boat. According to another account, Morton was on his way out of the submarine service before being assigned a berth on the *Wahoo* as prospective commanding officer (PCO). Captain John "Babe" Brown assigned him the duty, so one story goes, because he was impressed by the way Morton shook hands.[6]

The role of the PCO was largely that of an observer. Before being assigned their own boat, prospective skippers were required to take a four-week course at the New London Submarine School on tactics and were then assigned to make a patrol with a seasoned skipper in order to get firsthand experience. Morton, though, appeared to regard the *Wahoo*'s commander, Marvin G. Kennedy, as more a menace than a mentor. When the submarine terminated its patrol at Brisbane, Australia, on 26 December 1942, Morton harshly criticized Kennedy, allegedly calling him "a yellow-bellied S.O.B."[7] Specifically, Morton disputed Kennedy's claim that the *Wahoo* sank a Japanese submarine east of Bougainville.

As detailed by the patrol report, the *Wahoo* torpedoed a surfaced submarine from 800 yards, and despite problems of visibility due to rain squalls, Kennedy witnessed the Japanese craft go down with personnel still on the bridge.[8] Although Kennedy claimed the torpedoed submarine to be the *I-2*, official records indicate that the *I-2* was not lost until 7 April 1944, when it was attacked by the destroyer USS *Saufley*. Of course, it could have been another Japanese submarine; subsequent books—one published by the executive officer, Dick O'Kane, and another by yeoman Forest Sterling—corroborate that a submarine was indeed sunk. At the time, the commander of submarines at Brisbane, James Fife, confirmed the sinking in his endorsement of the *Wahoo's* patrol report and Kennedy received a Silver Star on the strength of the patrol.[9] Fife later claimed in his memoirs, however, that at least some of the *Wahoo* crew discredited the sinking.[10] Kennedy was more or less drummed out of the submarine service, and the command of *Wahoo* went to Morton.

In summary, the evidence of what happened on the patrol is confusing, suggesting either that Kennedy (wittingly or unwittingly) fabricated the sinking, or that he fell victim to a veritable coup. Somewhat ironically, Morton faced a similar ambush from his PCO following his second patrol in command of the *Wahoo*. Duncan Calvin MacMillan complained to the squadron commander that his experience on the *Wahoo* revealed a lack of planning and discipline in making attacks. In this instance, though, Morton retained his command and MacMillan took command of the USS *Thresher*.[11]

Soon after assuming command of the *Wahoo* at Brisbane, Morton made his own predilections known. He demonstrated a more democratic style than the reclusive Kennedy, and according to O'Kane, who stayed on as executive officer, soon "had his crew eating out of his hand."[12] Morton's avowed hatred of the Japanese also became obvious. Placards posted in the watch bill holders of each compartment proclaimed, "Shoot the Sunza Bitches." Also posted in the submarine were the words of General McNair: "We must shoot to kill for our enemies have pointed the way to swifter and surer crueler killing."[13] The *Wahoo* crew soon had the opportunity to put such admonitions into practice.

The *Wahoo* departed Brisbane at 9:30 A.M. on 16 January 1943.

Arriving at Pearl Harbor only twenty-four days later, it had made the shortest Pacific patrol to date but also the most successful. The *Wahoo* received credit for sinking five ships on the patrol, including an entire four-ship convoy. Later investigation eventually reduced the official tally to three ships, but for the time being news of the patrol created jubilation. While many in the submarine service were demoralized by defective torpedoes, the fact that Morton made his attacks with the controversial Mark VI magnetic exploder renewed faith in the weapon.[14] Confidence in the torpedoes proved short-lived, but Morton's patrol promised a new kind of aggression.

The timing of the patrol was serendipitous. In Europe the Axis powers had suffered reverses at Stalingrad and in North Africa, while in the Pacific the Japanese offensive had been stalled at Guadalcanal Island and at Buna in New Guinea. At a meeting of the Allies at Casablanca in French Morocco, President Roosevelt had just announced a policy of demanding "unconditional surrender."

Taking advantage of an enthusiastic reception on arrival at Pearl Harbor, the *Wahoo* flew a massive white pennant declaring in black letters Morton's slogan, "Shoot the Sunza Bitches." Charles Lockwood, newly installed as commander of Submarines Pacific, pronounced the *Wahoo* "The One-Boat Wolf Pack."[15] Morton received a Navy Cross for the patrol, and an impressed General Douglas MacArthur conferred on him the army's Distinguished Service Cross. The *Wahoo* also received a coveted Presidential Unit Citation. At the Mare Island Navy Yard, where the *Wahoo* was the first of seventeen fleet submarines constructed during the war, a huge billboard went up proclaiming: "Shoot the Sunzabitches! And the Wahoo did! Another Mare Island–built Champion!!"[16]

Morton became the first genuine superstar of the submarine service, giving numerous media interviews and appearing in *The March of Time* newsreel series. An article on the *Wahoo*'s patrol graced the pages of *Time* magazine under the leader "Clean Sweep."[17] A correspondent for the Associated Press, Walter B. Clausen, portrayed Morton as "the embodiment of American spirit, a devoted father, and easily approachable, kindly leader, with a quiet, deep enthusiasm that spreads confidence in his youthful crew until the moment of action, when he blazes forth like a tiger to kill."[18]

There was, though, a dark side to Morton's patrol that would dog his reputation to the present. On 26 January, at 11:35 in the morning, the *Wahoo* torpedoed a Japanese transport ship, the *Buyo Maru,* approximately 250 miles north of New Guinea. Using the graphic language that became a Morton trademark, the patrol report recorded: "The explosion blew her midships section higher than a kite. Troops commenced jumping over the side like ants off a hot plate. Her stern went up and she headed for the bottom."[19]

What happened next became the most contentious action by a U.S. submarine in the war. The *Wahoo* surfaced and opened its deck guns on the Japanese survivors, some in various small craft and others floating in the ocean. No one denies that the *Wahoo* fired on survivors, but debate has since raged over the intent and results of this event.

Did the *Wahoo* surface for the express purpose of killing survivors, or did it fire only in self-defense? Charles Lockwood, writing after the war, indicated the latter. According to his account, as the *Wahoo* approached the Japanese to pick up prisoners, the submarine received rifle and machine-gun fire. Lockwood concluded, "There was nothing to do but sink them all, which *Wahoo* promptly did."[20] The *Wahoo*'s executive officer, Dick O'Kane, also backed this version of events and remained a staunch defender of Morton's command throughout his life.[21] On the other hand, the *Wahoo*'s patrol report indicates the intention of attacking the Japanese from the beginning: "[W]e surfaced to charge the batteries and destroy the estimated twenty troop boats now in the water." According to this version of events, only after the *Wahoo* fired its four-inch gun at one of the craft did it receive return fire. The crew of the *Wahoo* then "opened up with everything we had."[22]

If the initial intention had ever been to pick up prisoners, this idea was quickly abandoned. According to one of the *Wahoo* crew, John Clary, when a Japanese survivor floated within twelve feet of the submarine, obviously "playing possum," some crewmen suggested taking the man alive. Morton ordered them instead, "Shoot the Sonza bitch."[23] Another *Wahoo* crew member, William Young, recalled, "We killed everyone we could."[24] Of course, even if the *Wahoo* had been fired on first, it could have simply steamed away, as other submarines did on occasion.

At the heart of many later discussions of the incident are the issues of how long the *Wahoo* actually fired on the *Buyo Maru* survivors and how many were killed. Morton claimed that the action lasted about an hour, but O'Kane challenged this as typical Morton hyperbole, insisting that the firing lasted no more than twenty minutes.[25] It is indeed likely that the action was shorter than many perceived, since combatants often describe an attenuation of time. The stress and excitement of battle speed up the participant's internal clock, making external events appear to be unfolding more slowly.[26] Of course, even a relatively brief period would have allowed the *Wahoo* to fire an immense amount of ammunition. In addition to the four-inch gun and two 20 mm guns, two Browning Automatic Rifles (BARs) were used to fire into the water. At one point Morton is credited with telling the crew, "Anyone who doesn't get up here and load the deck guns, I'll court-martial."[27]

According to some estimates, the massacre involved thousands of victims. Morton himself claimed that they killed most of the troops in the water, estimated at between 1,500 and 6,000. But again, O'Kane considered this a gross exaggeration, putting the number at more like 500 troops. Not until James DeRose published his research almost sixty years later were firmer statistics available. According to DeRose, the *Buyo Maru* carried a total of 1,126 men on board, and of these 491 were Indian prisoners of war being shipped from Singapore to New Britain for forced labor. The Indian POWs in fact took the main brunt of the *Wahoo*'s attack, with 195 killed, compared to 87 Japanese. Unfortunately, DeRose's documentation for these claims is vague, citing only that the information came from the Japanese Diet Library and U.S. Archives.[28] Until the information can be independently verified, the number of fatalities must remain questionable.

Whatever the number killed, the episode must be considered in context to understand both its motivation and the official response. As has been pointed out by some writers, for Morton and his crew the troops in the water represented a potential threat, for if rescued they might well have ended up facing Allied troops in the desperate island campaigns being fought at the time. Admiral Halsey's chief of staff, Rear Admiral Robert B. Carney, expressed a similar logic when commenting on the sinking of Japanese hospital ships. To his mind, "[T]hey were caring for NIPs which we failed to kill in the first attempt. Every one who is restored to duty potentially costs the lives of many of our people."[29]

Only a few weeks after the *Wahoo*'s action, the result of similar thinking manifested itself during the battle of the Bismarck Sea. American B-17s destroyed a convoy of eight Japanese transports and four destroyers sailing from Rabaul to reinforce forces at Lae, New Guinea, and then PT boats and aircraft systematically shot survivors on rafts or clinging to wreckage. According to a report in *Time* magazine, strafing U.S. A-20 Havocs along with Australian Beaufighters "turned lifeboats towed by motor barges packed with Jap survivors into bloody sieves."[30] Such actions were fueled by stories of Japanese atrocities. According to one account, for example, Morton was incensed by stories of Japanese planes bombing an Australian hospital ship, the *Manunda,* and strafing survivors when they attacked Darwin on 19 February 1942.[31]

Hatred, in part a lasting legacy of the attack on Pearl Harbor, goes far in explaining the killing of the *Buyo Maru* survivors. The *Wahoo*'s yeoman Forest Sterling recalls, "You have to remember how badly we hated the Japs and how far behind we were in the war then."[32] In a similar vein, Morton reportedly told news correspondent Richard Haller, "That's the only way we'll ever lick 'em. The Japs fight hard and use all the tricks and we've got to shoot, shoot, shoot."[33]

For some there were perhaps more personal motives for revenge. Only a few days before departing Brisbane on patrol, O'Kane had learned of the death of his former crewmates when the submarine *Argonaut* went down with all hands after an attack by Japanese destroyers in the waters southwest of New Britain.[34] But there were also those repulsed by the killing. David Veder, still a teenager when he served on the *Wahoo,* observed: "My view was that you sank ships, not people. There were humans in lifeboats. We were shooting them."[35]

While some in the submarine service were shocked by the incident, no official censure materialized. The lack of response may have resulted, as one writer suggests, from a "leadership gap" at the time of *Buyo Maru* incident. Rear Admiral Robert English died in a plane crash shortly before the *Wahoo* began its patrol, and Admiral Charles Lockwood assumed command of Submarines Pacific only after the *Wahoo*'s arrival at Pearl Harbor.[36]

In any case, there is no indication that Morton felt the slightest regret or remorse. On the *Wahoo*'s next patrol an incident took place that was in some ways more shocking than the gun attack on the *Buyo Maru* survivors. The *Wahoo* departed Pearl Harbor on 23 February 1943, heading for the Yellow Sea. On the morning of 21 March, at about 10 A.M., the *Wahoo* sank a 6,543-ton freighter identified as the *Nitu Maru*. The ship sank within minutes, and when two junks looked like they might attempt to rescue survivors, the *Wahoo* drove them off.[37]

This much is recorded in the official war patrol report, but there would be a chilling postscript that emerged only much later. Among the *Wahoo* crew was John Clary who, contrary to regulations, kept a diary of the patrol. According to Clary, when the *Wahoo* returned to the site where the freighter went down, the crew found three men amid the oil and debris. One of the men was on a raft, and two others were on an overturned lifeboat. The *Wahoo* approached slowly, striking the lifeboat with its bow and knocking one of the men into the water. Crewmen threw the man a lifeline, but he refused to come on board. Clary believed that the intended Japanese prisoner, who appeared to be about seventeen years old, was too stunned to understand their entreaties to board the submarine. Clary then records, "[H]e was riddled by machine gun fire & also the other Jap with him." The Japanese survivor on the raft met a similar fate, as the crew "held target practice on him & he soon sank beneath the sea."[38]

This time there could be no pretense of self-defense, immediate or potential, since the men in the water were not soldiers.

The kind of hatred that could take pleasure from others' misery reared its head again, if less graphically, four days later. On 25 March, with the mountains of Korea as a backdrop, the *Wahoo* attacked the 2,556-ton freighter *Sinsei Maru*. After missing the ship with torpedoes, the *Wahoo* surfaced for a gun attack. It claimed nearly ninety hits with the four-inch gun, while the 20 mm gun poured shells into the blazing vessel. When the submarine passed about a dozen survivors in the water, the crew called out, "So Solly, Please."[39] John Clary confided to his diary, "[I]t was very sad to hear them moan & sink."[40]

4

Atrocities

Mush Morton was not the only Allied submarine commander to order the shooting of survivors. Before the *Wahoo*'s assault on the *Buyo Maru,* the British submarine *Torbay* made analogous attacks in the Mediterranean. On its second patrol in the Aegean Sea during July 1941, the *Torbay* made a series of gun attacks on schooners and caïques carrying German troops, sometimes killing survivors. Paul Chapman, a *Torbay* officer, later described one of the attacks, tersely noting, "The troops were not allowed to escape: everything and everybody was destroyed by one sort of gunfire or another."[1]

The *Torbay*'s commander, Anthony Cecil Capel "Tony" Miers, resembled Morton in physicality and disposition. In a sense Miers, like Morton, might be characterized as a spiritual descendant of the berserkers—enraged Viking warriors who went too far in the heat of battle.[2] Like Morton, Tony Miers made no attempt to conceal the killings and received a hero's welcome when he returned to port. The recent battle for Crete, in which German aviators were accused of strafing British survivors in the water, created little mood for generosity toward the enemy. Andrew Cunningham, commander in chief of the Mediterranean Fleet, praised the patrol as "brilliantly conducted."[3]

The main concern arising from Miers's shooting of survivors was that the Germans might take reprisals. The Admiralty in London concluded some months later, "Commanding Officers of submarine can be trusted to follow the dictates of humanity and the traditions of service and it is unnecessary to promulgate general rules which may give the impression that they are not in the habit of doing so."[4]

While there was no official censure, privately Miers received instructions not to repeat the practice.[5]

The incident did little to hinder Miers's naval career. Whereas many believed that the attack on the *Buyo Maru* prevented Mush Morton from being awarded a Congressional Medal of Honor, Miers received the British equivalent, the Victoria Cross, for a daring raid on Corfu Harbor in March 1942. Following promotion, Miers embarked on a speaking tour of the United States and served as the Royal Navy submarine liaison officer at San Francisco and Pearl Harbor.

When Pete Galantin arrived at Midway with the USS *Sculpin* in 1943, he found Miers sharing his experiences with the Americans. Powerfully built, Miers sometimes challenged the U.S. officers to wrestling matches and usually won.[6] In 1944 Miers took command of the Eighth Submarine Flotilla based at Ceylon (now Sri Lanka), and later organized its transfer to Fremantle, Western Australia.

The fates of Miers and Morton offer a contrast to the only German U-boat commander accused of perpetrating an atrocity of comparable scale. On the night of 13 March 1944 the *U-852* under Heinz Wilhelm Eck torpedoed the 4,700-ton Greek freighter *Peleus,* under charter by the British Ministry of War Transport from Freetown to Buenos Aires. After sinking the *Peleus,* the *U-852* patrolled the waters for five hours, systematically shooting survivors and destroying any floating debris. From the original complement of thirty-five, including eight British seamen, only three *Peleus* crewmen survived the ordeal.

Whereas Miers and Morton appear to have acted out of a visceral hatred of the enemy, Eck seemed motivated by fear. The waters where he sank the *Peleus* were notoriously dangerous for U-boats, with four recent losses between Freetown and Ascension; Eck believed that any sign of the sinking would inevitably result in the loss of his own boat. Despite the efforts to cover up the sinking of the *Peleus,* however, the *U-852* came to grief during the same patrol. On 2 May 1944 a British bomber attacked the submarine and forced it to ground on the eastern coast of Africa, resulting in the capture of Eck, his crew, and the submarine's incriminating log. At the end of the war, Eck and two other *U-852* officers were sentenced to death by a British military court for killing of the *Peleus* survivors. They were the only submariners executed for war crimes committed during the Second World War.[7]

The punishment of Eck and his officers to a degree foreshadowed the Nuremberg war crimes trials. In part, Eck's killing of survivors had been motivated by the very efficiency of Allied countermeasures. At Nuremberg the German Navy mounted a similar defense for unrestricted warfare, claiming that the success of Allied antisubmarine forces made the picking up of survivors untenable.[8] The Eck case further figured in the trial of Admiral Karl Dönitz, who not only commanded Germany's submarines from 1935 but in 1943 replaced Erich Raeder as commander in chief of the navy. On the eve of his suicide, Adolf Hitler named Dönitz his successor as Führer, and in this capacity he arranged for Germany's surrender.

British prosecutors at Nuremberg claimed that Dönitz's so-called Laconia Order was tantamount to ordering the killing of survivors from torpedoed ships; the Eck case provided the most tangible outcome of this. Dönitz's instructions, issued by radio on 17 September 1942, did specifically instruct U-boats not to assist the survivors of sunken ships: "All attempts to rescue the crews of sunken ships will cease forthwith. . . . Such activities are a contradiction of the primary object of war, namely, the destruction of enemy ships and their crews."[9] There is no evidence, though, that Dönitz ordered the shooting of survivors. Indeed, the German Navy resisted suggestions by Hitler to do just that as a way of reducing the Allied merchant marine.[10]

At Nuremberg, Otto Kranzbuehler, a former naval judge, ably defended Dönitz. He elicited evidence from the American commander in chief of the Pacific fleet, Admiral Chester Nimitz, that U.S. submarines adopted the same policies of attacking merchant ships without warning and generally did not rescue survivors.[11] Indeed, the senior American judge at Nuremberg, Francis Biddle, concluded that the Germans had fought a "cleaner" submarine war than the Allies. According to Biddle, "[W]e would look like fools if we condemned Admiral Dönitz for doing towards the end of the war, what Admiral Nimitz had begun when the United States entered it."[12]

Although convicted of violating the London Protocol of 1936 and waging aggressive war, Dönitz received no direct punishment for violating the laws of submarine warfare. Indeed, he received the lightest sentence passed on a senior Nazi at Nuremberg, incarcerated at Spandau prison for ten years and twenty days before being released in October 1956.[13]

If Dönitz's punishment smacked of so-called victor's justice, a stronger case could be made for prosecuting the Japanese for atrocities at sea. In no other navy, Mark Felton claims, "was murder the rule rather than the exception."[14] This is no doubt an overstatement, and at least one writer argues that compared to atrocities by the Japanese Army, those committed by the navy "were very limited, and almost incidental."[15] Nevertheless, while Japanese submarines attacked far fewer ships than the Allies or Germans, they were involved in no fewer than a dozen documented atrocities against survivors. According to the Far East Tribunal, the commander of the First Submarine Force at Truk, Rear Admiral Takero Kouta, issued an order on 20 March 1943 instructing: "Do not stop with the sinking of enemy ships and cargoes; at the same time, you will carry out the complete destruction of the crews of the enemy's ships."[16]

Various explanations have been put forward for the Japanese propensity toward atrocities. It has been suggested that such relentless brutality, like their reputation for preferring death to surrender, served the purpose of intimidating their enemies. The Japanese purportedly worried, for example, that if they treated prisoners according to international conventions, American pilots might make one-way bombing attacks on Japan with little fear of being captured. In light of the institutionalized mistreatment dished out within the Japanese military, it is not surprising that the Japanese inflicted even greater cruelty on their prisoners. At the same time, a strong group ethic demanded absolute obedience and discouraged questioning orders or acting on individual conscience. But killing survivors, as in the Eck case, could also simply be a strategy to conceal a submarine's presence in hostile waters.[17]

One of the most notorious Japanese submarine commanders, Hajime Nakagawa, as skipper of the *I-177* sank the Australian hospital ship *Centaur* on 14 May 1943. The 3,222-ton ship had left Sydney two days earlier with 74 crewmen and 257 medical personnel for Port Moresby, New Guinea. Although the ship was painted white with red crosses and sailed with lights on, Nakagawa torpedoed it off the coast of Queensland. Australia's prime minister, John Curtin, denounced the attack as "barbarous" and made a formal protest to the Japanese government.[18] Only 64 of those on the *Centaur* survived. Some sixty-five years later one of the survivors, a twenty-year-old steward when the ship sank, professed that he still had nightmares about the event.[19]

Although the Japanese denied knowing that the *Centaur* was a hospital ship, Nakagawa's later career makes this claim doubtful. He subsequently took command of the *I-37* at Penang, and made a series of murderous attacks on survivors. The previous commander of the *I-37*, Kiyonori Otani, had already used the submarine's guns on survivors after sinking the Norwegian tanker *Scotia*.[20] Under Nakagawa the *I-37* torpedoed the 7,118-ton tanker *British Chivalry* after it departed from Melbourne in February 1944. The submarine crew then turned its 20 mm gun on the lifeboats. Despite the best efforts of the Japanese to kill them, thirty-nine of the fifty-nine crewmen eventually survived in a leaking lifeboat for thirty-seven days before being rescued.

The 5,189-ton British ship *Sutlej* became another victim of Nakagawa and the *I-37*. Carrying a cargo of phosphates and a crew of seventy-three, the ship was torpedoed on 26 February 1944. After the *Sutlej* sank, in under four minutes, the submarine surfaced and opened up its deck guns on the survivors. All but twenty-eight of the crew died in the attack.

The *I-37* next attacked the 7,005-ton steamer *Ascot*. Having departed Colombo for Fremantle, Western Australia, the ship was torpedoed on 29 February 1944. With the *Ascot*'s crew in lifeboats,

Nakagawa demanded that the captain of the British ship identify himself. Once the British officer was taken on board the submarine, Nakagawa reputedly shouted "English swine!" and slashed the captain's hands with a sword before pushing him into the sea. The submarine then began to ram lifeboats and machine-gun the surviving crew. In total, the *I-37* was responsible for the death of 118 seamen in its three attacks on British ships.[21]

Some idea of experiencing a Japanese submarine attack is conveyed by Harold L. Clark, seaman first class on the ship *John A. Johnson*. The 7,176-ton *Johnson* was one of the some 2,700 Liberty ships constructed during the war, and one of the 200 lost on active duty.[22] The ship departed from San Francisco on 24 October 1944 for Honolulu, carrying ammunition, trucks, and provisions; the *I-12,* under the command of Kaneo Kudo, torpedoed it four nights later. Clark had spotted a torpedo wake while standing on the starboard wing of the bridge; when the torpedo hit his ship, the concussion knocked him fifteen feet, showering him in water and oil. Within ten minutes the ship literally broke in two.[23]

All seventy crewmen managed to successfully abandon ship, gathering in three lifeboats and a raft. About a half hour later, however, a Japanese submarine surfaced within a couple of hundred yards of the small craft. After first circling the survivors, the *I-12* tried to ram the boats while its crew fired machine guns and pistols with the aid of a spotlight. Clark recalled being fired on from about 150 feet, close enough to see five American flags painted on the *I-12* bow, representing previous "kills." Another seaman, seventeen-year-old George A. Bushman from Minnesota, was hit by two bullets in the face and a third in the shoulder. The submarine continued to hunt the survivors for forty-five minutes, at times swerving hard in an apparent attempt to strike the men with the stern or screws. The sixty men who survived this onslaught were lucky to be spotted by a passing Pan American aircraft. A ship picked them up the next day, with five of the men requiring hospitalization for injuries from the attack.[24]

Under the Potsdam Declaration and the terms of surrender, Japan accepted that "stern justice" would be visited on war criminals.[25] The

International Military Tribunal for the Far East, which commenced 3 May 1946 and sat until 12 November 1948, tried a total of 5,700 suspected war criminals and convicted 920. Relatively few Japanese submariners faced the consequences of their actions. Some of the worst offenders were already dead, including Vice Admiral Takasu, accused of issuing orders to kill the survivors of submarine attacks. Also dead was Commander Tatsunoke Ariisuni, who had wreaked havoc in the Indian Ocean as skipper of the *I-8*. After sinking the 5,787-ton Dutch steamer *Tjisalak* some 500 miles south of Colombo on 26 March 1944, Ariisuni systematically murdered the survivors. Some were brought on board the submarine, where they were massacred with swords, rifle butts, a sledgehammer, and clubs. One group of prisoners was bound together and dragged behind the submarine before it dived. Only 5 of the 103 crew and passengers lived.

In another atrocity engineered by Ariisuni, over sixty crewmen from the U.S. merchantman *Jean Nicolet* were killed. The 7,176-ton Liberty ship was en route from Australia to Colombo when it was torpedoed on 2 July 1944. Many of the survivors had to run a gauntlet of swords, bayonets, and clubs on the submarine's deck before being knocked into the sea. Another group of survivors was left tied up on deck when the submarine crash-dived. Ariisuni shot himself after Japan surrendered, one of an estimated 500 Japanese officers to commit suicide.[26]

For those who survived the war, the penalties were not as draconian as might be imagined. Lieutenant Sadao Monontaka and Lieutenant Masanori Hattori, who served on the *I-8* at the time of the *Tjisalak* massacre, were sentenced to five and seven years of imprisonment respectively. Lieutenant Commander Kusaka, who as skipper of the *I-26* ordered the shooting of survivors from the *Richard Hoovey*, received a sentence of five years in prison. The notorious Hajime Nakagawa was arrested in Japan and tried as a B-class war criminal; those in the B and C class were accused of committing "conventional" war crimes and tried before some forty-nine tribunals both within and outside Japan. Far from expressing remorse for killing survivors, Nakagawa claimed that he had only fulfilled his duty. A British military tribunal sentenced him to eight years' incarceration, but the Japanese government released him after four years in Sugamo prison.[27]

Perhaps in part these relatively light sentences recognized that the Pacific war had been fought with extraordinary viciousness on all sides. Firing on maritime survivors paled in comparison to some of the horrors committed, such as the alleged beheading and eating of POWs.[28] There seemed, in fact, a common expectation by survivors on both sides that they might be shot in the water. When the Australian coaster *Iron Chieftain* was sunk in June 1942, for example, one of the survivors reported that "the submarine circled our raft and we thought that we might be machine-gunned so we lay still."[29] After the USS *Harder* torpedoed the frigate *Sado* in 1944, Japanese survivors were alarmed to see the submarine surface, assuming they were about to be massacred. Instead, crew on the *Harder's* deck only took photographs of the wreckage before cruising away.[30]

While the behavior of Mush Morton and Tony Miers was exceptional in the Allied camp, the two represented one extreme on a continuum. There were other U.S. submarines at least implicated in the shooting of survivors. After sinking a "fishing-patrol boat" in June 1943, crew on the USS *Sculpin* took potshots at Japanese clinging to wreckage in the water.[31] On one occasion the USS *Bergall* fired on a lifeboat with its 20 mm gun after dispatching a patrol boat in the early hours of 27 January 1945. The patrol report claimed that the crewmen believed the lifeboat empty when they opened fire, although the evidence of an eyewitness is ambiguous. He claimed that they destroyed the lifeboat in part to conceal the submarine's presence in the area.[32]

In 1944 the Japanese government lodged a formal protest against a submarine attack on the 130-ton *Taiei Maru*. The motor vessel carried a crew of six and seventy-seven civilian construction workers and their families on the morning of 3 July 1944, traveling between the islands of Palau and Yap. The Japanese claimed that after shelling set the ship on fire, a submarine circled the vicinity, firing machine guns at people in the water. Floating victims were allegedly probed with poles and if found to be still alive were shot with pistols. The accusations apparently emanated from the *Taiei Maru's* master, who said he escaped by feigning death and that the only other survivors were two women and two of his crew.[33]

There is no doubt that the submarine referred to in the Japanese allegations was the USS *Albacore,* although its patrol report described the wooden interisland steamer as nearly 1,000 tons, and not surprisingly made no reference to shooting survivors. The *Albacore's* commander, James W. Blanchard, gave a very different version of events when requested to respond to the accusations. According to Blanchard, the *Albacore* first fired at the vessel with its four-inch gun from some 6,300 yards away. The vessel took evasive action, and as the submarine gained ground it began firing with its two 20 mm guns and two .30-caliber machine guns. Blanchard insisted that guns were directed "at the target only" and that allegations of the crew firing at survivors in the water were "absolutely untrue."[34]

The fact that the *Albacore* picked up five wounded prisoners would seem to militate against the alleged atrocity. The five survivors (listed as Yakichi Tamura, I. Kubota, Eigoro Ota, H. Kitazano, and A. Seko) were turned over to the provost marshal at Los Negros in the Admiralty Islands. Blanchard also claimed that a rubber life raft stocked with food and water was left alongside two women and a young child clinging to a damaged lifeboat. Both the Japanese version and Blanchard's agreed that during the course of events incoming aircraft forced the submarine to dive a number of times. The Japanese alleged that the *Albacore* surfaced to continue killing survivors, while Blanchard insisted that they were attempting "to rescue other survivors."[35]

Leaving aside whether survivors in the water were shot, the *Albacore* had indisputably turned its considerable firepower on an unarmed craft carrying civilians. As is the case with many other gun attacks, it is possible to interpret the assault on the *Taiei Maru* as motivated partly by frustration. Earlier in the patrol, during what later became known as the battle of the Philippine Sea, the *Albacore* found itself in the midst of a Japanese carrier group south of the Mariana Islands. Blanchard managed to fire off six torpedoes at the 31,000-ton carrier *Taiho* before being driven deep by enemy depth charges. Believing he had failed to sink the carrier, Blanchard brooded over missing such a rare opportunity. He was subsequently ordered to intercept traffic between Palau and Yap, and it may have been the prospect of a barren patrol that spurred the ferocious attack on the *Taiei Maru*. Ironically, months later Blanchard received confirmation that he had indeed sunk the *Taiho* and he was awarded a Navy Cross.

There were other instances when individual submariners shot at survivors on their own initiative. In a postwar interview William Hazzard, skipper of the USS *Blenny,* related an incident in which his executive officer began shooting at a man in the water. After the submarine sank a gunboat in the Java Sea, one of the survivors began shouting and brandishing a knife. The executive officer responded by firing a .45-caliber pistol at the man before Hazzard stopped him and told him they weren't going to shoot anybody in the water.[36]

The impulse to inflict pain and suffering on the enemy at times seemed overwhelming. On the USS *Seahorse* one of the crewmen, who had lost a brother with the battleship *Arizona* at Pearl Harbor, begged the skipper to let him turn a machine gun on some Japanese survivors encountered at sea. In this case the request was refused.[37] Commanding the British submarine HMS *Thule* in the Malacca Straits, Alistair Mars professed, "At times I felt savage: I wanted to lay into some Japanese ship with the *Thule*'s gun, to smash her to pieces and massacre her men."[38] On at least one occasion Mars acted on these impulses; having driven a Japanese vessel onto some rocks, he ordered his gunners to shoot men as they abandoned ship.[39]

In an ecology of violence that not only condoned killing but encouraged it, such incidents can hardly be surprising.[40] American admiral Bull Halsey professed delight in the slaughter of Japanese troops, routinely ending messages with the admonition to "keep 'em dying."[41] As will be documented later, numerous submarine actions might be described as "atrocities" or "war crimes." Far less defensible than the killing of Japanese military personnel, these sometimes involved the death and maiming of civilians, whether Japanese fishermen or local seamen.

PART II

BATTLE STATIONS SURFACED

5

Sampans and Schooners

At least one American officer had made a patrol with Tony Miers and his British submarine *Torbay* in the Mediterranean. Reginald Marbury "Reggie" Raymond graduated toward the top of his class at the Naval Academy in 1933 and later assisted Charles Lockwood, then serving as American naval attaché to Britain. Raymond accompanied the *Torbay*'s eleventh patrol in April 1942 as an observer. One of Raymond's fellow officers, Paul Schratz, later recalled that the stories Raymond told about Miers's gun attacks "were enough to turn anybody's hair."[1] It was a gun attack by an American submarine, though, that cost Raymond his life.

Reggie Raymond, from Shreveport, Louisiana, served as executive officer on the USS *Scorpion* when it made its first patrol under the command of William Wylie. The submarine departed Pearl Harbor in March 1943, assigned to lay a minefield off Honshu. On the outward voyage the *Scorpion* crossed the path of a Japanese patrol vessel near Marcus Island, some 800 miles from Tokyo. With its mission in mind, the *Scorpion* avoided it, but there was brave talk among the crew about what would happen if they encountered the Japanese craft at the end of the patrol.

Later in the patrol, on 20 April, the *Scorpion* spotted a sampan in a streak of moonlight near midnight. Having previously practiced battle surface drills with no real target, Commander Wylie considered it an opportune time to put theory into practice. The *Scorpion* surfaced and riddled the craft at close range with the three-inch gun, 20 mm gun, and .45-caliber machine gun. Although the incendiary effect of the 20 mm ammunition proved disappointing, the explosive shells from the three-inch gun blew gaping holes into the sampan's hull each time they scored a hit. Some fifteen minutes after commencing the attack, the gunners secured from battle stations as their victim burned in the night.

Assuming the submarine's presence was now known, Wylie decided to start attacking any other sampans sighted, ostensibly to keep other small craft close to shore in future. On 22 April three more sampans, the largest estimated to be seventy tons and the smallest half that size, were destroyed with gunfire off northeastern Honshu.[2]

A week later the *Scorpion* began heading back to base at Midway, and on 29 April it used the guns to destroy a small patrol vessel. Although the patrol boat had an old-fashioned gun on its pilothouse, it sank without returning fire. The following morning the submarine encountered a more aggressive patrol vessel, described as about 600 tons and 175 feet long. When the patrol boat headed toward the submarine, the *Scorpion* opened up with its deck guns and managed to get off about fifteen rounds from the three-inch gun before it jammed, just as their adversary passed broadside within about 800 yards. Although the *Scorpion* knocked out the patrol boat's five-pound gun, it received heavy machine-gun and rifle fire. Reggie Raymond, manning a Browning automatic rifle from the bridge, died instantly when a machine-gun bullet passed through the center of his forehead. Also wounded were two other crewmen on the 20 mm guns. Paul Schratz got hit by a ricochet off the conning tower, but it struck his jacket zipper and left only a minor wound on his chest.

The fight continued, with Raymond's body laid out behind the bridge. The *Scorpion* finally backed off and fired its last remaining torpedo set for a depth of only two feet, blowing the patrol boat to bits. The arrival of an aircraft, however, forced the *Scorpion* to dive before the crew could get Raymond's body below. Raymond was an inspirational leader practically worshipped by his men, and his loss came as a devastating blow. The distraught crewmen held a memorial service for their fallen executive officer that evening. Raymond's loss continued to haunt the *Scorpion*'s officers. As Paul Schratz put it, "You can't have an episode like that not affect you for quite a long time, both ashore and in the wardroom."[3]

Other American submarines using their deck guns during 1943 attacked a miscellany of small vessels, which at times proved more dangerous than they first appeared. Having spotted a column of four apparently unarmed vessels off the northwest corner of Borneo, the USS *Finback* mounted a gun attack in the early afternoon of 19 August 1943. The *Finback* crew believed two of the ships, resembling mine planters, were between 500 and 1,000 tons. The other two craft were described as a small tug and an interisland steamer or barge.

Once the *Finback* opened fire, the lead ship turned and fired what was believed to be a one-pound gun. The vessel continued to close on the *Finback* before the submarine smothered it in fire from its three 20 mm guns and two .50-caliber machine guns. The second mine-planter vessel then began closing on the *Finback* firing a machine gun, but the bullets fell about 100 yards short. The *Finback* scored a number of hits with its four-inch gun, setting the ship on fire. In the meantime, the first mine planter came back into the fray, straddling the *Finback* with fire from 8,500 yards. The patrol report noted laconically, "[D]ecided the one pounder had gotten larger, and as we only had twenty rounds of 4 inch left, retired to westward."[4]

Most gun targets were less well defended. Out of a total of 121 craft attacked during 1943 in U.S. submarine gun actions, 48 were described as sampans.[5] As originally derived from the Chinese, *sampan* literally meant three planks. Although the term implied a rudimentary craft, it came to embrace a range of vessels that might be powered by sail or motor; they might be old and dilapidated or fairly new and large.[6] Some submariners believed sampans were employed as enemy decoys, either armed with formidable weapons or used as bait to expose submarines to lurking aircraft. At the least, American submariners regarded them as a nuisance, and some sank sampans as a matter of routine.[7]

Like the men of the *Scorpion*, there were others who saw attacks on sampans as an opportunity to practice their gunnery. Within days of the *Scorpion*'s first attack on a sampan, the USS *Snook* made a similar assault. Off Japan at Sandon Iwa Island on the afternoon of 25 April 1943, the *Snook* crew spotted a fifty-foot Japanese fishing vessel described as a diesel-powered sampan. Commander Chuck Triebel later reported that the target "was a little fellow and hard to hit outside 800 yards."[8] As this was the *Snook*'s first gun engagement, the gunners lacked experience and began by shooting wildly. In the absence of return fire, though, they quickly settled down and in twenty minutes had left the sampan a total shambles.

Pete Galantin affords a vivid account of some of the attacks in which he participated while serving on the USS *Sculpin* skippered by Lucius Chappell. Galantin joined the *Sculpin* as a PCO (prospective commanding officer) in order to gain experience with a more seasoned skipper before getting his own command. In the submarine's first gun attack during the seventh patrol, the *Sculpin* battle surfaced in early-morning darkness within 1,000 yards of a steel-hulled sampan estimated to be about 300 tons. The gun crews poured a deafening fire at the craft with the three-inch gun, two 20 mm guns, and two .50-caliber machine guns, sometimes circling within 100 yards. Despite a few flashes of small-arms fire from the sampan, it posed little serious resistance before it burst into flames and then slipped under the waves. The attack, as Galantin described it, represented "the crescendo of violence, the upwelling of fierce retributive emotion in men suddenly face-to-face with an enemy for the first time."[9]

Within twenty-four hours the *Sculpin* spotted another sampan, this time estimated at only seventy-five tons. One of the *Sculpin* officers, Corwin Mendenhall, described the vessel as a "fishing-patrol boat," noting that it had an impressive array of radio antenna.[10] Under cover of a fog bank, the submarine battle surfaced for a gun action; within forty minutes the vessel, identified as the *Miyashiyo Maru* on its stern, began sinking as it burned.

This time a small party boarded the sampan to inspect the damage. Armed with knives and .45 pistols, four crewmen jumped onto the wallowing Japanese boat. A fifth man, Lieutenant Joseph Defrees, missed the jump and ended up in the dangerous gap between the vessels. According to Mendenhall, some of the *Sculpin* men on the bow of the submarine were shooting at Japanese in the water at the time. He hurriedly stopped them lest they hit Defrees, who was yelling, "Don't shoot me!"[11] Defrees ran the additional risk of being crushed between the submarine and its victim.

Pete Galantin's account of the incident suggests that the boarding party found all five Japanese crewmen on board dead, but the *Sculpin*'s patrol report indicates that the Americans discovered two Japanese armed with rifles in the forecastle. Ambiguously, the report simply notes, "They were shot."[12] Although some small arms were found, the boarding party discovered that the machine guns mounted fore and aft were wooden replicas, so-called quakers. Presumably intended to deter attack, they had failed miserably.

Galantin reported that "exhilaration" pervaded the mess that evening, and that the attacks "lifted the spirits of the *Sculpin*'s crew."[13] The *Sculpin*'s commander, on the other hand, found the experience disheartening. It would be Lucius Chappell's last gun attack. Although the boarding party had presented him with a souvenir samurai sword from the sampan, according to one report he later tried to return it to the owner's family.[14]

Following a series of gun attacks on small schooners, the crewmen of the USS *Bowfin* exhibited a similar ambivalence toward their victims. The terms *sampan* and *schooner* were sometimes used interchangeably by submariners, but of the sixteen submarine gun attacks on craft described as "schooners" during 1943, the *Bowfin* made five.[15]

Today the restored *Bowfin* (SS 287) sits moored at Pearl Harbor, part floating museum and part memorial to the fleet boats of World War II. Because its keel was laid only eight days after the Japanese assault on Pearl Harbor and it was launched on the first anniversary of the attack, the *Bowfin* earned the nickname Pearl Harbor Avenger. Some of its most successful patrols, however, emanated from Australia rather than Pearl Harbor. Walter Thomas "Walt" Griffith took command of the *Bowfin* for its second patrol at Fremantle in Western Australia.

Griffith, a wiry five foot seven inches tall, with a ruddy complexion, pale eyes, and red hair, was born in Mansfield, Louisiana.

He graduated from the Naval Academy in 1934, and was thirty-three years old when he took command of the *Bowfin* in November 1943. To his crewmen he exuded so much confidence that they claimed his initials stood for "Water Tight," an assurance that they would never sink.[16]

When the submarine encountered a group of two-masted schooners off Indochina on the morning of 9 November 1943, Griffith showed no hesitation in attacking. The *Bowfin* sank three of the schooners within an hour using its guns, and then sank a fourth later in the afternoon. Each of the craft carried twenty to thirty people, and sank within minutes of being fired on. The patrol report marveled at "the abruptness with which they went down, taking masts, spars and sails with them."[17]

Griffith justified the attacks, claiming that the schooners must have been carrying something heavy, possibly construction materials, since they sank so quickly. For some men of the crew, though, the sight of not just men but women and children struggling in the water was more than they had bargained for. Griffith's executive officer on the patrol, William Thompson, stated that he would not have attacked some of the small craft. There were also those who subsequently claimed that Griffith expressed regret over the attacks in later years.[18]

At the time such actions caused little controversy. That the enemy was employing schooners to move supplies appeared to be confirmed, at least in Griffith's mind, by an incident on the *Bowfin*'s next patrol. On 16 January 1944, while the submarine was on a track for Balikpapan, the crew spotted a small craft in the distance. Its single mast and triangular sail gave the appearance of an ordinary fishing boat. On closer inspection, however, the craft proved to be a nicely painted schooner about sixty feet in length but without a schooner rig. A number of the vessel's crew jumped overboard when the submarine approached, although in the darkness the men of the *Bowfin* were unable to discern whether they were "natives." Griffith assumed the craft was probably "a spotter," and sank it with the 20 mm gun.[19]

Some other submariners were more circumspect. In June 1943, while patrolling off the north point of Jaluit in the Marshall Islands, the USS *Pollack* battle surfaced on a sailing schooner and began shelling the craft. As the submarine closed on the vessel, however, it looked considerably smaller than first thought and Commander Bafford Edward Lewellen ordered the crew to cease fire. When the submarine pulled alongside, the crew discovered five fishermen on a "small native craft."[20] The fishermen were given some bread and candy bars to compensate them for their scare. Even so, some members of the crew thought letting the craft go was a mistake. The following week, aircraft shadowed the *Pollack,* leading to speculation that the fishermen had reported its presence.

The Japanese did in fact often use small craft for transporting ammunition, fuel, and other supplies. As one *Bowfin* crew member put it, "If not subject to attack, they could get away with murder."[21] The Japanese had already turned to small vessels for logistical support during the Guadalcanal campaign in the Solomon Islands. The United States began its counteroffensive on the jungle-covered island by seizing the Japanese airfield, but then faced fierce resistance. The Americans, nevertheless, were largely able to cut off the Japanese supply lines. The last attempt to supply the Japanese garrison with ships of over 1,000 tons came in November 1942, when American aircraft managed to sink seven of eleven transports. The Japanese tried using destroyers and, as already noted, submarines, for delivering supplies. Far more cargo, however, could be carried by a wooden ship of only 250 tons than a submarine. Faced with difficulties of supply and growing numbers of troops dying of starvation as well as disease, the Japanese finally evacuated the island on 7 February 1943, exactly six months after the first U.S. Marines landed.[22]

A U.S. submarine bulletin issued in July 1943 put an official imprimatur on attacking small craft; while warning that "submarines are not suited to engage in gun fights with the enemy," it noted that guns could be effectively used against junks, schooners, and other small vessels. As the Japanese suffered mounting shipping losses, they increasingly resorted to such craft to transport equipment, supplies, and personnel. "Such damage," the bulletin claimed, "while small individually, in the long run will produce results."[23]

For most submarines, destroying small craft remained a sideline while much larger prey remained to be had. The burgeoning success of the submarine service at this time can be attributed to a number of factors. A key element was the cracking of Japanese codes and the consequent dissemination of intelligence generically referred to as "Ultra." At the beginning of 1943 American cryptanalysts had broken the "*maru* code," the Japanese Navy code for directing the merchant marine.[24] Although the code breakers were initially reluctant to share Ultra materials for fear that they might be compromised, submarines were soon receiving information on enemy ship movements directly through their own special code.

At Pearl Harbor, Charles Lockwood and his operations officer, Richard Voge, collected the latest intelligence every morning. In the vast reaches of the Pacific, the projected routes of Japanese merchantmen proved invaluable. Submarines were supplied with the estimated speed and course of Japanese vessels so that they could plot an interception. During 1943 the code breakers steered submarines toward over 800 targets, and although less than 100 of these were actually sunk or damaged, it still represented significant Japanese losses.[25] To paraphrase a saying that gained currency among submarine commanders, they went out "by the light of the Ultra and the dark of the moon."[26] Charles Lockwood estimated that the information was responsible for about half of all Japanese ships sunk by submarines during the war.[27]

Improvement in American torpedoes was another important contributor to the growing success of U.S submarines. In June 1943 submarines under the Pacific Command were ordered to deactivate the highly fickle magnetic exploders. Other problems with the navy's steam torpedoes were gradually worked out, and by late 1943 most of the defects had been rectified. A reliable electric torpedo also finally became available. The first enemy ship confirmed sunk by a Mark-18 electric torpedo came in October 1943. Although not without teething problems, the electrics could be fired in shallower water than the steam torpedoes, and left no telltale wake to disclose a submarine's location.[28]

In the meantime, the number of American fleet boats in the Pacific steadily increased, from 47 in February 1943 to 104 fifteen months later. Submarines were also being better supplied with spare parts as well as torpedoes. The net effect allowed them to largely sever Japan's supply lines to its overseas colonies and troops. By the end of 1943 Japan had lost merchant ships approaching a total of 3 million tons. Japan had started the war with an inadequate tanker fleet, and in 1943 less than one-third of the oil shipped from the south actually reached Japan.[29]

Such losses finally prompted the Japanese to begin using convoys, especially for tankers transporting oil from the East Indies. The belatedly created Japanese Grand Escort Command Headquarters began operations in November 1943. In a sense, though, the new escort system made convoys even more vulnerable; increased communications between vessels afforded American cryptographers more opportunities to determine their location. The Escort Command also remained grossly underresourced. By this stage of the war, Japan already faced a shortage of destroyers and aircraft to conduct antisubmarine warfare.[30] According to staff officer Atsushi Oi, "Japan failed in ASW [antisubmarine warfare] largely because her navy disregarded the importance of the problem."[31]

Given the precarious state of shipping lanes and the loss of so many large merchant ships, the Japanese turned increasingly to smaller craft for carrying supplies. Compared to America's mass production of Liberty ships, Japanese shipbuilding techniques had hardly evolved since prewar days. With shortages of steel and skilled labor, the production of wooden-hulled ships increased. The Wartime Shipping Control Act of 1942 allowed the government to requisition all merchant vessels over 100 tons and all sailing ships with engines over 150 tons. Shortages of oil also put a premium on ships that could travel under sail. Most of the vessels being turned out were between 100 and 200 tons.[32] According to one later claim, the Japanese used Chinese slave labor to mass-produce schooners for their depleted merchant marine.[33]

The use of wooden vessels offered some advantages in evading Allied submarines. They could operate in shallower waters, where submarines were much more exposed. Wooden hulls were also less vulnerable to magnetic mines. Although ships relying on sail moved more slowly, they were in a sense often safer. They left no telltale trails of smoke, frequently the first sign tipping off a submarine to a ship's presence. The use of smaller craft for short trips and coastal routes helped free up larger merchantmen for longer voyages.[34]

From the Allied side there was a continuing sense that attacking small craft not only damaged the enemy but served as a blooding for submarine crews. Late in 1944, for example, the USS *Barb* under command of Eugene Fluckey launched an early-morning attack on two schooners. Under an overcast sky and light drizzle of rain, Fluckey proclaimed the conditions "ideal for a small ship gun shoot."[35] The *Barb* made short work of the vessels with its four-inch and 40 mm guns, and sank a third schooner the same morning. In a personal message Charles Lockwood later sent Fluckey, he described the attacks not only as an "inspiring battle" but as "excellent gun practice."[36]

6

Pickets and the Picayune

The Allied submarine offensive continued to gather momentum during 1944, with Japan suffering its most catastrophic shipping losses of the war. In the first six months of the year U.S. submarines sank more than 300 enemy merchantmen, amounting to a million tons of shipping. By the end of the year the tally approached the combined total for 1942 and 1943.[1] In addition, U.S. submarines sank significant numbers of warships, including seven aircraft carriers and thirty destroyers.

In the assessment of submarine commander Lawson "Red" Ramage, the disruption of oil and other supplies from the Dutch East Indies did much to "throttle" the whole Japanese war effort. As Ramage saw it, the Japanese "depended so heavily on Indonesia and that area down there that anything we could do to intercept that logistic line was going to pay off heavily, and did."[2] Indeed, during 1944 Japan consumed over 19 million barrels of oil, but could only import 5 million barrels in compensation. Whereas Japan had been able to replace its tanker losses in 1942 and 1943, submarines quadrupled the number of tankers sunk in 1944.[3]

The South China Sea, extending some 1,500 miles from Singapore to Formosa, offered an especially rewarding hunting ground for submarines. In one month, February 1944, submarines wiped out an entire convoy of five tankers in the South China Sea. Shortages of fuel meant that Japanese warships often sailed at restricted speeds, which in turn increased their vulnerability to submarine attack. Japan suffered a similar decline of imports overall. In 1944 the total tonnage of Japanese imports was less than half that of 1941, falling from over 48 million tons to less than 22 million tons.[4]

With the capture of Saipan and other islands in the Mariana group in mid-1944, the Allies penetrated the so-called Absolute National Defense Zone once considered essential by Japan to continue the war and protect the home islands. The loss of the Marianas represented a huge psychological blow, prompting the en masse resignation of Prime Minister Tojo and his war cabinet.[5] With forward bases at Saipan and Guam, the American submarine blockade became more effective than ever. Japanese convoy routes became increasingly restricted to the South China Sea and East China Sea; by September 1944 the Japanese had abandoned convoy routes east of the Philippines.[6]

During 1944 American submarines made 520 war patrols, firing 6,092 torpedoes (more than the total fired during 1942 and 1943 combined).[7] The submarine onslaught also included an increasing number of gun attacks. In 1943, 37 different U.S. submarines made a total of 121 gun attacks, compared to 1944, when 83 different American submarines carried out 201 gun attacks.

At least one submarine made a gun attack on an oil tanker. On the evening of 27 March 1944, the USS *Hake* fired four torpedoes at an unescorted ship off Borneo estimated at 10,000 tons. Although damaged, the ship continued to circle at slow speed, so the *Hake* battle surfaced in an attempt to finish off its prey with gunfire. The gunners scored about thirty hits with common and high-capacity shells, putting holes in the ship's plating and rekindling fires. The *Hake* finally finished off the tanker with a torpedo from the stern tubes.[8]

The most common craft attacked, however, continued to be those described as sampans. These represented the targets in nearly one-third of submarine gun attacks in 1944, while over fifty attacks were made on "trawlers" (see the appendix). The USS *Finback,* for example, claimed the sinking of one trawler and damage on another in late January 1944. Returning from its patrol area in the East China Sea, the *Finback* elected to turn its guns on a vessel estimated to be 100 tons. Despite return small-arms fire and rough sea conditions, the *Finback* eventually managed to wipe out the trawler's superstructure. The *Finback* attacked another trawler the next day, finishing off the remainder of its four-inch ammunition.[9]

The USS *Jack* also made its first battle surface on a trawler, after spotting the vessel apparently patrolling Balintang Channel north of Luzon on the morning of 27 April 1944. Using the three-inch gun mounted some fifteen feet forward of the bridge, the *Jack* gun crew made a fairly impressive debut, scoring about twenty hits out of thirty rounds. The trawler, identified as *Dun Sai,* quickly burned. Inspired by this initial success, the *Jack* sank another trawler by gunfire the following morning.[10]

As Japanese freighters became scarcer, convoys of small craft became more common. In 1944 the Japanese constructed 254,000 tons of wooden ships.[11] Patrolling the area off the east coast of Okinawa on 3 May 1944, the USS *Halibut* encountered a group of eighteen wooden-hulled motor sampans. Many had sails rigged and were estimated to be about 150 feet long and 250 tons. Although the vessels might have been taken for a fishing fleet, they appeared to lack the requisite fishing gear and were escorted by a larger trawler. Given that its combined hull capacity was estimated to be about the same as a medium-sized freighter, the convoy represented a not insignificant potential source of supplies to the Japanese.

At 9:20 in the evening, the *Halibut* began firing its 20 mm gun and .50-caliber machine gun at the two trailing sampans. Return fire wounded two of the submarine's gun loaders, but the *Halibut* pressed the attack. One of the sampans exploded so violently that a piece of flying metal wounded a lookout on the *Halibut.* The explosion, as well as the heavy smell of gunpowder in the air, led the submarine's crew to conclude that the sampan carried munitions.[12]

The following month, in his endorsement of the USS *Tunny*'s sixth war patrol, the commander of Submarine Squadron Four, Charles Frederick Erck, noted, "The enemy's ever increasing use of 'targets not worth a torpedo' . . . effectively nullified our submarine warfare to the extent that cargoes are delivered."[13] Submarines, though, were taking an increasing toll on small craft with gun attacks.

The USS *Sunfish,* under Edward E. Shelby, carried out one of the most spectacular attacks off Paramushiro in the Kurile Islands. Officially described in a patrol endorsement as "an outstanding gun battle," the attack claimed the destruction of thirteen sampans as well as a larger trawler-type patrol vessel.[14] On 7 July 1944 the *Sunfish* emerged from a fog shortly after noon to investigate some radar contacts. With the deck guns manned, the crew first sighted a sampan estimated to be 250 tons about 500 yards off the starboard bow. Soon additional sampans were spotted ahead. The *Sunfish's* firepower, along with the element of surprise, gave it an immediate advantage, and as described by the patrol report, the action "[d]eveloped into a nice melee with us doing much circling until the entire group, including large flankers was wiped out."[15]

With the submarine's four-inch gun, 20 mm cannons, .50- and .30-caliber machine guns, and BARs firing simultaneously, both the noise and volume of fire from the *Sunfish* was horrific. High-capacity thin-walled shells from the four-inch gun obliterated large sections of the vessels, especially any upper works above deck. As described by the patrol report, "The terrible destructive power of the small guns literally cut the targets to pieces while the deck gun literally burst them apart at the seams."[16] Not surprisingly, the Japanese showed little will to fight back while being fired on; some preferred to jump into the freezing waters rather than risk being blown to pieces.

Even so, some of the Japanese craft charged toward the submarine as if to ram it. Most of the enemy fire either went overhead or fell harmlessly short. The only apparent damage to the *Sunfish* was a bullet hole in the periscope shears and a shot-down antenna. The greatest danger came from the debris of exploding sampans, which sometimes flew overhead.

Over the course of two hours, the *Sunfish* crew expended nearly 6,000 shells. At times the submarine's gun crews fired in several directions at once, and from distances of only thirty yards. Stationed in the conning tower, executive officer Paul Mansell passed radar information to Commander Shelby topside. According to some claims, the attacks represented "the most significant instance of submarine deck gun action of World War II."[17]

The Japanese fishing vessels sunk in the action included the *Hokuyo Maru No. 105, Kannon Maru No. 5, Ebisu Maru,* and *Kinei Maru.*[18] When the *Sunfish* later circled the wreckage the crew spotted no one still alive. The patrol report commented dryly, "Looked for survivors but they don't last long in water of 31 deg F."[19]

On other occasions Japanese resistance proved more effective. On its sixth war patrol the USS *Gunnel,* under skipper Guy E. O'Neil, unwittingly took on more than bargained for. Sailing off Mindoro in the Philippines, the crewmen of the *Gunnel* spotted numerous small wooden ships, but they kept to shallow water, leaving little prospect of a successful torpedo attack. Eventually the *Gunnel* tracked a convoy of sea trucks. Typically distinguished by their boxlike design, sea trucks could range from 100 to 1,000 tons. They could sail substantial distances in the open sea and, while primarily used for moving cargo, were sometimes armed.[20] To the *Gunnel* crewmen the craft appeared "fairly defenseless," and with no aircraft evident, they decided to "pick off a couple by gunfire."[21]

At 2:40 in the afternoon the *Gunnel* surfaced within several thousand yards of the sea trucks and opened up with its four-inch and 20 mm guns. Almost immediately both of the 20 mm Oerlikons jammed. Used extensively on British submarines, the Oerlikon became the most widely used automatic weapon of the U.S. Navy after initial testing in early 1943. The Bureau of Ordnance developed a twin-mounted version that first came into use in September 1944. Unfortunately, it remained prone to jamming.[22]

The four-inch gun proved no more effective, overshooting its targets by about 2,000 yards. At first there was some return machine-gun fire, which fell well short of the submarine. But then at least two of the sea trucks returned fire with large guns being towed behind them on barges. Initially covered by camouflaged tarpaulins, the exposed guns now offered a serious threat to the *Gunnel*'s survival.

The *Gunnel* cleared its deck and dived, but one of the crew was reported overboard. The missing crewman, Rudolph William Velle, motor machinist's mate first class from Irvington, New Jersey, was a *Gunnel* plank owner, having served with the boat since its commissioning. Velle also acted as the gun captain, and when the *Gunnel* had fired its last round from the four-inch gun, the recoil knocked him into the sea.

With an enemy patrol boat and aircraft arriving on the scene, the *Gunnel* remained unable to surface and search for Velle until evening. They found nothing. For skipper Guy O'Neil, the incident became the source of nightmares for some time. The crew did not give up all hope, however, since Velle was known to be a strong swimmer and perhaps capable of making the fourteen miles to land. Indeed, as was eventually discovered, Velle made it to the beach. After meeting some local Filipino guerrillas, he was evacuated on a schooner. As fate would have it, the schooner sank in a typhoon, but Velle again survived, this time in a lifeboat. The USS *Hake* finally picked him up on 4 December 1944 when the submarine retrieved over twenty evacuees off the island of Panay.[23]

As the experience of the *Gunnel* suggests, numerous factors had to be weighed before undertaking a surface gun action. These included not only the potential firepower of enemies but their potential to summon assistance and the proximity to enemy airfields.[24] When the USS *Barb* patrolled off the Japanese naval base of Sasebo on Kyushu, they encountered a large trawler equipped not only with radio antennae but a two-inch cannon, 20 mm gun, and fully-loaded depth charge racks. After a discussion in the wardroom, the officers decided not to make an attack lest the *Barb* expose its position and because rough sea conditions precluded accurate gunnery.[25]

Even with relatively light arms, small craft sometimes offered stiff resistance. On the morning of 19 April 1944 the USS *Finback* encountered a half dozen sampans, apparently carrying supplies to Nowin Island in the Caroline group. The *Finback* opened fire on the last sampan in the column. Despite hits from the *Finback*'s four-inch gun, the sampan continually attempted to close on the submarine, forcing it to turn away so that it could stay out of machine-gun range. Eventually the *Finback* demolished the sampan's deckhouse and engine, killing any crew members who didn't jump overboard.[26]

Patrolling off the Japanese home islands, the USS *Batfish* came across a large trawler with an escort on the morning of 1 July 1944.

Although the trawler appeared unarmed, the presence of the escort suggested that it might be carrying important cargo. Skipper John K. Fyfe ordered a gun action against the vessels. The *Batfish* sank the trawler with relative ease after scoring at least ten clean hits from the four-inch gun.

In the meantime the escort, described as "a yacht type patrol vessel," put up a valiant fight. Although the yacht carried three depth charges in racks aft, its main offensive weapons were three machine guns. It continually tried to move in on the submarine despite being strafed by 20 mm and .50-caliber machine-gun fire. Fyfe recorded a grudging admiration for the enemy's "intestinal fortitude."[27] Once the *Batfish* turned the four-inch gun on the yacht, though, its fate was sealed. The submarine demolished the vessel's topside, and then a fire set off its depth charges. The *Batfish* found no survivors in the wreckage.

The *Batfish* had also suffered a casualty. One of the gun loaders, Thomas F. Allen Jr., was hit by .30-caliber bullets in the knee and backside. Even so, for many of the crewmen the gun action provided a welcome diversion; Fyfe noted that most of the men, experiencing their first battle surface, responded "like a kid with a new toy."[28]

Just as the potential of targets to fight back varied enormously, so too did the attitudes of submariners toward their victims. Patrolling the Java Sea on its first war patrol, the USS *Bergall* launched a gun attack on a small sailboat on the afternoon of 2 November 1944. The craft appeared to be loaded with cargo, and from 1,000 yards the *Bergall* fired across the vessel's bow with the 20 mm and 40 mm guns. The sailboat's crewmen seemingly disappeared below deck, leading the *Bergall*'s skipper to reason "that if they were unarmed they would dive overboard where we could see them." The patrol report continued, "Opened fire and destroyed boat to protect our topside personnel from possible treachery."[29]

On closer inspection the sailboat proved unarmed. The crew, described as "seven Malays, one possibly Jap," had in fact jumped overboard on the side not visible by the *Bergall*. The patrol report re-flected a fairly cavalier attitude toward their survival. Although the men were twenty-five miles from land, the report stated, they could construct a raft from the debris of the boat and the men could subsist on the cargo of chickens and coconuts. The patrol report concluded, "Regret the whole affair as picayune."[30]

In this case, division commander Leon Joseph "Savvy" Huffman criticized the *Bergall*'s approach in his endorsement of the patrol report. Huffman earned his nickname at the Naval Academy, where he graduated toward the top of his class. Starting out as a submarine training officer on America's East Coast, Huffman had a reputation for thoroughness and for not letting anything get past him.[31] In this instance he commented: "Attacks on such craft in this area should not be made unless and until positive evidence of the enemy character of the vessel is established."[32]

Similar criticism was made on an endorsement of the USS *Hake*'s third patrol. Squadron commander John Meade Haines "regretted" an attack on a Malay sailboat during the patrol, although he also allowed that "the decision of the Commanding Officer to attack was justified."[33] The *Hake*'s skipper, John C. Broach, went to some lengths to justify the gun action against a forty-foot sloop estimated at fifteen tons. According to the patrol report, the vessel did not have the usual native rig, was not fishing, was eighty miles from land, and appeared to have an antenna. The *Hake* first fired "challenging bursts" from its 20 mm gun across the vessel's bow. At this point the sloop made the mistake of changing course and then hoisting a Japanese flag. Under fire from the 20 mm and two .30-caliber machine guns, the craft disintegrated and sank. The crew proved to be Malaysians, with at least one going down with the ship.[34]

Other submariners demonstrated greater discretion in dealing with noncombatants. A bit after noon on 6 December 1944, the crew of the USS *Segundo* spotted a group of five craft emerging from the passage between the islands of Fuga and Dalupiri at the northern extremity of the Philippines. The vessels included a junk with a large rising sun painted on the side, but although Commander James Douglas Fulp Jr. described it as a "big temptation," he decided not to attack since the other craft appeared to be Filipino.[35]

Patrolling the Philippines in mid-1944, the *Flying Fish* checked small fishing craft before determining whether to destroy them. On one vessel the crew found eleven frightened locals who "sat still as mice as we circled them."[36] Taking pity on them, the submariners traded some rice for bananas. When an investigated craft proved to be "innocent," submariners not uncommonly gave those on board some goods as a form of consolation. After checking a two-masted lugger near Bawean Island in December 1944, for example, the crew of the USS *Hawkbill* handed over a carton of cigarettes.[37] Patrolling off Singapore, the *Pintado* similarly bestowed rice, cigarettes, and matches on some "very friendly natives" once establishing that they were genuine fishermen.[38]

Exchanges of food were also not uncommon. After planting mines in the vicinity of the Yangtze River, the USS *Snook* waylaid a junk on 1 May 1943 looking for someone who could act as a Chinese interpreter. The crew found no one who could speak English but ended up trading a loaf of bread and a can of tomatoes for some dry salted fish.[39]

While patrolling the Sulu Archipelago in June 1944, the USS *Puffer* experienced similar communication problems. In the Sibutu Passage the submarine encountered three outrigger canoes, but apart from managing to trade two pounds of rice for a fish, a pineapple, and some breadfruit, the crews found little common ground. An attempt to "parley" with locals on a sailboat in the Molucca Sea a week later went little better. A list of Malay words prepared by the Bureau of Personnel appeared unhelpful. Nevertheless, according to the patrol report, "[A]ll parted best of friends, they with my peace offering of two or three pounds of rice and five packages of cigarettes and we with nothing."[40]

At times encounters at sea took on the character of humanitarian relief. In the Yellow Sea, the USS *Sunfish* pulled alongside to inspect a Chinese junk on the morning of 5 December 1944. Apparently blown far off course by storms, those on board were found in considerable distress. The patrol report noted, "We gave them a lot of food amid much grateful bowing."[41]

As the submarine pulled away, the Chinese on the junk frantically wailed and gestured that they also needed water. As the *Sunfish* started to transfer some water, however, a bomber appeared, forcing the submarine to crash-dive. According to the skipper, abandoning the junk at this stage was not an option: "My crew would have mutinied, I am sure, if I hadn't of [*sic*] planned to get the water, and other gear collected, aboard the junk." The submarine received a "royal welcome" when it surfaced again near the junk. Once the men had transferred supplies, those on the junk "all kneeled and bowed three times and then rose and cheered." The *Sunfish* crew cheered back, and so ended what was described as "a very touching incident."[42]

On 20 October 1944 the forces under General Douglas MacArthur began reclaiming the Philippines with landings at Leyte Gulf. As described by writer James Hornfischer, Leyte Gulf became "the most sprawling, spectacular, and horrible naval battle in history."[43] Involving nearly 500 ships, the battle offered Japan's last opportunity to score a major victory; instead, the Japanese lost most of what remained of their naval and air power. The Imperial Japanese Navy had already suffered the loss of forty-three submarines to Allied antisubmarine operations during the first eight months of the year. The Americans went on to take the Philippine's main island of Luzon, allowing them to further cut off the sea-lanes between Japan and the imports, especially oil, so desperately needed from the south.[44]

Destruction of Japanese shipping by U.S. submarines reached its peak in October, claiming 322,625 tons. When the USS *Halibut* sailed across the Philippine Sea that month, its crew found the waters thick with the remnants of sunken ships—oil drums, kegs, crates, and life belts.[45] Thereafter contacts with enemy ships and the "big bags" of earlier times fell off dramatically. According to Admiral Ralph Christie, the "golden age" of submarine warfare had come to a close by the end of 1944. With Allied air bases being established in the Philippines and the Mariana Islands, aircraft increasingly encroached on waters that had once been a submarine preserve. The remnants of Japanese shipping, in Christie's words, consisted mainly of "small stuff."[46]

At the same time, the number of U.S. submarines in the Pacific continued to increase, reaching 200 by the end of the year.[47] If it were not quite true that one was able to walk to Singapore on their periscopes, as some dispirited Japanese claimed, still, the toll they took on shipping became obvious in innumerable personal histories. When the soldier Takashi Namiki left Japan for Borneo, for instance, a submarine sank his transport outside Takao Harbor on 21 September 1944. He left Manila on another transport on 15 October, but a submarine sank this ship too. Finally, a month later, Namiki departed for Borneo with fifty-six other troops on a 150-foot wooden craft. This time they were sunk by an aircraft.[48]

The increasing use of small craft to transport both troops and supplies was directly noted by submarines. While "lifeguarding" for air strikes on Palau in July 1944, the USS *Balao* sank a 100-ton lugger with fifty Japanese marines on board.[49] When the USS *Hawkbill* destroyed a 300-ton sea truck in December 1944, the crew found about 100 oil drums in the wreckage.[50]

During 1944 Lew Parks, former commander of the *Pompano,* found the opportunity to resurrect his fascination with both gun attacks and photography. Now a squadron commander, Parks headed a wolf pack from Midway consisting of the *Parche,* the *Hammerhead,* and the *Steelhead;* Parks rode with the *Parche,* skippered by Red Ramage. The *Parche* made its first enemy contact south of the Bonin Islands when it came across a picket described as a brand-new steel ship of about 1,500 tons. The *Parche* began to attack with its four-inch gun at 3,500 yards and then added fire from the 40 mm guns. The submarine crewmen were lucky to get some early hits on the picket, knocking out its steering so that it circled aimlessly before going up in flames. To Ramage's bemusement, in the midst of the action Lew Parks came to the bridge laden with movie equipment and began filming the attack in color.[51]

With larger targets becoming scarce, some submarines were being deployed specifically to attack small picket boats. On 10 November 1944 a group of seven submarines left Saipan under Commander Thomas Burton Klakring, charged with clearing the area west and north of the Volcano and Bonin islands in the run-up to a carrier strike. Following a two-day briefing conference on the USS *Fulton,* the submarines departed to complete their mission in an eight-day period.[52]

Such missions, though, could prove dangerous for unexpected reasons. On 17 November the USS *Ronquil* carried out a gun attack in tandem with the USS *Burrfish* south of Honshu. In heavy seas and limited visibility, the submarines opened fire on a 400-ton patrol craft identified as the *Fusa Maru.* The *Burrfish* was hit by return fire, but the *Ronquil* suffered even more serious, self-inflicted damage when a five-inch shell accidentally exploded against a deck stanchion. Blowing two holes in the pressure hull above the after-torpedo room, the mishap put the *Ronquil* in serious jeopardy. Making repairs in the heavy seas proved difficult, but the crew managed to fix the hull sufficiently to dive the boat. Executive officer Lincoln Marcey later received a Navy Cross for his efforts in leading the repair party.[53]

Another submarine in the group, the USS *Tambor,* also sustained damage from enemy fire. Commanding the *Tambor* on its twelfth war patrol, Bill Germershausen ordered a battle surface after failing to sink a Japanese patrol vessel with six torpedoes. The submarine crew managed to sink the ninety-five-ton *Taikai Maru* and collected two wounded prisoners. One of the *Tambor* crewmen, however, had been injured in the return fire. Robert Eugene Baggett, motor machinist mate third class, acting as trainer on the five-inch gun, received a serious wound in the left leg; two days later he was transferred to the destroyer USS *Grayson* for medical treatment along with the two wounded prisoners. Germershausen later characterized the mission as "a masterpiece of confusion."[54]

Given more frequent gun attacks on small craft, submarine armament became more formidable. As described by British liaison officer Tony Miers, new-construction American submarines were fitted with five-inch guns in line with a policy to keep outside the range of "any small gun the enemy may have and of remaining out of range throughout the action."[55] On older submarines, larger deck guns were gradually phased in during refits. When the *Flying Fish* underwent maintenance at the Hunter's Point Shipyard in November 1944, for instance, a more powerful five-inch model replaced its four-inch gun. The submarine also had a 40 mm gun welded in place on the after portion of the bridge deck.[56]

U.S. ships began installing the Swedish-designed Bofors 40 mm gun in mid-1942. Primarily used as an antiaircraft weapon, it proved equally effective against shore and surface targets. By 1944, modified as a "wet" mount, the gun could be left locked down during dives, and increasingly replaced the 20 mm guns on submarines. It took shells about one and one-half inches in diameter and eight inches long, with a projectile weighing a little less than two pounds. Rounds could be armor-piercing, high-explosive, or incendiary. Fired by a foot pedal, the gun could pump out 160 rounds per minute.[57]

Following the anti-picket sweep off the Bonin Islands in November 1944, group commander Klakring declared, "If we are going to employ submarines to seek out and destroy these patrols, our gunnery equipment and technique should be greatly augmented and improved."[58] He recommended that five-inch guns be installed fore and aft, with more emphasis on training and practice firing. Even before this, a number of submarines were fitted with two large deck guns. When the USS *Snook* underwent overhaul at Hunter's Point in March 1944, a four-inch/50-caliber gun specifically designed for submarines was added to the aft deck; the original three-inch gun remained forward of the conning tower. At the end of the year, a more powerful five-inch/25-caliber gun replaced the *Snook*'s four-inch deck gun. A larger 40 mm gun mounted forward of the bridge also replaced the 20 mm gun.[59]

A similar transformation took place on the USS *Seal* during the first half of 1944. The three-inch gun was replaced by two five-inch guns, one forward and one aft of the conning tower, while a 40 mm gun displaced the 20 mm gun on the after-cigarette deck. While the *Seal* underwent refit at Mare Island, torpedoman John Ronald Smith overheard a conversation that seemed to explain the new guns. An admiral proclaimed: "We've got to get more aggressive with our tactics. The big targets are getting scarce. I think we should make more surface attacks."[60]

On the other hand, there were those who believed increased firepower might tempt skippers to take untenable risks. After receiving a new five-inch deck gun on the USS *Grayback,* Commander John A. Moore spoke enthusiastically about using it against the Japanese. When the *Grayback* went missing in February 1944, at least one fellow skipper speculated that "John was in a frame of mind to use that five inch gun in cases where the risk to the submarine and crew did not warrant it."[61] After the war Japanese records indicated that in fact the *Grayback* had fallen victim to an aircraft.

By late 1944 gun training had been stepped up. Submariners practiced using their deck guns at an AA Training Center at San Mateo, California, and at a similar range near Pearl Harbor. A practice range was also set up at Guam.[62] On 17 November 1944, for instance, the crew of the USS *Charr* practiced firing from various ranges at a target towed by the USS *Mallard.* According to reports, all of the *Charr*'s weapons functioned satisfactorily apart from the 20 mm gun, which jammed after firing fifty rounds of ammunition.[63] Gun jams remained a chronic problem. When the *Finback* mounted a gun action in April 1944, all three 20 mm guns on board jammed.[64]

On the other hand, the five-inch/25-caliber guns proved still more deadly with the introduction of VT-fused ammunition late in the war. Initially developed for antiaircraft guns, shells were fitted with electronic proximity fuses that could detonate the shell at a specified distance in front of a target. The submarine service was especially keen to deploy the ammunition against enemy gun crews and personnel on picket and patrol boats. Set to explode if they passed within 60 or 70 feet of a target, the shells had a burst area of 3,000 square feet. Armed with this ammunition, gunners on submarines could quickly and effectively decimate personnel on small vessels.[65] The USS *Balao,* under command of Cyrus Churchill "Cy" Cole, became the first submarine to experiment with the new ammunition. The USS *Charr,* commanded by Francis Dennis Boyle, also trained with proximity fuse shells before being sent on an anti-picket boat sweep.[66]

In attacking small craft, however, submarines were not simply relying on their deck guns. Given the extreme difficulty of sinking a shallow-draft vessel with a conventional torpedo, the Submarine

Operational Research Group (SORG) recommended developing a torpedo specifically for this purpose. The result was a small electric acoustic torpedo nicknamed "Cutie" designed to home in on the propeller noises of enemy vessels.

Submarines in the Pacific first took delivery of the new torpedoes in the summer of 1944, but they proved to be full of glitches. After a period back on the drawing board, they later functioned with more success. The *Sea Owl,* under command of Carter Bennett, became the first submarine to effectively deploy the new weapon, claiming the destruction of two enemy patrol boats.[67] The USS *Barb* claimed the only sinking of a merchant ship with the torpedo, but it had been fired from a distance of only seventy-five yards. About one-third of the Cuties launched found their target, and in total were credited with sinking twenty-four ships.[68]

Both Cuties and the new five-inch fused ammunition figured in an anti-picket sweep in February 1945. Early that month Charles Lockwood and his operations officer, Dick Voge, arrived at the advanced base on the island of Ulithi to discuss plans for a carrier mission with Admiral Spruance. In the lead-up to a Fifth Fleet strike on Tokyo, five submarines (*Sterlet, Pomfret, Piper, Trepang,* and *Bowfin*) armed with Cuties were to destroy any enemy picket boats capable of raising an alarm. At the same time, the *Sennett, Haddock,* and *Lagarto* were to create a diversion some 200 miles to the west, south of Honshu. Each of the submarines, in Lockwood's words, were "loaded for bear," fitted out with two five-inch guns and carrying ammunition with proximity fuses.[69]

As it happened, neither the *Sterlet* submarine pack nor the Fifth Fleet spotted any picket boats. The *Sennett, Haddock,* and *Lagarto* did attack two pickets, making short work of the enemy crews with their new ammunition.[70] It is possible, though, that such sweeps could be counterproductive, attracting attention to the very areas being cleared of boats. Following the submarine sweep off the Bonin Islands in November 1944, for example, enemy patrols appeared to increase.[71]

In the meantime, individual submariners continued to show a range of initiatives in dealing with small vessels. As the war progressed, running out of ammunition while on patrol became increasingly commonplace. A submarine might typically carry 100 rounds of five-inch shells, but a crack gun crew could fire nearly 20 shells in the space of a minute.[72] As a way of saving ammunition, some submarines blew up small vessels with demolition charges.

Others experimented with less conventional ways of sinking small craft. At one stage during the *Ronquil*'s attack on the patrol craft, detailed above, the crew fired rounds from "our new Bazookas," according to the patrol report.[73] The USS *Tambor* also carried a bazooka, but when crewmen tried to finish off a patrol boat with it they were unable to hit it after ten attempts. The crew decided machine guns were better suited to the task.[74] Thomas Wesley Hogan, who served on the *Haddock,* described another instance where extraordinary measures seemed necessary. After failing to sink a trawler with the deck guns, the crew resorted to throwing ignited balls of waste soaked in oil. The trawler finally caught on fire.[75] Such methods, as discussed later, often brought submariners face-to-face with their victims.

7

Straits of Malacca

Tony Miers, the former skipper of HMS *Torbay* whose exploits won him a Victoria Cross, arrived at Fremantle as British liaison officer in November 1943. He had sailed from Pearl Harbor on the USS *Cabrilla,* spending two months at sea with the American crew. In a letter to Admiral Claud Barrington Barry, Miers boasted, "I was easily the most aggressive officer on board (although the oldest)."[1] Perhaps in part because he was miffed at being forced to share a miniscule cabin with three junior officers, he gave a less than flattering report on the *Cabrilla*'s commander, Douglas Thompson Hammond, describing him as "utterly lacking in aggressive spirit and imbued with the idea of 'safety first.'"[2] The crux of his criticism was Hammond's refusal to mount a gun attack on two 200-ton trawlers spotted carrying cargo in San Bernadino Strait (between the Philippine islands of Luzon and Samar). The thirty-four-year-old Hammond did not wish to betray his position for such small vessels, whereas Miers believed coastal traffic could be attacked with relatively little risk.

Miers made the same point even more forcefully in a report sent directly to Hammond. Given that small vessels were known to be important providers of enemy supply, Miers wrote, "I think these craft should be sunk by gunfire even if it does give away the position. The bird in the hand is worth two in the bush."[3] Indeed, Miers seems to have reflected a philosophy shared more broadly by British submarine commanders. While the Americans dominated the submarine war in the Pacific, in terms of surface gun attacks the British surpassed the Americans by a considerable margin at one stage. During 1944, thirty-one British submarines carried out a total

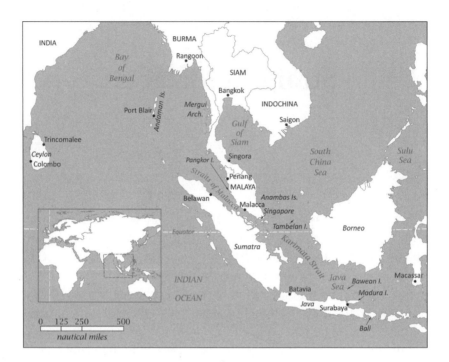

The Straits of Malacca

of 293 gun attacks (see the appendix). Most of these actions took place in the waters between Sumatra and western Malaya known as the Straits of Malacca, a vital corridor of supply that remains one of the world's busiest shipping lanes.

Initially, with the outbreak of war in Europe, all British submarines were withdrawn from the Far East. In 1940 ten submarines were transferred from the Pacific and Indian oceans to Alexandria. The *Trusty* and *Truant* briefly returned to Singapore, and even before the island fell in February 1942, the HMS *Trusty* sank a range of small craft with its deck gun.[4] By early March 1942 the remnants of British naval forces, including four Dutch submarines under British command, were based at Colombo on Ceylon.

When the Japanese first attacked Malaya in December 1941, the Dutch fleet included fifteen submarines based at Surabaya. As a minor naval power, submarines played a key role in the Royal Netherlands Navy strategy in the Far East. The Dutch submarines made a strong showing in the early days of the Pacific war, operating in three-boat wolf packs; as well as sinking a number of merchant ships, they claimed the first Japanese warship sunk by a torpedo. Indeed, between the surrender of the Philippines and the evacuation of Surabaya, the Dutch managed to sink more ships than U.S. submarines, claiming six to the Americans' three.[5] By Christmas 1941, though, the Dutch had lost four of their boats—three to the Japanese and one wrecked by a battery explosion. More submarines were lost in Japanese air raids on Surabaya, either bombed or scuttled before evacuation of the base in March 1942. The remaining seven Dutch submarines were dispatched to the bases at Ceylon and Fremantle.[6]

In Australia the Dutch sailors were generally perceived as good fellows, noted for their informal approach and prodigious drinking.[7] The Dutch submarines, however, were fraught with mechanical problems and mainly employed on "special missions"—landing and retrieving secret operatives on occupied islands. In September 1944 two additional Dutch submarines, the *O-19* and *Zwaardvisch*, arrived at Fremantle with the British Eighth Flotilla. These two boats were sent on conventional operations, as were another two Dutch boats that arrived with the British Fourth Flotilla in April 1945. In the meantime, the larger Dutch boats *O-21, O-23*, and *O-24* continued conducting numerous special missions from Ceylon under British command.[8]

Given their small numbers and the nature of their patrols, the Dutch boats made few gun attacks: one in 1942, one in 1943, fourteen in 1944, and ten the following year. Their victims included junks, coasters, and oilers, as well as seven *prau* (Malay sailing boats) (see the appendix). The *O-21*, under Lieutenant F. J. Kroesen, carried out the last Dutch submarine patrol of the war in July–August 1945. On patrol off Java, the submarine made only one attack, on 29 July, when it used its guns to engage two coasters. The action quickly ended after the submarine's gun jammed and the coasters headed for shallow water.[9]

Meanwhile, the commitment of British submarines in the Pacific theater only gradually escalated. Initially expecting a Japanese attack at Colombo, the *Trusty* and *Truant* were posted to guard the Straits of Malacca but were then recalled to England for refit, leaving only the Dutch submarines to patrol. In early 1943 only four submarines remained under British operational control, and three of these were Dutch. In March 1943 the sole British submarine in the region, HMS *Trusty,* carried out a patrol off Indochina, but mechanical problems resulted in it sailing back to the United Kingdom for refit on 5 April.[10]

After the capture of Sicily, the British presence in the Mediterranean as the main theater of submarine operations became less pressing, and in July 1943 eight submarines were detached for the Far East: *Tally Ho, Templar, Tactician, Trespasser, Taurus, Severn, Surf,* and *Trident.* With the arrival of reinforcements and the modern depot ship *Adamant,* the British subsequently stepped up operations in the Malacca Straits. By late 1943 the *Adamant* and submarines of the Fourth Flotilla had moved with the Eastern Fleet from Colombo to Trincomalee, an expansive harbor ringed by jungle. After an armistice with Italy in September 1943, more submarines from the Mediterranean found their way to the Indian Ocean. A second depot ship, the *Maidstone,* arrived at Trincomalee from Alexandria in March 1944, and the submarine force consequently split into two flotilla.[11]

A third depot ship, the HMS *Wolfe,* arrived at Trincomalee in August 1944. With twenty-six submarines based at Trincomalee, more than needed to patrol the Straits of Malacca, the *Maidstone* sailed to Fremantle, arriving on 4 September 1944. The Eighth Submarine Flotilla, consisting of nine British and four Dutch submarines, arrived a short time later after completing patrols in the Straits of Malacca. The Eighth Flotilla thus became the first unit of the Royal Navy to operate out of Western Australia, brought under American operational control and Admiral Ralph Christie. In the meantime, the Fourth Flotilla remained based at Trincomalee with the depot ship HMS *Adamant* until April 1945, when it too moved to Fremantle, leaving only the *Wolfe* and its flotilla in Ceylon. At the same time the Eighth Flotilla advanced from Fremantle to Subic Bay in the Philippines.[12]

In Western Australia proximity to the Americans inevitably led to invidious comparisons between the British boats and the U.S. fleet submarines. Having inspected the HMS *Clyde* after it arrived at Fremantle in August 1944, Ralph Christie professed he had never seen a filthier ship.[13] Edward Young, commander of the HMS *Storm,* arrived at Fremantle the following month, and after being guided through a U.S. fleet boat confessed, "I felt downright ashamed of the conditions [in] which my own able seamen and stokers had to live at sea."[14] Similarly, Tony Miers, although less than impressed with the Americans' offensive spirit, had no doubts about the superiority of their submarines for all forms of patrol except in very shallow water. In fact, Miers's suggestion that the British immediately adopt a similar design got him into some hot water; not only was this impractical, it implied that the British boats were hopelessly outmoded just when they were concentrating their efforts in the Pacific.[15]

In the Mediterranean, with the distance between Gibraltar and Alexandria only a couple of thousand miles, fuel had not been a problem for the British submarines. In the vast expanses of the Pacific, on the other hand, the British boats had a limited range. Production of the Swordfish or S-type boats, intended for operations in confined waters, began in the early 1930s. They had a cruising range of 3,800 miles doing nine knots on the surface. From Fremantle the S-boats could patrol only as far as the Makassar Strait or the Java Sea.

The Triton or T-class submarines, dating from 1937, had been designed with the possibility of war with Japan in mind, anticipating operation from bases in Singapore and Hong Kong. From Western Australia they could make it to Singapore or the north coast of Borneo.[16] T-class submarines carried just over fifty officers and crew members. The average duration of a T-class submarine patrol was twenty-five days, compared to twenty days for the S-class boats.[17]

The American boats were not only bigger, they were better equipped, with amenities including air-conditioning. Although some British boats had dehumidifiers, these were so noisy and used so much electricity that they proved more or less useless.[18] As described by the British submariner Ian Nethercott, on patrol "you were just one mass of prickly heat and sweat rash. Between your legs and under your arms it was just great running sores of blood and sweat."[19] The HMS *Surf* had to return to base after only eighteen days at sea because of five cases of heat stroke.[20] Eventually these problems were somewhat rectified; new-construction submarines sent to the Far East were fitted with air-conditioning and ballast tanks converted for carrying fuel to give them greater range.[21]

The one advantage of the smaller British submarines was an ability to operate in shallower and more confined waters, making them better suited to attacking the small coastal craft that increasingly supplied Japanese troops. This was especially so in the treacherous Straits of Malacca, where abundant sandbanks, unpredictable currents, and low-lying coasts offered innumerable hazards for a submarine. On tropical nights spice-scented breezes reached those on patrol, but the proximity of land also meant that enemy airfields and naval bases were close at hand.[22]

Like their Dutch counterparts, British submarines were often deployed on clandestine "special" operations behind enemy lines. In May 1943 a submarine landed the first agents of Force 136 on the island of Pangkor, destined to serve as a base of operations in Malaya.[23] However effective such operations, British submariners inevitably bridled against what they saw as distractions from their proper role—sinking enemy shipping. From Ceylon, the commander of the Fourth Submarine Flotilla, Captain H. M. C. Ionides, confided to Ralph Christie, "We envy you your freedom from having to use your submarines for these side-shows."[24]

Once turned loose on Japanese shipping, though, the British found only limited success. By late 1943 the British had nineteen submarines operating in the Straits of Malacca, mainly attempting to cut off supplies to the Japanese in Burma. They managed to sink only one ship and one submarine before the end of the year. During the first six months of 1944 the British sank only eight merchant ships, totaling some 16,000 tons.[25]

In the absence of larger prey, the British increasingly focused their attention on smaller craft. Lurking like crocodiles, the submarines were often stationed near headlands and channels waiting for unwary coastal traffic. The HMS *Storm,* under Edward Young, encountered its first victim in the Straits of Malacca in March 1944, a 500-ton coaster on course for the port city of Belawan on the northeast coast of Sumatra. The *Storm* sank it with gunfire. As with the Americans, such actions served partly as morale-raising exercises. Young, the first Royal Navy Volunteer Reserve (RNVR) officer to command a submarine, noted that although the victim was small, sinking it "acted as a tonic to our spirits, and all was cheerful in the messes as we sat down to our evening meal."[26]

By May 1944 the British Admiralty gave submariners permission to attack junks as well as other coastal craft believed to be carrying supplies from Malaya to Burma, and they began taking a heavy toll on local shipping.[27] During the first three weeks of June, the HMS *Stoic* claimed the destruction of a coaster, two junks, and a landing barge; the *Sirdar, Truculent, Sea Rover, Sturdy,* and *Spiteful* reported between them the sinking or damage of another ten junks and eight other assorted vessels. In October 1944 the HMS *Tantivy* rampaged through Makassar Strait, sinking eighteen vessels with gunfire in four days. By the end of October British submarines had sunk nearly 100 small craft.[28]

With most attacks being made with the deck guns, additional ammunition was carried in spaces previously used for torpedoes. On patrol off the Malaya coast in April 1945, the HMS *Statesman* sank 10 landing craft, a schooner, and 8 junks without firing a torpedo. It did, though, fire nearly 500 rounds of three-inch ammunition, along with innumerable rounds from its Oerlikon gun and Vickers machine guns.[29] Commander F. W. Lipscomb notes, "[M]atters got to such a pitch that submarines sailed with gun ammunition stowed in every possible place, including under the wardroom table!"[30] Most of the vessels attacked in submarine gun actions were described as junks, totaling 121 in 1944, followed by 75 coasters and 32 schooners (see the appendix).

Chinese junks usually had at least three masts and were distinguished by their high sterns and batten-stiffened sails. Even before America went to war, the secretary of the navy, Frank Knox, predicted that the only neutral shipping in the Pacific was likely to be conducted by Chinese junks.[31] The status of neutral, however, proved ephemeral. Prisoners captured from junks confirmed that the Japanese were using them to ship rubber, timber, tin, rice, and tea.[32]

When crewmen from the HMS *Tantivy* boarded a junk they found a cargo of tin ore; thereafter British submarines were given permission to sink junks of twenty tons or more.[33] Partly because junks were constructed with watertight compartments, they often proved difficult to sink. Indeed, even fifteenth-century junks were designed to stay afloat with flooded compartments, and were sometimes deliberately flooded for transporting trained sea otters. On one occasion the HMS *Statesman* required nearly fifty rounds of three-inch ammunition to destroy a single junk.[34] When the U.S. Navy called for ideas on how to sink junks, Lew Parks from the *Pompano* suggested using phosphorous shells to facilitate burning them.[35]

From early 1943 the Japanese had begun employing junks from the Yangtze River capable of hauling up to 800 tons of cargo for military service in the south.[36] With the increasing naval supremacy of the Allies, junks crewed by "drafted" Chinese and Koreans, as well as Japanese, regularly carried supplies.[37] In the Straits of Malacca the Japanese depended on junks to transport rice from Siam to Singapore, and Alistair Mars, skipper of the HMS *Thule,* believed that junks moved thousands of tons of rice south every day.[38]

It was apparently a similar story off the east coast of Malaya, where junks transported huge amounts of food. Although the food was mainly for local consumption, it was claimed that 10 percent of everything went to the Japanese. Most of the junks were owned by Chinese and operated by mixed crews of Chinese, Malays, and Indians. According to some reports, such crews were often fairly cavalier about having their cargoes destroyed, and it was even rumored that the Chinese sometimes gambled on how many rounds would be needed to sink their craft.[39] At least some junks, though, were run by Japanese firms and under direct orders to carry supplies to the military.[40]

Edward Young speculated that junks carried more than cargo, believing that they might be equipped with radio transmitters or even with torpedo tubes.[41] At least some submarine commanders, though, considered the task of destroying junks disagreeable. Alistair Mars thought most of the junks were manned by Chinese crews from Malaya, impressed into service by Japanese threats against their families. Certainly the Chinese in Malaya and Singapore, having once sided with the British, were a special target of Japanese abuse, and an estimated 50,000 were murdered.[42]

Mars nevertheless carried out attacks on junks, believing that duty required it. Within the calculations of Mars's moral economy, a 100-ton junk might carry enough rice to feed 2,000 Japanese soldiers for three months. When the *Thule* sank nine junks on a single day, Mars claimed that the actions had destroyed enough rice to feed 5,000 Japanese troops for months.[43]

Affectionately nicknamed "Mars Bars" and "Marvelous" by his crew, Mars made special efforts to pick up survivors when possible.[44] Even so, witnessing the aftermath of a close-range gun attack could be a life-scarring experience. When the *Thule* attacked a junk on 19 December 1944, most of the junk's crew members jumped overboard. The submarine continued firing until the vessel sank, and then moved in to collect survivors. They found one of the Chinese badly wounded: "a sack of blood drenched crumpled limbs with a hole at the base of his chest as large as a cricket ball."[45] There was some talk of amputating one of the man's legs with a hacksaw, but given his other injuries that seemed pointless. Offered a cigarette as he lay dying, the man literally exhaled the smoke through his chest wound with his dying breath. Little wonder that Mars referred to attacks on defenseless craft as "atrocities," and that Edward Young once described such actions as "like murder."[46]

There were certainly some actions generally acknowledged as atrocities, the most notorious involving the HMS *Sturdy* under William St. George Anderson. In waters north of Australia on 25 November 1944 the *Sturdy* encountered a 350-ton Indonesian coaster suspected of supplying the Japanese. Although hit with some forty shells, the craft refused to sink, and some crewmen from the *Sturdy* boarded the vessel to finish it off with demolition charges. By this time the coaster's crew of about fifty had already abandoned the ship in lifeboats, but about fifty women and children were left on board. Despite protests by the sailor setting the charges, Anderson instructed him to "get on with it": the women and children were blown up with the vessel. Anderson later stated, "Owing to the nature of the cargo (oil) and the use of this type of vessel to the enemy, I disregarded the humanitarian side of the question."[47]

There is some evidence that Ralph Christie pressed for an investigation of the incident, but that the British demurred.[48] No one condoned the action, however, and the British submarine flotilla commander at Fremantle, Captain Lancelot Shadwell, declared that the incident would be "viewed with distaste and repugnance by the whole submarine service."[49] Nevertheless, Anderson still received a Distinguished Service Cross and Bar at the end of the war.

In reality, submarines often sank vessels with no knowledge of their cargoes and little regard for crew and passengers. The prospect of being spotted by enemy planes tended to deter hanging around to help survivors. When the HMS *Shakespeare* made its first Far East patrol in January 1945, it tried to sink a small merchant ship with torpedoes off Port Blair in the Andaman Islands. After the torpedoes missed, the *Shakespeare* attacked with its gun, but the merchant vessel scored a direct hit that penetrated the submarine's pressure hull. Unable to dive, the *Shakespeare* was hit four more times, wounding four men of the crew. Forced to head back to base on the surface in full daylight, the *Shakespeare* had, by sunset, miraculously survived twenty-five attacks by Japanese aircraft, but at the cost of fifteen men wounded and two killed. Although the submarine made it back to its base at Trincomalee, its fighting career had ended.[50]

Despite such dangers, some British skippers adopted measures to minimize the costs in human lives. Alistair Mars, disgusted by the carnage, began trying to use the *Thule* to ram his victims instead of sinking them with the deck guns. In theory this would allow the crews of targeted vessels to jump clear into the water, leaving the submarine positioned to pick up survivors or to dive quickly if an aircraft appeared. The *Thule* first put the theory into practice on 22 December 1944, ramming a number of junks and then collecting survivors.

Mars, according to one of his crewmen, "wouldn't go to gun action if he thought he could sink it in some other way, and that's what he did."[51] On one occasion the *Thule* cut a fifty-ton junk cleanly in half.[52] On another occasion, in December 1944, the *Thule* stopped a sampan, pulling the unwilling crew onto the submarine. The men of the *Thule* destroyed the sampan, which Mars described as a "little pisser" not even worth a gun shell, with fused charges.[53] The use of boarding parties was a practice increasingly adopted both to destroy vessels and to ensure the safety of their occupants.

The idea of forming boarding parties on submarines seems to have developed more or less spontaneously, rather than as the result of uniform policy. As the British increased the number of surface gun attacks on small craft, so too did the use of boarding parties become more commonplace. In mid-1944 the British submarine *Storm* organized a boarding party while patrolling the Mergui Archipelago. Instructed to search and blow up small craft used for supplying the Japanese garrison at Rangoon, a young sublieutenant, Richard "Dicky" Fisher, was appointed "boarding officer." Fisher put together a group of five crewmen equipped with grappling hooks, demolition charges, revolvers, and a lethal-looking collection of knives.

Edward Young, *Storm's* commanding officer, described the group as resembling "as bloodthirsty a crowd of pirates as ever slit throats on the Spanish Main."[54] An element of boy's own adventure certainly pervaded such parties, and like their pirate antecedents they offered a serious threat to merchant shipping. Despite the fierce appearance of the *Storm's* boarding party, however, Young regarded it primarily as a way to save lives. Patrolling the Gulf of Boni in October 1944, the *Storm* had authority to sink local schooners carrying nickel ore from the port of Pomelaa. Since these craft were manned entirely by "native" crews, Young determined to try to avoid killing anyone. The first schooner the submarine encountered, a wooden two-masted craft, carried ten Malays. The *Storm's* boarding party under Dicky

Fisher searched the schooner and found the hold empty, but given that the vessel had orders to take back a load of nickel on its return to Macassar, Young felt compelled to sink it; "[S]he was useful to the enemy and we had no alternative."[55] Initially he brought the Malay crew on board the *Storm,* and then later transferred it to a fishing boat. In the course of the patrol the *Storm* managed to sink eleven schooners, all without loss of life or limb to their crews.

Boarding vessels, though, involved risks. In one action off Point Blair in the Andaman Islands, the HMS *Taurus* stopped a small steam ferry. When the ferry was secured alongside the *Taurus* with grappling hooks, eighteen Indian passengers boarded the submarine before the boarding party could move onto the ferry. Once the submarine's boarding party got on the steamer, however, the grappling hooks separated and the ferry began speeding toward Point Blair. Eventually the *Taurus* men gained control of the ferry and headed back to the submarine, but only as an enemy aircraft approached. The *Taurus* dived with the Indians still on deck.[56]

The HMS *Statesman* fired the last torpedo of the war by a British submarine, after departing Trincomalee on 9 August 1945. In these final days of the war, the *Statesman* used torpedoes to finish off a derelict ship and then sank five junks in the Malacca Straits with gunfire. Over the course of nine patrols, the *Statesman* claimed the destruction of forty-nine vessels totaling about 10,000 tons.

The tactics of British submarines were in some ways a microcosm of the Pacific submarine war. There was often an appalling loss of life and disregard for noncombatant lives. On the other hand, there were those who tried to minimize civilian casualties. In the end British submarines accomplished their mission to establish control over traffic in the Straits of Malacca and cut off supplies to Japanese troops in Burma.[57]

8

Boarding Parties

Like the British, the crews of U.S. submarines frequently made use of boarding parties. In the opening years of the war this most often involved inspecting craft in the aftermath of an attack with a view to retrieving any intelligence-worthy material or prisoners. After the USS *Pompano* attacked a patrol boat on 2 September 1942, for example, skipper Willis Thomas directed a party armed with revolvers to row over in a rubber boat to get a prisoner for interrogation.[1]

Again like the British, American boarding parties were often fond of casting themselves in the role of pirates. Some submariners had their left ears pierced with gold rings to reinforce the image.[2] They presumably had in mind a fairly romanticized version of piracy, as opposed to what some jurists have termed the first international criminals and terrorists. In fact, submarine boarding parties might more accurately be compared to privateers, the state-sponsored pirates who directed their activities toward a specific adversary.[3] Submariners carried out similar activities during the First World War, sometimes boarding small craft to search for contraband. In one instance during the Dardanelles campaign in 1915, British crewmen not only boarded a sailing vessel but lashed their submarine to it to disguise their presence.[4]

Submarine boarding parties were typically heavily armed, either anticipating resistance or to intimidate the people on board. At times small arms were used to kill those on boarded vessels. In the early morning of 18 April 1944, for example, the USS *Tambor* opened fire on a 250-ton wooden vessel said to resemble a crab tender. The ship carried fresh vegetables and other food apparently intended for Japanese soldiers on Wake Island. Although the submarine received some return fire, the *Tambor* quickly suppressed this by raking the craft at point-blank range with its 20 mm gun. As the vessel settled in the water, four men from the *Tambor* boarded to search it.

Initially there was no sign of life, but as the water rose, a half dozen crew members began moving. One man was taken prisoner. The rest of the crew were shot, including a badly wounded man found in the pilothouse. One of the *Tambor* men who boarded the vessel, John Clausen, described to a crewmate how blood pumped from the bodies of the Japanese each time a bullet hit them. Clausen told his friend that he "wished the whole thing had never happened."[5]

On 7 April 1945 the *Spadefish* battle surfaced on a Chinese junk, later identified as the 198-ton *Tenshin Maru No. 3*. After shelling the craft at a distance, the submarine raked the junk at close quarters with the 20 mm and .50-caliber guns. As the junk slowly sank, five of the *Spadefish*'s crew boarded it carrying machine guns, rifles, pistols, and hand grenades. Those on the junk who survived the shelling, mainly Koreans, got on their knees and begged for mercy.

A search of the junk's living spaces by the *Spadefish* men revealed someone hiding under the covers in the skipper's bunk. The men, believing the Japanese captain might be armed, shot him to death with .45-caliber pistols; he proved to have been unarmed. The junk's cargo consisted mainly of grain, but the boarding party found some charts of mine fields. In the words of Lieutenant Decker, the men also took "all the souvenirs that they could pocket," including some Japanese flags.[6] The ship's mate, the only other Japanese aboard apart from the deceased captain, was taken prisoner. The *Spadefish*'s skipper, William Germershausen, noted in his report, "The action and subsequent piracy were enjoyed by all hands."[7]

By the latter stages of the war, boarding parties were frequently being used to spare lives rather than take them. Some submarines sailing out of Fremantle carried Australian commandos, who lent a more professional character to the operation of inspecting suspect craft. An extraordinary Australian major, William Thomas Lloyd

"Bill" Jinkins, largely forged the role of commandos on Allied submarines in the Pacific. After being captured with the Australian Army on the island of Ambon in January 1942, Jinkins managed to escape a Japanese prison camp and, after a perilous voyage, make his way back to Australia in early May of the same year.[8] Jinkins then became involved with the Allied Intelligence Bureau, joining its special operations branch, the Services Reconnaissance Department (SRD). Numerous SRD operatives were inserted (and later extracted) behind enemy lines by Allied submarines.

Although most submariners saw their main business as sinking enemy ships, only reluctantly becoming involved in these so-called special missions, once commandos were on board a strong bond inevitably developed between them and crews. Bill Jinkins became actively involved in an operation known as Python, and in June 1944 played a key role with the USS *Harder* in extricating Australian operatives from northern Borneo as the Japanese closed in on them.[9] The success of this mission helped convince Admiral Ralph Christie at Fremantle to frequently assign Australian commandos to U.S. submarines operating under his command.

In an exercise dubbed Operation Politician, pairs of Australian commandos began to be routinely carried on some submarine patrols in 1944. Their special equipment included foldboats, lightweight kayaklike craft some seventeen feet long with a rubberized canvas skin.[10] Armed with magnetic limpet mines, the commandos were capable of blowing up targets that were inaccessible to submarines, such as ships in shallow water, behind reefs, or beached. Australian commandos Cecil H. Anderson and Clifford J. Owens made several patrols with the USS *Bluegill* commanded by Eric Barr, and on one mission blew up a tanker beached on Hon Doi Island off Indochina near the present border of Vietnam and Cambodia. The men paddled nearly a mile through rough seas to the island and set six delayed-action limpet charges on the 5,700-ton ship's undamaged hull. They were surprised to find on board a Colt Browning antiaircraft gun manufactured in Harford, Connecticut, as well as a box of silk stockings made in the U.S.A.[11]

More often, the duties of commandos included boarding suspect vessels. Bill Jinkins made two successive patrols with the USS *Redfin* skippered by Marshall "Cy" Austin between August and October 1944. On the first patrol, he and another commando, Alec Chew, boarded local sailing boats to search for Japanese soldiers and radio transmitters that could be used to report the positions of U.S. submarines.[12] Jinkins later made patrols with the USS *Flounder,* USS *Pargo,* and USS *Hawkbill.* In an extraordinary ethos of cooperation, Australian commando Cecil Anderson described the American submariners as "magnificent people," while another commando, Rowan Waddy, proclaimed that they "treated us with such high respect, it was embarrassing."[13] Uniquely, Bill Jinkins even studied for qualification on U.S. submarines and eventually won the submarine combat insignia.[14]

Since they were trained in speaking Malay, Australian commandos had a much better chance of communicating with local seamen than the typical submariner. On patrol with the *Bluegill* in the Java Sea, for instance, the commandos reported no problems communicating with the crew of a sailboat boarded and searched on 30 March 1945. That was until they asked whether the Japanese used the boat; "From this point the crew ceased to understand."[15] The commandos confiscated the sailboat's log and papers. When they inspected another sailboat the same day, they found nineteen emaciated people on board, including two women and eight small children. The people begged for food and water, dutifully supplied from the *Bluegill.* It is likely that such interactions saved lives, not only through supplying provisions but by not indiscriminately sinking craft considered of potential use to the Japanese.

Apart from the periodic use of commandos, at least some boarding parties received formal instruction. A group of five men from the USS *Barb* took training in hand-to-hand combat and using grenades from Marines at Midway in late 1944. On the *Barb's* next patrol this group, led by Tom King from Nashville, boarded a small Japanese weather ship on 1 January 1945 using grapnels to pull alongside the vessel. Commander Gene Fluckey described the party as a "swashbuckling group of modern pirates," and indeed it returned to the *Barb* with bags of "loot" containing not only potential intelligence materials but binoculars, barometers, rifles, and flags. The crew celebrated this exploit with a cake inscribed "Jappy New Year 1945!"[16]

By 1945 the decline in Japanese antisubmarine capabilities made operating on the surface far less risky. When conditions appeared safe enough, vessels that might once have been sunk on sight were inspected before being destroyed and measures taken for the safety of their crews. On the USS *Tirante*, Lieutenant Endicott "Chub" Peabody led a ten-man boarding party. A future governor of Massachusetts, Peabody had graduated from Harvard in 1942 and wore his letter sweater when boarding vessels.[17] The boarding party was more practically equipped with .45-caliber pistols, knives, hand grenades, flashlights, whistles, and life jackets. The group's activities were backed on the *Tirante* by a so-called fire support party, led by Ensign Ledford, charged with setting fire to craft marked for destruction.

Peabody made his first boarding on 6 April 1945, off the south coast of Korea near Shori To. After stopping a schooner by shooting a large hole in its sail, Peabody, along with H. W. Spence, gunner's mate first class, hopped on board. The *Tirante*'s patrol report recorded, "The dignity of the boarding party was considerably shaken when Lt. Peabody landed in a pile of fish."[18] Peabody's men fired a machine-gun burst to intimidate the crew, then searched the schooner. One Korean was wounded after jumping over the side, hit by a machine-gun bullet in the left arm. Peabody and Spence returned to the *Tirante* with a clock and pipe as souvenirs. Like the original pirates, many boarding parties indulged in oceangoing plunder, and souvenir hunting often became an integral part of the process. In a later incident, Peabody would take not only a Japanese flag but a vessel's nameplate.[19]

On the evening of 22 June 1945, as the *Tirante* patrolled off the western coast of Korea, the crew sighted a four-masted junk. Rather than simply destroying the vessel, the plan was to board it to see if it carried enemy cargo and possibly to recover charts and a prisoner. After firing warning shots, the submarine pulled alongside the junk and, as described by the patrol report, "[M]en swarmed aboard like Hollywood pirates."[20] The boarding party was surprised when a voice called out, "Don't shoot!" several times. The skipper of the junk, although of Japanese-Korean parentage, proved to be able to speak English. The remaining dozen crewmen were described as "nondescript" Koreans or Manchurians. The *Tirante*'s crew identified the junk, 108 feet long and 132 tons, as the *Antung Maru No. 293.* Interrogation of the skipper revealed that the junk had departed the Chinese province of Antung with a cargo of dried peas for Reisui on Korea's southeastern coast.

The junk's crewmen were put into its twenty-foot lifeboat and pointed in the direction of the nearest land. The English-speaking skipper, kept prisoner, proved a useful interpreter in later encounters. In the meantime, the *Tirante*'s fire party began setting the vessel alight with the aid of spirits and fuel oil. Even when seven miles away, those on the submarine could still see the ship furiously burning.

Two days later, in the early hours of 24 June, the *Tirante*'s boarding party inspected a small schooner. The vessel proved to be only a fishing craft and on this occasion was left unharmed. The same afternoon the submarine came alongside another junk, identified as *Antung Maru No. 284.* Using the *Tirante*'s prisoner-interpreter, the boarding party established that the junk's skipper came originally from Nagoya, and that again this craft carried a cargo of dried peas. The junk's crew was put in a lifeboat and headed toward land ten miles to the east, while the junk's holds were then set on fire, and the hull blasted with 40 mm shells to ventilate the blaze.

Several more junks were destroyed during the night, following what was by now described as "standard procedure."[21] After daybreak, however, the *Tirante*'s submariners' methods changed. The boarding party had been exhausted by a busy night's work, and in daylight the submarine became more vulnerable to attack by aircraft or patrol vessels. When crewmen sighted another junk at about 6:00 A.M., they opened up with the five-inch and 40 mm guns. The first shots were aimed high with the intention of allowing those on board to abandon ship. Once the junk's lifeboat was away, the *Tirante* pulverized the wooden vessel along the waterline. Not surprisingly, other junks in the area began sailing at their best speed for shallow water.[22]

William T. Kinsella, skipper of the USS *Ray*, took a similar approach. When attacking junks, Kinsella believed in giving crews a chance to abandon ship. At the same time, though, he proclaimed that "none of them are worth one of my men, so will not take unnecessary chances by boarding to inspect cargo or to persuade crew to abandon. A few well placed 40 mm. shots convince them much quicker."[23]

Not infrequently, what started out as an act of war could turn into humanitarian relief. Patrolling off the coast of Hainan on the morning of 23 January 1945, the USS *Batfish* battle surfaced on a fleet of twenty-eight Chinese junks to see whether the boats carried cargoes valuable to the Japanese. After the *Batfish* opened fire at 2,000 yards and hit one of the junks several times, the junks hove to. A quick inspection by a boarding party revealed that the junks were manned by "harmless Chinese fishermen" and that most carried entire families. For two of the Chinese, though, the *Batfish* had caused more than a scare, wounding them with the initial gunfire. One man had been shot through the thigh and another hit in the back and arm, so the *Batfish* pharmacist's mate boarded the junk to treat their wounds. The patrol report concluded, "We stocked their larder with cigarettes, beans, and rice and parted best of friends."[24]

Similarly, when patrolling off Hainan in March 1945, the USS *Puffer* observed hundreds of junks, many of which appeared to be crewed by families. With the aid of a Chinese-English dictionary, the *Puffer's* crew tried to learn the whereabouts of Japanese ships. The men proved more successful at bartering flour and canned fruit for fish, crab, and lobster. For some of the *Puffer's* crew, these cross-cultural encounters were consolation for an otherwise monotonous patrol. One of the *Puffer* officers, Lieutenant Frank Golay, credited the experiences with instilling an interest in the Far East. A math teacher in Kansas before the war, Golay later pursued research on Asia as a professor at Cornell University.[25]

Often eking out a marginal existence, those on junks appeared understandably keen to take advantage of any offers of food. When the USS *Balao* closed on a couple of junks in May 1945, the men found they could elicit a response just by holding up a bag of canned goods. The patrol report noted, "They didn't know what was in it, but they sure did want it."[26] The Chinese were prepared to reciprocate. Even before examining the contents of the bag, they began throwing fish to the *Balao*, about half of which skidded across the deck and over the other side.

As noted previously, submariners sometimes proffered food and cigarettes as compensation for the trauma of being stopped and boarded. On patrol in May 1945, the crew of the USS *Segundo* spotted five Chinese junks and boarded the one nearest. The boarding party found a crew of eighteen men and one elderly woman, with little on board other than fish and flour. The patrol report concluded: "They were a funny, scared lot. We passed them some Spam, bread, cigarettes and matches."[27] The following month the *Segundo* crew inspected some single-masted sailboats, noting the Chinese crews were "scared to death until we passed them some presents of tinned peaches and cigarettes."[28] This time the Chinese reciprocated by offering some fish in return; having determined the fish was either dried or rotten, the submariners threw it overboard once out of sight. The men of the USS *Icefish* took a similar tack. When they inspected a large junk off Hong Kong in August 1945, they found only ten frightened crew and a cargo of maggoty dried fish. The *Icefish* crew gave them a carton of cigarettes "to soothe their nerves."[29]

By the closing months of the war, inspecting and destroying junks had become the principal activity of many submariners. When the USS *Hawkbill* departed Subic Bay in July 1945 for the Gulf of Siam, Tonkin Gulf, and South China Sea, its directives included the discretionary investigation of junks. The HMS *Selene* had discovered an organized traffic in the area, and on one junk found a three-pounder gun under camouflage. The *Hawkbill*'s orders authorized it to attack junks found carrying contraband for the enemy, but also stipulated that the commanding officer assume "responsibility for this action."[30]

In Malaya, large Japanese firms controlled much of the economy, including shipping and rice distribution. It seems that some junks had new auxiliary engines installed in Singapore, where they were operated by a Japanese company or directly by the Japanese army.[31] On the morning of 17 July the *Hawkbill* intercepted a junk off Malaya headed south for Singapore, and an inspection found it loaded with 50,000 pounds of rice. Before the *Hawkbill* sank the junk with its 40 mm gun, its nine-man crew was transferred to the submarine's deck. About an hour later, the junk's crew was transferred to a smaller junk in the area.[32]

Using boarding parties involved some obvious risks. As the crew of the USS *Spot* discovered in January 1945, boarding an already damaged vessel created the possibility of going down with an enemy craft. At the end of an unsuccessful patrol along the China coast, the *Spot* used its guns to disable an auxiliary patrol vessel. A group of seven submariners subsequently boarded the craft with the intention of retrieving any intelligence material and finishing it off with demolition charges. While this party was on board, however, the ship suddenly heeled over by the stern and sank. The *Spot*'s crewmen were lucky to float clear and make it back to the submarine.[33]

Being caught on the surface by an enemy aircraft posed another risk. On the morning of 20 July 1945 the USS *Hawkbill* surfaced to inspect a junk that was found to be loaded with 62,500 pounds of rice bound for Singapore. Since the junk's lifeboat wasn't big enough to carry its eight-man crew, the submariners decided to dump the cargo into the sea rather than sink the vessel. As they were in the process of bringing the crewmen back on board the submarine, though, they spotted four aircraft closing from about four miles away. The *Hawkbill* made a stationary dive, leaving five crewmen still on the junk. After an anxious ten minutes, the *Hawkbill* surfaced to recover the rest of the boarding party.[34]

A little over a week later the USS *Cod* illustrated even more graphically the dangers of conducting boarding operations while inspecting vessels off the coast of Indochina. Operating in the Gulf of Siam between 21 July and 1 August 1945, the *Cod* made twenty gun attacks, mainly on junks and sampans. These vessels were discovered to be carrying a range of cargoes, from rice to crude rubber to horseshoes. The *Cod* managed the destruction of this shipping, though, with little loss of life. Endorsements of the patrol praised skipper Edwin M. Westbrook for the careful system of inspection he carried out and the consideration he took for the lives of friendly locals. Squadron commander Chester Carl "Chet" Smith enthused that the *Cod* symbolized "the type of action which has made the United States respected the world over."[35]

Nevertheless, the *Cod* demonstrated the risks of such an approach even this late in the war. On 21 July the submarine was bombed twice while in the process of diving and, even more dramatically, on 1 August a fighter aircraft strafed the *Cod*, forcing it to dive while part of the crew was inspecting a nearby junk. The *Cod* had pulled alongside the junk at 8:30 in the morning while patrolling south of Pulo Tenggol off the Malay Peninsula. The submarine's five-man boarding party, led by Lieutenant (junior grade) Franklin S. Kimball, included also John Babick (chief electrician's mate), George McKnight (motor machinist's mate first class), William Tolle (torpedoman's mate third class), and Sam Kinfroe (seaman first class). Also accompanying this team was a Chinese interpreter, Tom See, picked up from another junk five days earlier. The party found a cargo of army blankets, knapsacks, and canvas tarpaulins, but was now left stranded on the junk.

Because of the arrival of more aircraft and a destroyer, the *Cod* remained submerged until 2:35 in the afternoon. By this time the junk had blended into a mass of other craft in the area. Although the boarding party was well armed (carrying a Thompson machine gun, carbine, and four pistols in addition to knives and flashlights), there were grave fears for its safety. Other submarines in the vicinity, including the *Ray, Cobia, Lamprey, Boarfish,* and *Lizardfish,* were called in to help search for the men. Eventually, on the afternoon of 3 August, the *Cod* received a message from the USS *Blenny* that the men had been recovered and were okay; the *Cod*'s patrol report noted, "Everyone's spirits have been wonderfully lifted."[36]

The *Blenny* had spotted the junk with the *Cod* crewmen at a little after noon, some two miles east of the island Pulo Kapas. As it turned out, the leader of the boarding party, Lieutenant Kimball, was an old shipmate of the *Blenny*'s skipper, William Hazzard. The men stranded on the junk had been well treated, and they implored Hazzard not to harm its crew. Even though the junk clearly carried materials for the Japanese, the *Blenny* crew let it go unmolested, even leaving the junk crew some canned goods and fresh bread. The war, Hazzard reasoned, was almost over anyway.[37]

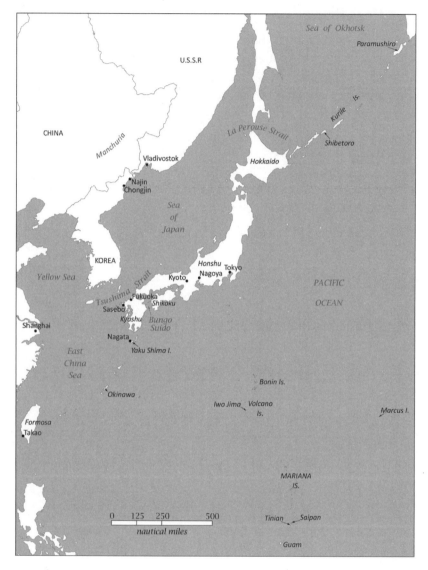

Japan

9

Mopping Up

The USS *Blenny* epitomized the tactics adopted by submarines in the closing months of the war, departing Fremantle on 5 July 1945 to patrol the Java Sea and off the eastern coast of Malaya. The *Blenny*'s skipper, William Hazzard, graduated from the Naval Academy in 1935 and became one of the last in his class to get a command. Having arrived in the Philippines in February 1940, he made ten war patrols before putting the *Blenny* in commission in September 1944. Under Hazzard, who characterized himself as full of nervous energy and an "eager beaver," the *Blenny* disrupted trade between Singapore and Saigon.[1] Crewman Frank Toon described the *Blenny*'s patrol as "a merry-go-round for the gun crews."[2]

During the course of the patrol numerous junks were boarded and inspected, and in most cases subsequently sunk. Some were bound with rice from Singora in Siam (today Thailand) to Terengganu on the east coast of Malaya. Some sailed from Singapore to Bangkok or Singora to collect rice. Others carried cargoes of coffee, sugar, salt, or grain. Junks traveling from Singapore with sugar could exchange their cargoes for rice at Menara in Malaya.

Sometimes the crews from these vessels were temporarily brought on board the *Blenny* while their junk was destroyed, and then later transferred to another local craft. If no other vessels were in the vicinity, the junk's crew would be enlisted to throw the cargo into the sea and its craft left intact. Preserving life sometimes required more proactive measures. When the *Blenny* boarded a sampan bound for Singora with a load of rice, six Chinese men on board hastily took to their boat. Unfortunately for them, the boat swamped; the *Blenny* crew hauled the men out of the water, and a short time later off-loaded them onto a local sailboat.[3]

Some small vessels were sunk with a single five-inch shell, or "five-inch bullet," as Hazzard liked to call them, to the bemusement of his crew.[4] Even with such parsimonious use of ammunition, however, the *Blenny* had to borrow additional shells from other submarines returning to port. On 24 July 1945 the crew transferred by breaches buoy about 250 rounds of five-inch and 40 mm ammunition from the USS *Hammerhead,* also taking the opportunity to exchange movies. A week later, on 2 August, the *Blenny* again took on more ammunition and swapped movies, this time with the USS *Lizardfish.* The next day more ammunition, including a box of shotgun shells, was received from the USS *Boarfish.*[5]

On occasion the *Blenny*'s boarding party used a twelve-gauge shotgun to blast holes in the bottom of junks, which would then be left to sink or set on fire using buckets of fuel oil. In one incident, crewmen from the *Blenny* boarded a thirty-ton junk already abandoned by its Chinese crew, and blew it up with a half pound of TNT.[6] By the end of the patrol the *Blenny* claimed the sinking of sixty-three craft, including forty-two described as junks and nine motor sampans, along with a miscellany of sea trucks, schooners, tugs, and barges. Arriving at Subic Bay on 14 August, the *Blenny* ended the war having sunk more small craft on one patrol than any other U.S. submarine.

In 1941 Japan was the world's third-largest ship-owning nation. By August 1945, including only merchantmen of 500 tons or more, Japan had lost nearly 9 million tons of shipping. Over half of these ships were sunk by submarines, while less than 1 percent were destroyed by surface gunfire.[7] In the case of shipping under 500 tons it was a different story, for although there are no official figures, hundreds of smaller vessels fell victims to gun attacks.

By the closing months of the war, guns had displaced torpedoes as the primary weapon for many submarines. Before the cessation of hostilities in mid-August, 91 different American submarines had carried out gun attacks on 641 vessels during 1945. British submarines made 393 gun attacks during the same period, while Dutch submarines carried out 10 attacks. Thus gun attacks by Allied submarines during 1945 totaled over 1,000 (see the appendix).

More and more submarines carried more and more armament. When the USS *Jack* underwent refit in early 1945, a five-inch/25-caliber gun replaced its old three-inch model. The *Jack* also got a 40 mm gun installed on the cigarette deck and twin 20 mm guns on the forward bridge platform, leading James Calvert to conclude that the submarine had become "a floating arsenal."[8] By July 1945 the *Flying Fish* had been declared a "gunboat," equipped with two five-inch guns that operated with a basic computer-controlled firing system.[9] At least some submarines also began sacrificing the number of torpedoes carried in order to take on additional ammunition. Gunnery training continued to be ratcheted up; at Guam submarine crews honed their skills firing at radio-controlled drone airplanes and targets towed by tugs. Before departing Subic Bay for patrol in July 1945, the USS *Hawkbill* practiced firing all of its guns at a target towed by the Chanticleer-class submarine rescue ship the USS *Coucal*.[10]

By 1945 the seas around Japan, as Pete Galantin put it, seemed crowded—not with potential targets but with other submarines.[11] When the *Pintado* patrolled the waters off Singapore in March 1945, Corwin Mendenhall compared the location to Grand Central Station, with so many U.S. submarines in the vicinity but no Japanese ships.[12] During 1945 an additional 39 U.S. submarines joined the fleet in the Pacific, bringing the total number of American boats to 252. At the same time the enemy tonnage sunk, after reaching a peak in October 1944, fell off sharply.[13] By January 1945, according to Charles Lockwood, most of Japan's remaining shipping consisted of small craft that skulked near the coasts carrying food and raw materials from Manchuria and Korea.[14] On its seventh war patrol in early 1945, Slade Cutter's former command, the USS *Seahorse,* made its only attack of the patrol on a fifty-ton fishing junk. The next patrol uncovered nothing even worthy of gunfire.[15]

One crew member described the USS *Puffer*'s seventh war patrol, completed in April 1945, as "kind of like going deer hunting on the last day of the season."[16] The same month the USS *Tunny* found only one vessel to attack, a wooden sampan estimated at 200 tons. On a rough sea, sinking even this meager target seemed hard work. From its rolling deck, the *Tunny* fired forty-four rounds of five-inch, forty-eight rounds of 40 mm, and fifty-seven rounds from the 20 mm gun. During the half-hour attack the crewmen detected no human activity on the sampan, although they later found a naked dead body floating in the debris.[17] Those vessels left afloat sometimes adopted elaborate camouflage in an effort to escape detection. In May 1945 the *Blenny* encountered a 100-ton lugger in the Java Sea disguised with palm fronds and mounting a machine gun on top of its deckhouse.[18]

After completing a patrol in June, the USS *Icefish* reported, "Hunting is very poor when a wolfpack considers a 600 ton, 230 ft. minelayer a large target."[19] Norvell G. Ward, working as assistant operations officer to Dick Voge, recalled, "The last month of the war we practically had nothing to work against. We were trying to make up targets. I think they found very few in the last two or three weeks of the war."[20] The majority of submarines were deployed on lifeguard duty for aircraft strikes. In May 1945 the USS *Jack* found itself stationed just south of Honshu for such duty, with no contacts worthy of a torpedo and the occasional wooden craft too close to shore to attack with its guns.[21]

Much of the competition for Japan's remaining shipping during the final stages of the war came from aircraft. Whereas submarines dominated the destruction of Japanese shipping during 1943 and 1944, aircraft overtook them in January 1945. After the Americans reoccupied the Philippines, aircraft were able to effectively control Japanese convoy routes in the South China Sea. The last imports of iron ore were cut off in March 1945, as were virtually all coal imports. The last shipment of oil to reach Japan from the south was also in March 1945. Without fuel, the remaining Japanese warships were either retired or employed solely as antiaircraft batteries.[22]

The increasing presence of aircraft also created added danger for submarines. In a scenario that became almost prosaic, a U.S. B-24 strafed and depth charged the *Seahorse* about 600 miles northeast of Luzon as it made its way to its patrol area. Despite the designation of areas reserved for submarine operations and strict protocols for aircraft, "friendly fire" remained a very serious danger throughout the war.[23] Under regulations issued in September 1944, aircraft were to refrain entirely from attacks on submarines in so-called havens and submarine patrol zones, but still submarines were attacked by their own side's planes.[24]

American aircraft could access waters too shallow or close to land to be efficiently patrolled by submarines. In the bluntly named Operation Starvation, B-29s operating from Tinian in the Mariana Islands dropped some 900 mines in Japanese harbors and waterways. These would eventually account for about half of Japanese ships sunk after April 1945. During the five stages of Operation Starvation, over 12,000 mines were laid, claiming over a million tons of shipping. Both Japanese civilians in the home islands and troops abroad were figuratively strangled by having their supplies cut off. By June and July 1945, the U.S. Third Fleet combed the Japanese coast looking for any remaining shipping, and Japan had to fall back on its insufficient railways for transport.[25]

Even before America entered the war, Japan's food supplies were strained by bad harvests in Korea and the demands of the military. Rice was rationed from 1940, and from October 1942 the Japanese government vested neighborhood associations and community councils with responsibility for the distribution of food and clothing. By 1944 distributions of fish had all but ceased in some areas. In August 1944 one Japanese factory reported that one-third of its workforce suffered from beriberi, the result of a white rice diet with little else of nutritional value.[26] By 1945 millions of Japanese suffering from malnutrition faced the prospect of something worse. It is claimed that at least 10 percent of Japan's population would have starved to death if the war had continued for another year. Allied commanders increasingly believed that the combined effects of blockade and aerial bombing would force Japan to surrender without the necessity of an invasion.[27]

With a dearth of larger freighters, the Japanese relied increasingly on small wooden vessels, often constructed by forced labor. At Pare Pare on the west coast of Celebes (today Sulawesi), 3,000 laborers turned out a dozen 170-ton ships per month. In the Menado district of northern Celebes the locals were subject to press-gang parties that forced them to leave their homes and work at shipyards, while large swathes of forest were cut down to provide timber.[28]

At times submarines were able to target vessels still under construction. On 26 July 1945 the USS *Barb* sighted a sampan-building yard at Shibetoro in the Kurile Islands. The yard had sixteen cradles for construction, and rows of newly built craft sat at the water's edge not far away. Using its 20 mm and 40 mm guns, the *Barb* started a fire that consumed much of the area and destroyed thirty-five new sampans.[29]

The closing months of the war saw an increasing number of bombardments on shore targets. The Japanese had initiated the first submarine-land bombardments, beginning with an attack on the American base at Johnson Island in mid-December 1941. Japanese submarines briefly shelled Midway on 23 January 1942, but were quickly forced to dive by shore batteries. The following month, on 24 February 1942, the *I-17* made the first attack on the U.S. mainland, shelling the Richland Oil refineries south of Santa Barbara, California.

At this stage of the war submarine bombardments were mainly intended to terrorize civilian populations rather than cause genuine damage. On 8 June 1942 the Japanese submarines *I-24* and *I-21* surfaced off Australia's eastern coast and shelled the suburbs of Sydney and Newcastle, and on 28 January 1943 the *I-165* fired about ten shells at the tiny community of Port Gregory on the western coast. Since such actions caused relatively little damage and exposed submarines to considerable danger, they were generally unpopular with Japanese skippers.[30]

Early in the war the oversized USS *Nautilus,* armed with six-inch guns, provided supporting fire for commando landings. In August 1942 the *Nautilus* fired its huge guns at Makin Island in the Gilberts to provide cover for landing Marines. In the course of the action, planned partly as a diversion for the invasion of Guadalcanal, the *Nautilus* lobbed twenty-four shells at a Japanese post, and then sank a freighter and patrol boat with its guns. In November 1943, during Operation Galvanic in the Gilbert Islands, the *Nautilus* carried seventy-eight Marines charged with capturing Apamama. Despite friendly fire from an American destroyer and cruiser, the *Nautilus* landed the Marines and supported the assault with its guns.[31]

Most American skippers, though, like their Japanese counterparts, at least initially took a cynical attitude toward the bombardment of shore targets. Pete Galantin believed that at best this was an irritant to the enemy. Nevertheless, while commanding the USS *Halibut,* Galantin fired fifty high-explosive shells into two warehouses on a pier at Kume Shima on Okinawa in 1944.[32] By late 1944 some submarines were rehearsing night bombardments. The *Piper, Sennet,* and *Blower* held exercises on the night of 24 November 1944, firing at Valladolid Rock in Panama Bay before departing for Pearl Harbor, with the *Sennet* proving the best shot.[33]

U.S. submarines in the vicinity of Fais Island near Ulithi Atoll in the Caroline Islands regularly bombarded the phosphate plant at Refinery Point. Given the use of phosphate in the manufacture of ammunition and explosives, this seemed a worthy target. On 24 April 1944 the USS *Tang* fired thirty-three rounds of four-inch shells at the island, reporting that the "detonations were nicely visible."[34] The *Tang* found another use for its deck gun six days later, turning it on shore batteries in order to facilitate retrieving downed aviators off Ollan Island.

In the Straits of Malacca, British submarines regularly fired their deck guns at shore targets such as trains or fuel dumps.[35] Gun attacks on Pratas Island, a small dot in the South China Sea some 180 miles southeast of Hong Kong, became more or less a matter of routine. The island served as a radio and weather base for the Japanese, and after departing Guam, the *Puffer, Piranha,* and *Sea Owl* were ordered to attack the island's radio installation. On the morning of 26 March 1945, forming a column some 1,500 yards from shore, all three submarines trained their five-inch guns on a radio tower and shelled the island as dawn broke. According to the *Puffer*'s patrol report, it was "probably the first submarine divisional bombardment on record."[36] Eventually the *Bluegill,* with the aid of two Australian commandos, declared the island abandoned and hoisted an American flag there.[37]

At times submarines turned their guns on entire towns. Patrolling off the southeast coast of Kyushu in July, the USS *Batfish* surfaced near the village and barracks of Nagata on the pentagon-shaped island of Yaku Shima. From a distance of 3,500 yards the submarine first opened up on the village with its 40 mm gun, firing 128 rounds. The five-inch gun then fired at the barracks and camp, apparently demolishing a frame building, although smoke made it difficult to assess the damage.[38] In the Sea of Okhotsk on 2 July 1945 the USS *Barb* bombarded Kai Hyo To. The submarine claimed the destruction of an observation post and an oil dump with its 40 mm gun, while the *Barb*'s five-inch gun destroyed a new radar and radio installation.[39]

The USS *Hawkbill*, under Francis Scanland Jr., departed Subic Bay for its last patrol of the war on 28 July 1945. With five Australian commandos on board, the submarine combed the islands between Borneo and Singapore. The commandos were landed on Terampah, the capital of the Anambas Islands, where they claimed an abandoned Japanese compound. On 9 August the *Hawkbill* used its two five-inch guns to demolish a radio tower on Tambelan Island, located about 200 miles south of Great Matoena Island in the South China Sea. The following day it destroyed a radio tower and building on Jemaja Island in the Anambas group.[40]

On 28 April 1945 Slade Cutter assumed command of the brand-new USS *Requin*. Judging from the submarine's armament (two five-inch guns, two 40 mm guns, eight .50-caliber machine guns, and bow rocket launchers for five-inch shells), clearly things had changed since his days on the *Pompano* and *Seahorse*. After completing shakedown cruises and training, the *Requin*'s crew received orders to bombard a patrol boat base at the island of Hokkaido. To Cutter the mission appeared "stupid," but it seemed that in the absence of enemy shipping submarines had little left to do.[41] The *Requin* set off on 13 August, but before it could reach its objective the war was over.

In addition to bombardments, 1945 also saw an increasing number of "coordinated" gun attacks with two or more submarines acting in concert. In February the USS *Bashaw* combined with the *Flasher* in several gun attacks on sea trucks in the waters off Indochina.[42]

In his endorsement of the USS *Blenny*'s third war patrol, James Fife declared that "coordinated gun attacks, under conditions of tactical advantage and after careful planning, are encouraged."[43] On its next patrol the *Blenny* made an attack with the USS *Cod* in the early morning of 27 July 1945. Discovering up to twenty small cargo-carrying vessels anchored off the western coast of Pulo Kapas, Terengganu Island, the submarines made a simultaneous attack. After first firing warning shots so that the crews could abandon ship, the submarines claimed the destruction of three vessels each.[44]

In May the USS *Lamprey* teamed up with the *Blueback* to make a surface gun attack on a sub chaser.[45] On patrol in the Java Sea the night of 29 June, the USS *Baya* picked up a small convoy of sea trucks and patrol boats on radar. The *Baya* waited for the arrival of the USS *Capitaine* at about 1:30 the following morning before it moved in to attack. Despite return fire, the submarines claimed the sinking of a sub chaser and damage on two of the sea trucks.[46]

According to naval historian and former submarine commander John Alden, submarines were authorized to go after coastal traffic in shallow waters and narrow straits only in the last few months of the war.[47] In the relative absence of Japanese defenses, submarines often operated close to ports and land with impunity. In May 1945 the USS *Bergall*, along with the *Bullhead*, *Cobia*, *Hawkbill*, and *Kraken*, explored every inlet of the Gulf of Siam, sinking numerous small craft with their guns. On one night alone, 30 May, the *Bergall* claimed the destruction of two small tugs and five barges estimated to be about seventy-five feet long each.[48]

The same month half a dozen U.S. submarines operated in the Yellow Sea, with the USS *Ray*'s skipper, William T. Kinsella, acting as the group commander. Because of its shallow depths, averaging just 120 feet, the Yellow Sea's murky waters presented special hazards to submarines and made it a difficult hunting ground. Operations were further inhibited by a lack of accurate charts. This in itself provided an incentive for submarines to operate largely on the surface, destroying craft carrying coal and other cargo.[49] The *Ray* received credit for sinking twenty-one miscellaneous craft in what one patrol endorsement described as "well planned and expertly conducted gun attacks."[50] During the patrol the *Ray* expended all of its five-inch and 40 mm ammunition. The total tonnage claimed, slightly over 6,000 tons, was the equivalent of one medium-sized freighter.[51]

The *Ray* illustrated the desperation for targets on its next patrol in the Gulf of Siam, when in order to sink seven junks found anchored north of Lem Chong Pra, six men from the *Ray* paddled two rafts to the vessels and blew them up using demolition charges.[52] Torpedoes were also occasionally resorted to in destroying small craft. During the *Aspro*'s sixth war patrol in April 1945, Commander James "Jungle Jim" Ashley unleashed a torpedo on a vessel described as about the size of a seagoing tug. It was customary for the skipper to be presented with a "victory cake" following successful attacks; on this occasion the *Aspro*'s baker presented Ashley with a cupcake.[53]

The Sea of Japan—frequently referred to in Allied naval circles as Hirohito's private bathtub or pond—appeared to be the last haven of Japanese shipping on any scale. Stretching some 900 miles from Tsushima Strait in the southwest to La Perouse Strait in the northeast, the sea is 250 miles at its widest point. With most other routes cut off, the bulk of Japan's remaining imports crossed the Sea of Japan from Manchuria and Korea. With the entrances to the sea guarded by dense minefields, no submarine had tried to gain entry since the loss of Mush Morton and the *Wahoo* in October 1943. Tokyo Rose, the Japanese radio propagandist with an American accent, warned Allied submariners that these waters could not be penetrated, and if they were there was no escape.[54]

Despite these warnings, in June 1945 nine submarines equipped with a new technology for detecting mines made their way into the Sea of Japan through Tsushima Strait. Dubbed Operation Barney, the mission paid tribute to Barney Sieglaff, who had been instrumental in putting it together. Sieglaff, a former skipper of the *Tautog* and the *Tench,* joined staff at Guam as an assistant operations officer. The Sea of Japan operation, though, was very much the brainchild of Charles Lockwood. From the outset Lockwood had followed the development of mine-detection equipment, visiting the Naval Research Laboratory at San Diego (part of the University of California's

Division of War Research) in April 1943. He personally checked out the frequency modulated (FM) sonar operators and rode on many submarines when they later made training runs against dummy mines planted off Saipan.[55]

The USS *Spadefish* became the first submarine to have FM sonar installed for detecting mines. When William Germershausen relieved Gordon Underwood as commander of the *Spadefish,* he inquired about the FM sonar gear on board, but was told not to worry about it because he would never need to use it. The next thing he knew, Germershausen was sent to map the minefields at Tsushima Strait, but the FM sonar equipment constantly broke down. The *Spadefish* was withdrawn, and the mapping assigned to the *Seahorse.* On his next patrol, though, Germershausen received instructions to penetrate the minefield at Tsushima Strait with eight other submarines.[56]

Deliberately sailing into a minefield was not high on most submariners' agenda, and a number of skippers expressed cynicism about the plan. It "wasn't a very appealing mission," Alexander Tyree recalled, with some understatement.[57] Red Ramage considered that the risks were greater than the chances for real success. He believed the main rationale behind the operation, as envisioned by Admiral Lockwood, was to demonstrate that Japanese ships had no place to hide. "He wanted to prove that we could even penetrate minefields and to do this before the war was over."[58]

By Lockwood's own account, his haste to enter the Sea of Japan was in part politically motivated. With Germany's surrender, Russia's active engagement against Japan appeared imminent, and Lockwood felt little enthusiasm about sharing operational areas with the Soviets. At a more personal level, Lockwood saw the operation as a way of avenging the loss of Mush Morton and the *Wahoo.* He acted against the advice of his own Submarine Operational Research Group (SORG), which warned that the mission was likely to result in heavy losses for relatively little gain.[59]

The FM sonar installed on the Operation Barney submarines made an eerie screeching noise when in the proximity of mines, instantly putting crews in a state of alarm.[60] Not trusting his FM sonar equipment, Germershausen took the *Spadefish* under the mines rather than around them as instructed. Once inside the Sea of Japan, the USS *Crevalle* celebrated the second anniversary of its commissioning with a huge cake. It bore the inscription "Was this trip necessary?"[61] It was a question many of the submariners no doubt pondered.

Working in groups of three, the submarines were scheduled to begin their attacks at sunset on 9 June, with orders to sink anything and everything Japanese. Lockwood hoped the attacks would strike a fatal blow to Japanese morale and undermine any remaining confidence in the country's leaders.[62] Almost inevitably, the mission proved an anticlimax, since even in the Sea of Japan the amount of shipping proved disappointing. The USS *Bowfin,* patrolling the Korean side of the sea, found few targets and sank only two small ships. As the *Bowfin*'s skipper, Alexander K. Tyree, put it, "The Japanese just did not have that many anymore."[63] At one stage, when the submarine's crew was inspecting a small craft outside Joshin Harbor, some smiling Koreans handed over a mess of freshly caught fish.[64]

Also designated an area off Korea, the *Flying Fish* had instructions to patrol the northern coast between the ports of Seishin (now Chongjin) and Rashin (now Najin). As the submarine headed toward Seishin in fog, its radar picked up a number of small targets. The crewmen sighted three sailing vessels, and when they approached the lead boat the *Flying Fish*'s commander used an American-Japanese translation book to call on the crews to abandon their craft. After receiving no response, they fired .50-caliber bullets into the hull, followed by some 40 mm rounds into the bow. Finally persuaded to abandon ship, the crew pushed off in a small boat. The *Flying Fish* finished off the vessel, loaded with lumber, with its five-inch gun.[65]

After firing on the other two sailing vessels, the *Flying Fish* spotted a tug with two barges as the fog lifted. The barges, loaded with bricks, were close enough for pieces of shattered brick to reach the submarine's deck when the crew opened fire with the 40 mm gun. Dale Russell, a gunner on the submarine, recalls the action as "unpleasant." One of the men on the tug managed to scramble over the bow, but another fell to the deck. According to Russell, "None of us took pride in the miniscule dent we may have put in Japan's war supplies," and he felt sympathy for the "poor bastards" killed.[66]

When the *Flying Fish* encountered a fishing fleet, it sank ten to fifteen of the craft with its deck guns. The executive officer, Julian T. Burke Jr., later described the attacks as "terrible." Although he did not protest the skipper's decision at the time, he concluded that such attacks were "not good psychology with the crew and the officers."[67]

The USS *Tunny,* along with the *Skate* and the *Bonefish,* prowled the southwestern sector along the coast of Honshu. The *Tunny's* skipper, George E. Pierce, was highly motivated, having lost his older brother on the USS *Argonaut.* The *Tunny* made two torpedo attacks, neither successful. The submarine returned empty-handed apart from two prisoners, apparently survivors of a ship sunk by the *Bonefish.*[68]

The *Spadefish* worked its way north to La Perouse Strait, but found the ships off Hokkaido disappointingly small, with its first three victims about 1,000 tons each. On 12 June at 3:30 A.M., the *Spadefish* made its first gun attack after spotting a motor sampan with sails rigged, quickly setting the sampan on fire. One of the *Spadefish* crew jumped overboard to capture a souvenir, a glass fishing ball from the vessel. The *Spadefish* destroyed another fishing vessel by gunfire later the same morning. Although the vessel appeared to have a machine gun on its bow, this proved to be only a wooden mock-up. Later in the day two more vessels were sunk by gunfire. Following one of the attacks torpedoman Lundquist, manning a machine gun, confided to his journal: "Got myself a Jap with .30 caliber."[69]

More attacks on freighters followed, but the *Spadefish's* largest kill proved a case of mistaken identity. In the Soya Strait between Hokkaido and Karafuto, the *Spadefish* torpedoed a 10,000-ton freighter. Germershausen, who had already been called on the carpet for mistakenly firing on a Russian ship in the Sea of Okhotsk during a previous patrol, hesitated to attack, but was egged on by his junior officers. The ship indeed later proved to be Russian—the *Transbalt* sailing out of Vladivostok. Having expended all of the *Spadefish's* torpedoes, Germershausen sought to make more gun attacks on small craft, but was denied permission by the pack commander.[70]

After sixteen days in the Sea of Japan, the submarines were to rendezvous at midnight on 24 June. When they assembled at the designated point just inside the bleak waters of La Perouse Strait, one of the submarines was missing. The USS *Bonefish,* last spotted on 18 June, had disappeared with all hands. The submarines had sunk a total of twenty-eight ships and another sixteen small craft on the mission.[71]

The destruction of junks and coastal traffic continued in other parts of the Pacific. Patrolling the Gulf of Siam, Tonkin Gulf, and the South China Sea, the USS *Hawkbill* found two junks at anchor only 1,000 yards offshore in the vicinity of Pulo Tenggol on the evening of 20 July 1945. Despite the proximity of land, crewmen from the *Hawkbill* boarded the larger of the two junks, finding it loaded to the gunwales with about 25,000 pounds of rice for Singapore. After putting the junk's crew in their lifeboat, they set the junk on fire. It burned slowly until raked with a pan of incendiary 20 mm shells, which set some fuel drums alight. The patrol report noted approvingly that after this the junk burned "very nicely."[72] More junks were boarded and burned using similar procedures.

The same month, July, after a fruitless search in the East Java Sea, the USS *Puffer* made a surface sweep along the northern coast of Bali, determined to see some action before heading back to base at Fremantle. When the submarine arrived at Chelukan Banang in the early hours of 5 July, the crew was surprised to find another submarine, the USS *Lizardfish,* already shelling the bay with its deck gun. The *Lizardfish* had left a couple of boathouses and a wooden lugger on fire on the beach. It had missed, however, five well-camouflaged barges, and the *Puffer* opened up on these with its five-inch gun from 1,400 yards. When hit the barges, apparently loaded with aviation fuel, sent flames 300 feet into the air. The *Puffer*'s skipper, Carl R. Dwyer, described it as "the most amazing sight I have seen in four years of submarine warfare."[73]

The *Puffer* continued its sweep along Bali's northern coast looking for more targets, and at Buleleng found a bay full of small craft. From 1,100 yards it opened up with the five-inch gun on a wooden sea truck anchored near the waterfront. After the submarine scored three quick hits in the middle of the vessel it broke in two, and with continued fire it disappeared entirely. Dwyer noted, "At this close range it was a revelation to see the power and destruction of this 5 inch High Capacity ammunition."[74]

The *Puffer* crew next shelled a freshly painted landing barge beached at the water's edge, and then trained the guns on a steel sea truck and motor sampan camouflaged with foliage. Finally a shore battery opened fire on the submarine, putting a round fifteen feet off the starboard side. The *Puffer* crew cleared the decks and submerged the boat, but hung around long enough to fire two torpedoes. One of the torpedoes hit the sea truck, while the other ran up the river to explode near a hub of activity at a bridge.

With the *Puffer* claiming damage on harbor installations as well as the sinking of two sea trucks and six landing craft, the patrol was judged "successful" on the basis of this one day's work. The gun actions, however, had been made at enormous risk. According to some of the crew, at least forty men were topside when the Japanese returned fire. Just clearing the deck before the submarine dived presented a major hazard that could have gone horribly wrong.[75]

The USS *Barb* similarly took enormous risks in pursuing shipping during its twelfth war patrol. In order to raise his crew's morale, Commander Gene Fluckey declared that they would sink fifteen vessels "of some kind" during the patrol. Hugging the east coast of Karafuto, near the town of Sakayehama, the *Barb* pursued a lugger into waters too shallow to dive. Although the *Barb* managed to sink the lugger, it was lucky to avoid counterattack by an aircraft and coastal defense cannons.[76]

The final U.S. submarine gun attacks of the war were made by the *Balao* as it patrolled east of Honshu. On the afternoon of 14 August the submarine spotted two luggers or picket boats hugging the coast, estimated to be a little over 100 tons each. After the *Balao* opened fire, one of the vessels beached itself. Although the submarine's five-inch shells appeared to fall short of the other vessel, they may have inflicted underwater damage since it began to sink. Both craft were believed armed, but the *Balao* received no return fire. Most of the *Balao*'s efforts on the patrol, though, were devoted to lifeguarding for downed aircraft crews, and the submarine returned to Pearl Harbor two days after the gun attacks.[77]

PART III

FACE-TO-FACE

10

Survivors

The German U-boat skipper Reinhard Hardegen once observed, "We were waging war against merchant ships, not against the crews, and there is a great difference."[1] No doubt many submarine commanders agreed, but there was also a great difference between not actively trying to kill survivors and doing something to assist them. Acts of compassion tended to be selective and fickle. Commander Otto Kretschmer of the *U-99* once became so haunted by the sight of a single man on a raft that on the following day he backtracked his submarine until he found the man. His crew provided the survivor with warm clothes and brandy, then transferred him to a lifeboat stocked with food and water.[2] Such singular attention to an enemy's survival, however, was rare. In both the Atlantic and the Pacific most survivors of submarine attacks had to rely on being rescued by their compatriots or sheer good fortune to stay alive. Even rescue by friendly ships could be in doubt, since those traveling in convoy were routinely instructed not to stop to help torpedoed merchantmen.[3]

In the Atlantic theater over 30,000 British merchant mariners perished during the war, a higher fatality rate than any of the armed services. The odds of survival tended to improve the longer the war lasted, because of innovations such as protective clothing and life jackets with lights. Much depended on how long a ship took to sink and the conditions of the sea; a slow-sinking ship on a calm sea during daylight in warm latitudes provided the optimal situation for survival. At least the last condition was much more likely to prevail in the South Pacific than in the North Atlantic, but while one might be less likely to die from hypothermia in tropical waters, the problems of thirst and sharks were accentuated. By one estimate, 116,000 seamen in the Japanese merchant marine were killed or wounded, with 70,000 casualties the result of U.S. submarine actions.[4]

Since submarines typically went deep to avoid counterattacks after firing their torpedoes, their crews tended to remain oblivious to the death and human misery left in their wake. Charles Andrews, skipper of the USS *Gurnard,* claimed never to have seen a Japanese survivor.[5] As with many other modes of mechanized twentieth-century warfare, a distant torpedo attack made killing easier and more impersonal. In contrast, gun attacks and boarding parties frequently brought submariners face-to-face with their victims; how they reacted in such situations illustrates a range of attitudes as well as the vagaries of naval warfare.

More than was true of other warships, the lack of space on submarines and their vulnerability on the surface provided two obvious disincentives for rescue operations. Admiral Chester Nimitz, in a statement to the war crimes tribunal at Nuremberg, emphasized the lack of room for passengers, while rescue operations could cause "undue additional hazard" and interfere with a submarine's mission.[6] German submariners made a similar case for not assisting survivors, emphasizing that they faced the added dangers posed by the Allies' effective use of radar and long-range aircraft patrols.[7]

Arguments about lack of space were in fact somewhat overstated, since submariners frequently managed to cram considerable numbers on board when rescuing comrades and allies. For example, after the USS *Sealion* and the USS *Pampanito* sank two Japanese transports in a convoy from Singapore in September 1944, the crews discovered that most of the passengers were Allied prisoners of war. The men of the *Pampanito* managed to pull seventy-three Australian and British survivors from the water and add them to the eighty-nine crew members already on board. The *Pampanito*'s skipper, Paul Edward Summers, noted the problem of habitability with so many men on board, but they were able to berth most in the after-torpedo room. Saving these men would be remembered as one of the *Pampanito*'s most illustrious actions of the war. Summoned to the scene, the

Sealion, Barb, and *Queenfish* assisted in the rescue, picking up over 100 more survivors despite the threat of an impending typhoon.[8]

The evacuation of soldiers and civilians from behind enemy lines also involved transporting considerable numbers of people by submarine. In April 1942, for instance, the USS *Searaven* evacuated thirty-one Australian aviators from Timor.[9] The USS *Gato* under Bob Foley picked up some fifty coast watchers, scouts, and refugees (including a half dozen Catholic nuns) from Teop Harbor on the northeastern coast of Bougainville for transport to Tulagi. Foley's executive officer, Norvell G. Ward, would later carry out many similar missions in command of the USS *Guardfish.* Ward believed a submarine could handle up to 100 additional passengers, as long as extended dives weren't required. In this sense air quality rather than space proved the main limitation.[10] Gene Fluckey of the *Barb* also believed that up to 100 survivors could be accommodated on a submarine if every square foot were used.[11]

Beginning in October 1943, nineteen different submarines evacuated nearly 500 civilians from the Philippines. In 1944, for example, the USS *Angler* made a rendezvous off Panay expecting to take on about twenty passengers, but found fifty-eight people waiting to be rescued. Not wanting to disappoint people who had been stranded for two years, the crew packed them into the torpedo rooms and lived on short rations until the submarine could reach Australia.[12]

Such missions exposed submarines to extraordinary dangers, as did rescue efforts to recover downed aircrew. The idea of submarines "lifeguarding" for Allied aviators originated with Admiral Charles Pownall after he led air attacks on the Gilbert Islands. With their ability to penetrate deep into enemy waters, submarines appeared to be a splendid means of recovering downed pilots and crews. Charles Lockwood claimed that the *Skate,* under Gene McKinney, carried out the first "effective lifeguard duty" when fighters and bombers attacked Wake Island in early October 1943, but the episode also highlighted the dangers involved.[13] Diving out of an overcast sky, a Japanese Zero surprised the submarine during the operation and one of the *Skate*'s officers, Lieutenant (junior grade) Willis E. Maxson, was shot. Maxson died the following day. In a similar incident, the executive officer and five crewmen of the USS *Plunger* were wounded by a diving Zero in late 1943 while lifeguarding in the eastern Marshall Islands.

On one patrol alone the USS *Tang* under Richard O'Kane rescued twenty-two aviators. In line with O'Kane's recommendations, a special air patrol subsequently worked with submarines to locate downed aircrews and provide air cover for the rescuers. In 1945 the USS *Tigrone* under Hiram Cassedy set a record by rescuing 31 downed aviators in the space of five days. By the end of the war U.S. submarines had pulled over 500 airmen out of the drink.[14] The Japanese had nothing comparable, and indeed were astonished by American efforts to recover their men.[15]

On occasion submarines also effectively doubled the number of men on board by rescuing the crews of other Allied submarines that ran aground. When the USS *Darter* grounded in October 1944, the 85 officers and enlisted men were transferred to the USS *Dace*. With 165 men on board, provisions were quickly depleted, but the men reached Fremantle on a diet of mushroom soup and peanut butter. Similarly, after the Dutch submarine *O-19* grounded on a reef in July 1945, the USS *Cod* picked up the entire crew. In yet another dramatic incident, after the USS *Bergall* received damage from an enemy shell, all hands but a skeleton crew were transferred to the USS *Angler*.[16]

There was, of course, a difference between having cooperative comrades on board and the potential dangers of an enemy. At least in the early stages of the war, any rescue operation could likely expose submarines to considerable danger, and attempts to aid survivors remained relatively rare. Some submariners, however, did assume responsibility when they endangered noncombatants. After accidentally ramming a sampan in Makassar Strait on 31 May 1943, for example, the crew of the USS *Gurnard* temporarily took on board fourteen Moros (Muslims indigenous to the southern Philippines). Although the Moros carried some Japanese money on them, the crew did not ask for payment; they were given food and later transferred to another sampan.[17]

As previously noted, submariners tended to do more to assist survivors, or at least minimize loss of life, as the war progressed and more gun attacks were made. William Robert Anderson, who served on the USS *Trutta,* recalled that if women and children were spotted on junks, the crew would allow the passengers to abandon the vessel before firing along its waterline.[18] As skipper of the USS *Bluefish,* Lieutenant Commander George W. Forbes Jr. recommended that submarines be equipped with additional life rafts in order to accommodate people off-loaded from vessels sunk.[19] William Kinsella, skipper of the USS *Ray,* explained that when he and his men sank small ships they tried to knock out the engine first, allowing crews to get in lifeboats before they sank the craft with the five-inch gun and fire.[20]

Some other submariners were more proactive in assisting survivors. On 13 February 1944, the USS *Hake* used its guns to attack a sailing sloop estimated to be fifteen tons. After the *Hake* fired some "challenging bursts" from its 20 mm gun, the sloop changed course and ran up a Japanese flag, at which point the submarine destroyed the craft with a withering fire kept up for nearly ten minutes. The *Hake* pulled four Malaysian survivors from the water, but two broke away and jumped overboard. According to the patrol report, the two men who remained on board responded to "dry clothes and kind treatment." The *Hake* returned to the site of the sinking about an hour later, and crewmen managed to coax the two other Malaysians back on board; they also responded to "decent treatment," but had little information to impart.[21]

In another incident, the USS *Hawkbill* used its deck guns to sink a small coastal steamer in the Gulf of Siam on the night of 29 May 1945. The crew subsequently discovered twelve Siamese survivors, including one young woman, in a sinking lifeboat. Some of these people were temporarily brought on board the submarine, but four men were too badly wounded to move. After the *Hawkbill's* men bailed out the survivors' half-flooded lifeboat and accommodated some of them in the submarine's rubber boat, they towed the Siamese ten miles toward land before cutting them loose some four miles from the coast of Thailand. At this point the survivors were given some bread, fresh water, a medical kit, and directions to the nearest land.[22]

As discussed in the next chapter, Japanese survivors were almost invariably treated as a distinct group. The status of Koreans, and more so "native" Malays, Indonesians, Indians, Chinese, and Filipinos, proved more ambiguous. At least initially, many local peoples in Southeast Asia accepted Japanese occupation with equanimity. The Greater East Asia Co-prosperity Sphere proclaimed in August 1940 promised liberation from Western control, while "pan-Asian" rhetoric appealed to the nationalist instincts of Indonesians, Malays, and Indians. At least initially, for example, Indonesian elites widely collaborated with the Japanese. By the end of the war, however, most had been alienated by the privations, forced labor, notions of racial superiority, and outright cruelty they endured under Japanese rule. An estimated 5 million people died in Southeast Asia as a result of Japanese invasion and occupation.[23]

The problem for Americans often involved distinguishing between friend and foe. Shortly after the attack on Pearl Harbor, *Time* magazine offered hints on distinguishing the Japanese from other Asians, but it is doubtful that this helped much in practice. *Time* observed, for example, that the Chinese were less hairy than the Japanese and likely to have a "more placid" expression.[24] It appears that some U.S. submariners drew little distinction between Koreans and Japanese. Dale Russell, a gunner on the *Flying Fish*, reports that one of his crewmates wondered out loud "what good we did by shooting up those small Korean boats." Another crewman, however, retorted, "Remember what the bastards did at Pearl Harbor? . . . Some of the planes flown on that Pearl Harbor attack were probably flown by Korean pilots."[25]

In truth, thousands of Koreans had joined the Japanese armed forces, although often through coercion. After Korea was annexed by Japan in 1910, Koreans remained second-class members of the Empire and resisted assimilation policies, which by the 1930s included a ban on using the Korean language in schools. A further move toward cultural domination came in 1938 when Koreans were forced to adopt Japanese surnames. The veneer of volunteer recruitment ended in August 1943 when full-scale conscription began, and more than 200,000 Koreans were drawn into the Japanese Army and Navy. At least some would develop a reputation for brutality comparable to that of the Japanese. Over another million Koreans were forced to work in Japanese factories, construction sites, and mines during the war, and throughout the war they were conscripted into labor battalions in support of Japanese troops.[26]

There is some anecdotal evidence that American submariners treated Koreans more leniently than they did the Japanese. Conducting its fourth patrol in the Yellow Sea and East China Sea, the USS *Segundo* attempted to discriminate between vessels manned by Koreans and those crewed by Japanese, attacking only the latter. On the afternoon of 29 May 1945, the *Segundo* pulled alongside a Korean craft, motioning for one of the crew members to board the submarine. Apparently the whole crew wanted to come on board; however, all but one were turned away. According to the *Segundo*'s patrol report, the submariners reasoned that a Korean prisoner "would be just as well informed as the Japanese and would be more inclined to part with his information." The report added, "Besides he was cleaner and was not wounded."[27]

After stopping and boarding a fishing schooner in April 1945, the USS *Tirante* crew found "three thoroughly scared and whimpering fishermen." The men, all apparently Koreans, were taken prisoner. Interrogation later revealed that a fourth Korean on the schooner had evaded the Americans, because "he thought we were Japs, thus putting his days as a 'draft-dodger' to an end."[28] In another incident, the *Tirante* fired on a two-masted schooner, estimated at thirty to forty feet long, when patrolling off the western coast of Korea in June 1945. The vessel quickly hove to, and when inspected was found to be manned mainly by old men who were assumed to be Korean. The only man of military age on the schooner was taken prisoner. The rest of the schooner's complement received some bread, Spam, and cigarettes, for which the *Tirante* crew "received much bowing to express their thanks."[29]

A confidential letter from the Pacific Fleet in December 1944 instructed that whenever it was practical to do so, Korean and Formosan prisoners should be segregated from the Japanese, noting, "The hostility which many Formosans and Koreans feel for the Japanese makes them particularly valuable as a source of intelligence."[30] At least occasionally, it appears that Japanese prisoners tried to trade on the distinction. As described by the *Barb*'s commander, Gene Fluckey, one of their Japanese prisoners "was smart enough to claim he was Korean, knowing full well none of us could tell the difference."[31]

Generally, the ethnic Chinese elicited greater sympathy than other groups in the Pacific. Japan had occupied Manchuria in 1931 and seized much of China's coast in 1937, nearly two full years before Germany invaded Poland. Following the Doolittle bombing raid on Japan, the Chinese aided in the recovery of sixty-seven American airmen, suffering massive retaliation from the Japanese for their efforts. During the course of the war an estimated 15 million Chinese were killed.[32]

Chinese who were living overseas tended to view the war as an extension of Japanese aggression in China and formed the main element of resistance. At least on occasion, Chinese fishermen helped land Allied agents from submarines in Malaya.[33] Throughout Southeast Asia the Chinese also suffered the main brunt of occupation. After the conquest of Singapore, thousands of Chinese were tied up and dumped at sea or machine-gunned. Japanese Army administrative policies for Sumatra and Malaya stipulated that hostile Chinese be executed, and that noncooperation be met with property confiscation and deportation. Many Chinese were massacred in Malaya, and other massacres occurred in Borneo, where the money and businesses of local Chinese were appropriated. Thousands of Chinese were sent to Japan to work in mines or on construction works, where many perished.[34]

With ships frequently manned by mixed crews, the Chinese often became unintended casualties. On the afternoon of 19 March 1945 the USS *Balao* battle surfaced and attacked a group of trawlers. In one of the attacks four men were blown over the side of their vessel after being hit by a five-inch shell. The *Balao* crewmen left a rubber boat for the survivors. With prisoners already on board, they were not keen for more, but nevertheless took on board a young man who swam to the submarine.

Those left in the lifeboat yelled pitifully as the submarine sailed away. The *Balao*'s commander, Robert Kemble Worthington, confided, "Poor devils probably would have been better drowned than dying of exposure."[35] In fact, as the *Balao* sped away, it dawned on him that one of the men in the lifeboat had been yelling, "Me Chinesieman." Sure enough, the young man picked up by the *Balao* proved to be Chinese. With this information, Worthington elected not to attack another group of trawlers spotted later the same day.

The USS *Ray* further illustrated the dilemma of sorting out the relatively "innocent" from belligerents during its seventh war patrol, when it attacked small ships transporting rice from Korea to Japan in the Yellow Sea. The patrol got off to a poor start due to defective torpedoes. In one attack a torpedo literally jumped out of the water, resulting in the *Ray* being punished by a severe depth charging in shallow waters. In order to compensate for the torpedo problems, the submarine began gunning for diesel luggers and sailing vessels.[36]

When the *Ray* pulled alongside one of its victims, a four-masted schooner, on 24 May 1945, water was already washing over the sinking craft's deck. Eight frightened Chinese emerged from the aft end of the schooner, and they were brought onto the submarine's deck with the idea of transferring them to a fishing boat. A couple of the Chinese spoke enough English to explain that the vessel was bound from Daimen to Kyushu under the command of two Japanese. The *Ray*'s attack killed one of the Japanese, while the other reportedly took the schooner's only life ring and jumped overboard when the first shots were fired.

For skipper William Kinsella, the interrogation was a revelation: "[W]e realized that in sinking these ships we had killed innocent, although mercenary Chinese and Koreans."[37] Kinsella still believed the ships had to be sunk, however, since the vessels and their cargoes of rice were of value to the Japanese. He resolved, though, that in future he would give crews every chance to abandon their vessels before destroying them.

Having given the Chinese some food and transferred them

to a fishing sampan, the *Ray* attacked another schooner the same morning. This time the crew fired only a few rounds from the 40 mm gun into the ship's rigging. The patrol report jubilantly noted: "Our tactics work! The crew lowered the lifeboat and abandoned ship."[38] The *Ray*'s boarding party subsequently set the vessel on fire, but only after discovering the Korean master in the hold and taking him prisoner. This system of subduing by gunfire, putting crews in lifeboats, and then destroying the craft with fire saved not only lives but ammunition. Nevertheless, Kinsella emphasized that he would not put a single member of his crew in jeopardy for the sake of a survivor.[39] Some submariners adopted a policy of boarding ships only if the crews refused to leave, fearing that otherwise there might be a danger of booby traps.[40]

Allied submariners, along with fate, sometimes dealt survivors extremely cruel hands. After the USS *Spadefish* sank a Japanese freighter in February 1945, the submarine surfaced to look over the survivors. According to torpedoman John Schumer, "When you got topside after a sinking and saw the group in the water, you felt sorry for them." In the freezing waters of the Yellow Sea, Schumer observed, "you'd know they weren't going to last long."[41] Interested in finding a useful prisoner, the crew of the *Spadefish* nosed up to a lifeboat, and an armed deck party coaxed a couple of men on board the submarine. One was so young that the submariners initially mistook him for a woman. This youth could speak some broken English, but once the men were identified as Chinese instead of Japanese they were thrown overboard into the icy waters. The episode haunted some of the crewmen long after.[42]

Many ships had ethnically mixed crews, frequently overseen by one or two Japanese officers.[43] After sinking a small freighter in May 1945, the USS *Blenny* acquired a detailed profile of its crew, noting that in addition to twelve Japanese from Batavia, the crew consisted of seventeen Javanese, three men from Borneo, two each from Ambon and Madura, two Chinese from Singapore, and one Dyak. The ship itself, the 520-ton *Hokoku Maru,* was formerly the Chinese ship *Li Liang.* After the sinking the *Blenny* crew spotted eighteen men in the water, and persuaded a dozen to board the submarine. These included four Japanese and eight Indonesians. Most of the Indonesians were later transferred to a small prau and given some tinned goods for their trouble. The three Indonesians who elected to remain on board the submarine were identified as Wasio Soewito, a Javanese and the ship's second machinist; seaman Said Abdullah, a Javanese-Madurese; and Max Adam, the fireman from Ambon.[44]

While mixed crews might function harmoniously when a vessel was afloat, the battle for survival following a submarine attack sometimes revealed ethnic tensions. After sinking a junk on its next patrol, the crewmen of USS *Blenny* discovered that the junk's skiff was unable to hold the entire crew; two men, Indians, were in the water until rescued by the submariners. The other crew members were Chinese who, as explained by the patrol report, "not having room for all, had drawn the race line."[45] The *Blenny* transferred the survivors to a sampan headed for Terengganu with a load of dried fish two days later, compensating them with a sack of canned goods.[46]

Some Southeast Asians apparently served willingly within the Japanese military organization while others were incorporated under duress. In these cases, the lines between survivors and prisoners often seemed blurred. When in late 1942 the USS *Tautog* came across a seventy-five-ton fishing schooner in the Sulu Sea, it fired across the vessel's bow. After the schooner hoisted a Japanese flag and hove to, the *Tautog* crew found that the craft was manned by a dozen Japanese and four young Filipinos. In this case the Japanese were treated kindly; after they abandoned ship in a small boat, they were given food, water, and directions to land. The four Filipinos were brought on board the submarine, where they claimed that the Japanese had impressed them into service from Zamboanga and kept them prisoner with no pay.[47] Charles Lockwood suggested that the young men might be employed as submarine mess attendants, claiming, "I have been urging all skippers to do a little recruiting and this is our first batch."[48]

As Lockwood's comment suggests, submariners sometimes demonstrated an inherent sympathy for the people of the Philippines, millions of whom had been killed or dislocated by the Japanese occupation.[49] The USS *Gudgeon* collected more Filipinos after using its deck guns to sink a small trawler off Nogas Island in the Sulu Sea on 4 May 1943. The ship, identified as the *Naku Maru,* carried a load of lube oil, ice, and fishhooks. From among the twenty people left in the water, the *Gudgeon* crew picked up three Filipinos, who claimed they had been forced to work for the Japanese. Perhaps believing there were further Filipino survivors still in the water, skipper Bill Post had a rubber boat with provisions put over the side.[50]

On the way back to Fremantle at the end of its second war patrol in January 1944, the USS *Puffer* encountered a trawler and fired a warning shot across its bow. Instead of stopping, the vessel turned away and increased its speed. After being hit about fifteen times, the craft finally stopped and hoisted a white rag of surrender. The *Puffer* signaled for men on the deck of the trawler to swim over to the submarine, and the two who complied proved to be Javanese. One of the young men could speak a little English, and he indicated that most of the sixteen left on board were Japanese. The *Puffer* then sank the craft with gunfire but also left an inflated rubber boat stocked with water, canned goods, and a can opener for survivors.

The English-speaking Javanese identified himself as Abdul Hamid, and the trawler as the *Nansing Maru No. 16* out of Surabaya. He had apparently learned to read and write at Dutch schools. The *Puffer*'s patrol report noted that "the two Javanese are apparently very happy to be aboard, Abdul professing a distinct dislike for the Japs and great friendship for the Americans and Dutch."[51] Just how genuine these sentiments were, of course, is questionable, but the Javanese appeared to fit easily into the *Puffer*'s routine. They were assigned to cleaning duties and impressed the crew with their hard work.

Survivors picked up by the USS *Raton* on its fourth patrol were similarly put to work. After sinking a small freighter with gunfire, the submarine picked up the Japanese engineering officer as well as ten islanders from Celebes. It picked up an additional eight Chinese after sinking a small sampan. The Chinese were employed as mess cooks, while the others were put to work cleaning en route to Fremantle. One of the *Raton* officers, Donald "Pete" Sencenbaugh, later boasted that "we had the cleanest, polished submarine that ever landed in Australia."[52]

Keeping survivors in such large numbers was rare, however, and posed potential management problems both on board and back at base. On one patrol in the Straits of Malacca, for example, the HMS *Thule* accumulated thirty-five survivors on board, close to half the number of British crew. When the *Thule* was depth charged, the survivors threatened to mutiny and had to be beaten back by the crew with spanners.[53]

Early in 1945 the *Bashaw* operated in tandem with the USS *Flasher* off the east coast of Hainan. On 21 February the submarines attacked two boats described in the *Bashaw*'s patrol report as "pathetically small." When one of the craft capsized, twenty people were left in the water; desperately clinging to debris, they "set up a terrific wailing." The men of the *Bashaw* were not prepared to take all the survivors on board, deciding that two "was the greatest plenty."[54] In the meantime the *Flasher* picked up one man from the water, but as the submarine backed away the crewmen discovered another person clawing his way aboard. The patrol report commented, "Didn't have the heart to push him back, so took him too."[55] Both the people picked up by the *Flasher* proved to be Chinese teenage boys who spoke some English. According to their information, each of the boats sunk had carried about fifteen Japanese troops, but about half of the crew members were Chinese.

With increasing numbers of small craft boarded and sunk during the closing months of the war, it became common practice for some submariners to off-load the occupants before sinking their vessel. The USS *Bugara,* under command of Arnold F. Schade, searched and destroyed a total of fifty-seven junks, schooners, and other coastal vessels in the Gulf of Siam during July–August 1945. Armed with two five-inch/25-caliber guns, the *Bugara* expended more than 200 rounds of five-inch ammunition in addition to nearly 700 rounds of 20 mm and 40 mm ammunition.

The *Bugara* crew began the patrol by boarding and releasing a number of craft unharmed, but Schade received permission from the Commander Task Force 71 to attack vessels carrying supplies. On 24 July the submarine sank a schooner loaded with spare parts for aircraft. Most of the craft attacked carried food as part of a Bangkok–Singapore supply line. The crew of one coaster from Singapore was reportedly delighted to be boarded and begged to remain on the submarine. The *Bugara* did retain one of the men, apparently educated at a British university, to act as an interpreter. There were other crews that cheered when their vessels were sunk, saying such things as "The Japs are finish—no more work for Japs."[56]

In one notable incident, on 2 August, the *Bugara* approached a 150-ton schooner at anchor, surrounded by Malay canoes. The schooner proved to be a Japanese vessel with a Chinese crew hauling rice to Singapore, while the Malays turned out to be pirates. The pirates had already killed two of the crew on the schooner before being driven off by the *Bugara*. The submarine then off-loaded the Chinese and sank the schooner with its cargo. Schade believed that those Chinese who lost their ships would be killed if they returned to Singapore, so most "took to the hills" once put on shore.[57]

In the *Bugara*'s experience, any Japanese aboard a vessel usually jumped overboard as soon as he spotted a submarine. Before the *Bugara*'s crew destroyed a craft, the local crews were either allowed to get into lifeboats or were temporarily taken on board the submarine with their personal belongings until they could be transferred to another boat or to shore. This was apparently the preferred method of operation by this stage of the war, since an endorsement of the *Bugara*'s patrol praised: "Excellent judgment was used in following the force policy of examining all cargoes and providing for the safety of friendly native crews."[58] "Friendly" was the operative word, however, and often determined by submarine crews on tenuous evidence within a matter of seconds.

A similar pattern is illustrated by the actions of the USS *Icefish* when it encountered a lugger in the Hong Kong area during the late afternoon of 7 August 1945. The boat, estimated at fifteen tons, carried building bricks, rice, and oil and was apparently traveling from Singapore to Borneo. One of the Japanese crew jumped overboard rather than be taken. The remaining crewmen (described as "five

Chinese, two Malaccans, and one Jap") were brought aboard the submarine. The *Icefish* then destroyed the lugger using the deck guns.

Once on board the *Icefish*, the men from the lugger were cleaned up and given clothes from new Red Cross survivor kits. The lone Japanese prisoner remained isolated, but the others messed in the after-torpedo room and were given access to a head in the maneuvering room. According to the patrol report, the Chinese and Malaccans "kept very clean and worked hard, specially the two Eurasians who were excellent mess cooks and tackled their work with pride and gusto."[59] The *Icefish* subsequently received instructions to transfer the lugger's crew to another submarine or put all but the Japanese on a local craft. On the morning of 11 August all eight were transferred to the USS *Croaker* for transport to Subic Bay, where they arrived a few days later.[60]

Although space for survivors was at an even greater premium on British submarines than on the American boats, some British captains adopted similar practices. When the HMS *Storm* under Edward Young attacked a small wooden two-masted schooner on 1 August 1944, most of the schooner's crew jumped overboard. The submariners discovered later that the captain, first mate, and chief engineer were Japanese, while the rest of the crew consisted of five Malays, two Chinese, and two Indians. The Japanese had already shot some of the crew when they attempted to abandon ship.

The surviving Japanese avoided being picked up, but the submarine took on board two men described as Indians, both with serious wounds. Young's attention was then drawn to a young Malay man who waved and shouted excitedly. Against the advice of his executive officer, Young directed for him to be brought on board. As it turned out the fellow, named Endi, spoke excellent English. Expressing joy at coming under British authority, he quickly proved himself useful. When the *Storm* attacked another coastal vessel the same day, Endi warned that it might be an ammunition ship; luckily the *Storm* kept its distance, because the craft exploded in a shower of potentially lethal debris.[61] Endi represented a small select group of survivors who actively served as intermediaries between Allied submariners and local seafarers.

11

Japanese Prisoners

In the Hollywood movie *Destination Tokyo,* released shortly before Christmas in 1943, theatergoers were given a rare glimpse into the world of the "Silent Service." The film, starring Cary Grant, focused on the fictional submarine *Copperfin* as it carried out a mission of reconnaissance for the Doolittle bombing raid on Tokyo. In one action sequence Japanese Zeroes attacked the *Copperfin* as it traveled on the surface through the Aleutian Islands. The *Copperfin*'s crew managed to shoot down the planes, but when one of the sailors tried to assist a downed Japanese pilot, he was stabbed to death. The submariners promptly retaliated by machine-gunning the pilot.[1]

The navy's technical adviser for the film was none other than Mush Morton. As a reward for his outstanding patrol in January 1943, Morton was given leave in Hollywood while the *Wahoo* underwent refit at the Mare Island Navy Yard. Possibly influenced by Morton, *Destination Tokyo* reflected a common view of the Japanese as fanatics who preferred death to surrender. Although a stereotype, it was far from unfounded.

The Japanese Field Code issued in 1941 bluntly declared: "Do not be taken prisoner alive."[2] The Japanese refused to ratify the Geneva Convention on the treatment of POWs partly on the grounds that such provisions would be entirely one-sided; Japan's vice minister of the navy explained that his men had no concept of being captured.[3] As an additional disincentive to surrender, the government informally warned that any prisoners of war returning to Japan would be executed. At the end of the war, the United States held only about 5,500 Japanese POWs.[4] Admiral Charles Lockwood claimed that the

Japanese "fought so long as they had a weapon and, even when found helpless in the water, refused to be rescued."[5] In his statement to the International Military Tribunal at Nuremberg, Admiral Charles Nimitz similarly referred to "the known desperate and suicidal character of the enemy" when explaining the reluctance of submariners to pick up survivors.[6]

There are abundant examples of Japanese refusing rescue by submarines. At least one involved the USS *Haddo* commanded by Chester Nimitz Jr., the Pacific Fleet commander's son. After sinking a ship on the night of 21 September 1944, the *Haddo*'s crew tried to induce some of the forty or so Japanese survivors to come aboard. On two occasions the submarine's spotlight trained on swimmers within six feet of the hull, only to watch the men sink and apparently drown themselves. The *Haddo*'s war patrol report recorded, "Got so disgusted we depth-charged one of them with a hand grenade as he went deep."[7]

Those Japanese captured were often taken by force. On the USS *Gudgeon,* crewman Albert Strow recorded in a diary his role in the acquisition of a survivor for interrogation. Whenever the submarine got close enough to pick up a prospective prisoner, the Japanese would dive under the surface. As related by Strow, "Finally we flooded down to where the deck was just awash and with two sailors hanging on to my feet I was able to grab on to him and the 2 of us were dragged on board."[8] Submariners occasionally had explicit orders to obtain prisoners and formed swimming teams for the express purpose of capturing them.[9]

Japanese resistance to being captured did not result simply from a sense of duty; they also feared that they would be tortured and killed. Stories of alleged Allied atrocities circulated widely among the Japanese forces. John W. Clary, who kept a secret diary during his time on the *Wahoo,* noted, "It strikes me that the Japs are taught we will torture them so they prefer death instead."[10] After the USS *Balao* sank a trawler on 18 March 1945, the crew found that despite the freezing waters survivors were reluctant to be rescued. But, the patrol report noted, "when we put away the tommy gun, several began to clamor to come on board."[11]

For many prisoners, their first introduction to submarine life could hardly have been comforting. They were invariably stripped in a search for concealed weapons and as part of the "delousing" process. Prisoners also had their hair shaved or closely clipped to prevent the spread of lice. Since this process could include shaving their pubic area, sometimes at gunpoint, the situation proved rife for misunderstanding.[12] Some prisoners also feared being poisoned. After the *Flying Fish* picked up a prisoner in the Sea of Japan, the man refused the offer of soup until one of the crew took a swallow.[13]

Occasionally it seemed that a prisoner's worst fears might be realized. In September 1944 the USS *Seahorse* spotted a group of four downed Japanese aviators who had already spent five days adrift in nothing more than life jackets. Skipper Charles "Weary" Wilkins had one of the men brought on board for interrogation. He proved to be badly injured and, while being treated by the pharmacist's mate, a large torpedoman menaced him with a machete. Whether this played a role is unclear, but the prisoner died a short time later, at which point he was unceremoniously put over the side in a mattress cover weighted with a five-inch shell.

Still determined to get a prisoner, the crew of the *Seahorse* returned to the group of drifting aviators. As the submarine approached, two of the Japanese swam away, but a third waved his arms. The new prisoner, suffering from exposure and burned almost black from the sun, was confined in a torpedo room. Eventually the crew warmed to the young man, identified as Seiza Mitsuma, a seventeen-year-old bomber radio operator. When the *Seahorse* made an attack, Mitsuma was handcuffed to a bunk in the crew's quarters and kept under armed guard. After several weeks, though, he was given a degree of freedom and put to work cleaning and cooking. As described by one of the *Seahorse* crew, yeoman Dell Brooks, he was "really a nice kid and the entire crew took to him."[14]

As in this case, a number of prisoners picked up by submarines were downed aviators. Given that Japanese aircrews had no parachutes until mid-1943 and an acute shortage of flying boats, rescue by their own forces was unlikely.[15] On the morning of 1 April 1944, the USS *Tunny* came across a Japanese airman swimming some thirty miles west of Palau. The crew maneuvered the submarine alongside him, but despite having no life jacket and being circled by two large sharks, he refused rescue. The same morning, however, the *Tunny* crew persuaded another downed aviator to board the submarine. The prisoner, a nineteen-year-old Zero pilot shot down the previous day, proved "a model prisoner and quite willing to talk."[16]

When in April 1945 the USS *Tirante* encountered an overturned Japanese floatplane with three aircrew members, one of the men, identified by his goggles as the pilot, threw a lit flare at the submarine. Lieutenant Commander Edward Beach replied with a warning rifle shot, while the gunners on deck had to be restrained from opening fire. The submarine had previously taken on board several Koreans from a sunk fishing schooner; these men were employed to try to persuade the Japanese onto the submarine. One of the Japanese shouted, "Kill, Kill, Kill" before drowning himself. Another of the men gave himself up, while the pilot was brought on board after apparently losing consciousness.[17]

Once assured that they would not be tortured or killed, Japanese prisoners often became highly cooperative. After sinking a Japanese fishing vessel, the *Nanko Maru,* near the Telaga Islands, the crew of the USS *Redfin* resorted to tangling up the feet of one survivor in a line so he could be dragged on board. The patrol report noted that as soon as the prisoner realized he wasn't going to be killed, he quickly settled down and tried to answer the questions put to him.[18]

The Japanese refusal to consider capture as an option meant that troops had received no indoctrination on their "rights" as POWs or on the safeguarding of information under interrogation.[19] After the USS *Barb* picked up a prisoner in 1944, a secret report by skipper Eugene Fluckey noted that the man "was extremely grateful for being rescued from a certain death in icy waters, was always affable, and apparently did his best to get the information we wanted across to us." After a week of interrogation, however, the prisoner expressed concern that if the Japanese became aware of his cooperation he would be beheaded. Once assured that this wouldn't happen, the man continued to supply intelligence. At one stage the prisoner, according to Fluckey's report, announced "that when we took him aboard he was a Japanese Navy man, but now he was an American Navy man, and sincerely never intends to return to Japan."[20]

Prisoners were often most compliant in the anxious period immediately after capture.[21] On the other hand, interrogations were generally inhibited by language difficulties. The USS *Jack* picked up two prisoners after sinking a trawler north of Luzon in April 1944; over several days of interrogation the crew discovered that the vessel sunk was the *Dun Sai* and that it carried eight crewmen and a radio. Lacking anyone with interpreter skills, however, the submariners found "a nearly dry well" when it came to intelligence information.[22] When Gene Fluckey questioned a prisoner picked up in the Sea of Okhotsk north of Hokkaido in 1944, he had only a one-page phonetic vocabulary taken from a Bureau of Personnel bulletin. He later procured an English-Japanese dictionary while on leave, which facilitated questioning.[23]

Understandably, Japanese survivors from merchant ships or fishing vessels tended to be more compliant than those in the military.[24] Even survivors from the same vessel, however, might react in quite different ways. When on 23 June 1945 the USS *Barb* made a gun attack on a wooden diesel trawler, setting the craft on fire, some of the crew preferred to burn with the vessel rather than abandon ship. According to the *Barb*'s patrol report, one of the men "committed Hari-Kari by slitting his throat." Another five of the crew, however, volunteered to be taken on board the submarine. The *Barb* crewmen selected only one prisoner, and when they revisited the site a couple of hours later, they found that the rest had "joined their ancestors."[25]

Indeed, picking up survivors frequently became a process of selection rather than simply taking all who volunteered. After the *Barb* sank a trawler during a gun action the following month, the patrol report noted, "Selected two prisoners who appeared to be in fair shape."[26] A similar approach was evident after the USS *Bowfin* sank a small ship with gunfire on 4 September 1944. With about a dozen Japanese survivors in the water, the *Bowfin* captain planned to take a single prisoner. As it turned out, two men grabbed for a proffered life ring "and held on for all they were worth," despite both being

The USS *Sculpin* at Mare Island in 1943, armed with a three-inch gun and a 20 mm gun. (U.S. Navy photo #NH97305, courtesy of the Naval Historical Center, Washington, DC)

A sampan burns in the Sulu Sea in the aftermath of an attack by the USS *Gar*. (U.S. Navy photo, courtesy of the USS *Bowfin* Submarine Museum, Pearl Harbor)

Mike Harbin, torpedoman's mate third class on the USS *Silversides,* became the first submariner killed in a surface gun action. (Courtesy of Charles R. Hinman, On Eternal Patrol Web site)

Dudley "Mush" Morton in his stateroom on the USS *Wahoo*. (U.S. Navy photo, courtesy of the USS *Bowfin* Submarine Museum, Pearl Harbor)

rewmen of the USS *Wahoo* assault a disabled trawler with Molotov cocktails. (U.S. Navy
hoto, courtesy of the USS *Bowfin* Submarine Museum, Pearl Harbor)

A billboard at the Mare Island Navy Yard pays tribute to the USS *Wahoo* following its successful patrol in January 1943. (U.S. Navy photo, courtesy of USS *Bowfin* Submarine Museum, Pearl Harbor)

A lookout on the deck of the USS *Albacore;* note the 20 mm gun in the foreground and the four-inch gun in the background. (U.S. Navy photo, courtesy of the Submarine Force Museum, Groton, Connecticut)

The *Taiei Maru* burns after being hit with gunfire by the USS *Albacore*. (U.S. Navy photo, courtesy of the Submarine Force Museum, Groton, Connecticut)

Japanese POWs from the *Taiei Maru* on the deck of the USS *Albacore*.
(U.S. Navy photo, courtesy of the Submarine Force Museum, Groton,
Connecticut)

An Australian commando on board the USS *Gar* at Exmouth
Gulf. (U.S. Navy photo, courtesy of the USS *Bowfin* Submarine
Museum, Pearl Harbor)

Submarine gun action, possibly on the USS *Bugara*, in July 1945. (U.S. Navy photo, courtesy of NavSource Online: Submarine Photo Archive)

Eugene Fluckey, wearing a Navy Cross, poses on the deck of the
USS *Barb*. (U.S. Navy photo #NH103534, courtesy of the Naval
Historical Center, Washington, DC)

The Barb Strikes, an artist's depiction of the *Barb* battling patrol craft and junks. (Courtesy of the USS *Bowfin* Submarine Museum, Pearl Harbor)

Mush Morton (*right*) and his wife with Cary Grant on the set of *Destination Tokyo,* 1943. (Dudley Morton Papers, courtesy of the USS *Bowfin* Submarine Museum, Pearl Harbor)

Oil-covered Allied prisoners of war rescued by the USS *Queenfish* after the *Rakuyo Maru* was sunk in September 1944. (U.S. Navy photo, courtesy of NavSource Online: Submarine Photo Archive)

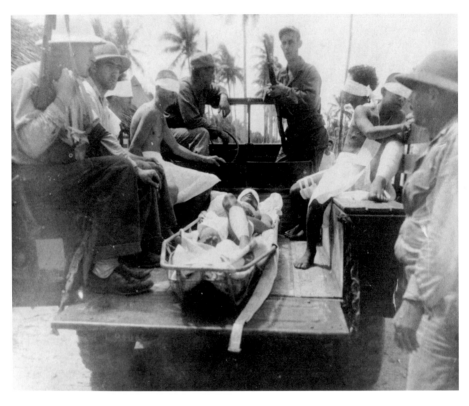

Japanese prisoners taken by the USS *Albacore* on arrival at Los Negros, Admiralty Islands. (U.S. Navy photo, courtesy of the Submarine Force Museum, Groton, Connecticut)

wounded.[27] On one occasion the USS *Ray* under William Kinsella took a Japanese prisoner who didn't want to be left in a lifeboat with Chinese survivors.[28]

Ultimately, the relatively small numbers of prisoners taken reflected Allied submariners' disinclination as much as Japanese resistance. If prisoners were collected at all, there was a preference for picking them up toward the end of a patrol so they would not require lengthy supervision. For example, after sinking a ship a little after midnight on 6 July 1944, the USS *Sunfish* crewmen inspected wreckage and found a number of Japanese on rafts. According to the patrol report, they "heard much moaning and sing-song shouting Jap," but since it was still early in the patrol they elected not to pick up any survivors.[29]

The USS *Parche*, under Red Ramage, illustrated a similar lack of enthusiasm about prisoners. In 1944, in its first enemy contact of the patrol, the *Parche* attacked and sank a picket boat south of the Bonin Islands. The crew spotted about five survivors in the water, but showed little inclination to bring them on board since the submarine had just arrived at its patrol area. As Ramage later explained, "[W]e had no place for them aboard and to try and keep them under surveillance in a submarine during the patrols would be a very difficult problem."[30] As it transpired, those in the water exhibited no interest in being rescued, with one of the men trying to hide by putting his head in a bucket.

Potential prisoners who had injuries were generally left to their fates. After attacking a small freighter manned mainly by Indonesians, the USS *Blenny* picked up four Japanese among the survivors. One, though, had been badly wounded, suffering a broken leg and "critical injuries in the groin."[31] After the man's leg was put in a splint and he was administered a shot of morphine, he and some of the other survivors were transferred to a local prau in the area. Although the *Blenny*'s commanding officer, William Hazzard, later expressed some guilt at abandoning the wounded Japanese, he saw no point keeping him aboard when he was not expected to live.[32]

Some submariners were more generous in taking on prisoners for humanitarian reasons. The USS *Tambor* stopped a thirty-ton sampan in the Sulu Sea on 10 November 1942 and found it crewed by ten fishermen ranging in age from an elderly man to a boy of about ten. The vessel lacked not only arms but a lifeboat, so the Japanese were all taken on board before the *Tambor* sank their sampan with machine-gun fire and three rounds from the three-inch gun. The prisoners were kept under guard in the forward torpedo room before being turned over to authorities in Australia.[33] As the war drew to an end, more submariners were prepared to take prisoners in larger numbers.[34]

Almost inevitably, submariners rationalized picking up prisoners for "intelligence purposes."[35] There could also be more pragmatic reasons, however; a prisoner afforded tangible proof that a submarine had actually sunk his ship. In the case of James Blanchard, skipper of the *Albacore,* a prisoner served to confirm the sinking of a ship previously thought only damaged, garnering Blanchard a Navy Cross.[36] In at least one instance, a submarine crew coached its prisoner to exaggerate the tonnage of his former ship when interrogated at Pearl Harbor.[37] Prisoners could also serve as a source of labor while on board. Perhaps sensing that their survival depended on proving their usefulness, most prisoners proved willing workers if given the opportunity.[38]

Once on board a submarine, some prisoners remained recalcitrant. The USS *Trout* had been the first American submarine to take a Japanese prisoner, picking up a survivor from the cruiser *Mikuma* at the Battle of Midway in June 1942. A year later the *Trout* took five Japanese prisoners after attacking a "small cargo-fisherman" with its deck guns. The submariners set three of the prisoners adrift in a dinghy, while two were retained "for possible intelligence value." One of the men, identified as S. Itshakawa, later died on board. After the *Trout* attacked a Japanese submarine, the patrol report noted that the "prisoner became morbid and sullen and refused all food."[39]

Captured Japanese commonly expressed a profound sense of disgrace and evinced a belief that they had dishonored their families in Japan. Many prisoners stated that they preferred their families to believe they were dead. On the USS *Seahorse,* Seiza Mitsuma confided to one of the crew that if he were forced to return to Japan he would have to take his mother's maiden name since he had dishonored his own.[40] A prisoner on the *Flying Fish,* Siso Okuno, professed in a letter to his captors, "I died on the day on which I was captured."[41]

U.S. naval personnel were instructed to follow the "letter and spirit" of the 1929 Geneva Convention in their treatment of prisoners. Handcuffs and leg irons were to be resorted to only in order to maintain a vessel's security. Reprisals against prisoners were explicitly prohibited, as was coercion to obtain information.[42] In practice, these guidelines were not always adhered to and the treatment of prisoners on board submarines varied. Cruising in the Bonin Islands, the USS *Archerfish* came across a Japanese pilot adrift who had been shot down near Iwo Jima. Unlike the fictional pilot in *Destination Tokyo,* this one offered no resistance, but he still spent the journey to Midway manacled to a bunk in the torpedo room and was constantly guarded by the submarine's electricians.[43] As discussed in chapter 4, the *Albacore* took five Japanese prisoners after sinking the *Taiei Maru.* Skipper James Blanchard insisted that the men were given medical attention and "treated humanely at all times" before being turned over to the provost marshal at Los Negros in the Admiralty Islands. The prisoners' journey, however, could not have been comfortable since they were confined to the submarine's empty four-inch shell magazine.[44]

After sinking a patrol vessel, the *Pompano* under Willis M. Thomas obtained a prisoner with considerable difficulty. When approached by a rubber boat containing the *Pompano*'s boarding party, some of the Japanese drowned themselves. The *Pompano* party finally got one of the survivors, described as a regular navy enlisted man, by hitting him over the head with a .45 pistol. Once he was taken belowdecks, the crew began shoving and knocking the man around until an officer intervened. In this case the crew's wrath was raised by the wounding of fellow crewman Herbert Calcaterra during the preceding gun battle. Calcaterra, who remained conscious for some hours before dying, told his crewmates to kill the prisoner. They ignored this request, eventually developing a close affinity with the prisoner, whom they nicknamed Tojo. Before he was handed over to

Marines, the *Pompano* crew collected cigarettes and sweets for him, and pinned a note to him: "Tojo is a good guy. Treat him right."[45]

If Japanese prisoners were abused on submarines, the evidence suggests that this usually occurred immediately after capture. When a Japanese prisoner was transferred on board the USS *Spadefish*, for example, one of the crew offered the man a knife, saying, "Hari Kari?"[46] In a similar incident on the USS *Flying Fish*, a crew member imitated committing hari-kari with a knife and then offered it to the prisoner, who refused to take it. As one of the crew recalled, during the first few days they tried to demonstrate their dislike for the prisoner.

On the *Flying Fish* it was not long, however, before the crew "began to accept him as a suffering human being."[47] Crewmen nicknamed the prisoner Charlie, claiming he resembled the actor Charles Boyer. Indeed, some officers believed that the crew spoiled him, constantly communicating with him through sign language. In time they discovered that Charlie was thirty-four years old, with a wife and four children. The *Flying Fish*'s executive officer, Julian T. Burke Jr., later credited the prisoner with having a big impact, noting, "I had never been that close to a Japanese."[48]

The fate of prisoners often followed a similar pattern on other submarines. When the USS *Spadefish* took a Japanese prisoner after sinking the junk *Tenshin Maru* in the Yellow Sea, there was initially a phase of intimidation. One of the crew recounted, "We had some fun with him. I'd take my .45 out and hold it on him. He would say, 'No! No!' But it was empty."[49] At first the prisoner remained confined in the bilges, but it wasn't long before the crew warmed to him. The same man who had threatened him with a pistol started treating him to ice cream. The prisoner, nicknamed Joe, began assisting one of the torpedomen in cutting the crewmen's hair.

After sinking a freighter in the Gulf of Tonkin in May 1943, the crew of the *Tambor* was able to secure a Japanese officer only after spraying the water around him with machine-gun bullets. On board the submarine a crewman pointed a .45 pistol at his head, but once the prisoner indicated a willingness to die by pointing his finger at his temple, the pistol was lowered. Nicknamed Gus, the prisoner was put to work and became popular with the crew. His only outburst involved yelling, "Banzai!" during a *Tambor* attack, but even this was interpreted as possibly in support of the Americans.[50]

Given the difficulties of eliciting and pronouncing prisoners' real names, they were almost invariably nicknamed by the crew at an early stage. When Gene Fluckey interviewed a prisoner on the USS *Barb,* he made a show of placing a .45 pistol on the table. This quickly overcame the prisoner's initial reluctance to give his name, and Kitojima Sanji henceforth became known to the crew simply as Kito. He was kept busy on the submarine doing some of the dirtiest jobs.[51] When the USS *Jack* recovered two prisoners, they were called Freddy and Adam. James Calvert comments, "They seemed to like these names and answered to them freely."[52] They were even fonder of the food available on the submarine, and quickly gained weight.

The man pulled on to the *Gudgeon* by Albert Strow became known as Tojo, a nickname that proved popular among submarine crews in reference to Japan's war minister, General Hideki Tojo. Initially the *Gudgeon*'s prisoner was chained to a skid in the forward torpedo room and kept under twenty-four-hour guard. The prisoner protested these conditions by going on a hunger strike, a tactic that seems to have worked since he was transferred to kitchen duties. With his new status came a new nickname, Jamoke—slang for coffee. When the *Gudgeon* stopped at Midway, it is claimed some of the crewmen defended their prisoner against drunken Marines, and when he was removed at Pearl Harbor on 11 December 1943 some openly wept.[53]

Despite naval regulations banning fraternization between prisoners and a ship's crew, this seems to have rarely been enforced on submarines.[54] Younger prisoners were the most likely to become crew favorites. One of the Japanese prisoners taken by the USS *Balao* proved to be a nineteen-year-old apprentice mate, described as a "very scared boy." The skipper professed, "Won't be able to keep the men from spoiling him, so will put him in crew's mess."[55] The two other prisoners taken at the same time were segregated in the torpedo rooms.

Living in such close proximity, often for over a month or more, prisoners and crew frequently became integrated to some degree. After crewmen from the USS *Tang* dragged a survivor aboard on 4 July 1944, they nicknamed him Firecracker to commemorate American Independence Day. Although handcuffed to a bunk during attacks, he in some ways appeared to be treated as a guest. Skipper Richard O'Kane once found the boat's cook in the galley putting some effort into preparing the prisoner's rice the way he liked it. The crew also took him along to movies screened in the forward torpedo room. Eventually the men discovered that the prisoner's name was Mishuitunni Ka and that he originally came from Kyoto. When he was turned over to Marines at port, blindfolded and handcuffed, one of the *Tang* crew demanded a receipt stating that he was delivered in good health.[56]

The USS *Spadefish* collected a prisoner, after sinking the freighter *Tairai Maru* in February 1945, who proved to be the ship's third officer. As described by one of the *Spadefish* crew, John Brewer, the man "was real polite." "He had a wallet and showed us pictures of his folks."[57] The crew nicknamed the prisoner Sugo because he loved sugar.

Even on Mush Morton's *Wahoo,* there appeared to be a certain amount of bonding between prisoners and crew. After the *Wahoo* sank a fishing vessel on 20 August 1943, six survivors were brought on board. According to the patrol report, the "[p]risoners seem to be grateful for being picked up," and they were each given clean clothes, a bath, and a round of Canadian Club whisky to warm them up.[58] One of the survivors was a youngster, described as no more than about ten years old. The prisoners, who quickly learned some English, mainly stayed on mats in the after-torpedo room but were also employed cleaning. One of the *Wahoo* crew, yeoman Forest Sterling, concluded: "It's hard to believe those stories about the butchery of the soldiers after seeing these guys." Indeed, he said, "We became so attached to our prisoners that we began to feel they were part of the crew."[59]

The treatment of prisoners on British submarines followed similar patterns. After sinking by gunfire a small ship crewed mainly by Malays and Indonesians, the HMS *Tantalus* recovered a Japanese soldier who had served as an armed guard on board. He was put to work cleaning and polishing for the remainder of the patrol, a job he did so effectively that by the time the submarine arrived back in Fremantle one sailor claimed that it was ready for an admiral's inspection.[60]

Familiarity, however, went only so far. More often than not a prisoner's status was that of a mascot or a pet, and they served largely to break the monotony of long voyages.[61] While submariners taught the Japanese some English, they often did so at the prisoner's expense. On the *Seahorse,* for example, Seiza Mitsuma was taught to respond to "Good morning" with "Fuck you."[62] On the USS *Threadfin* prisoners were taught to say "Bum Chow" when they finished eating.[63] Some of the crew further tormented Mitsuma by telling him he would be tortured and beheaded when they arrived at Pearl Harbor.[64]

A survey of U.S. soldiers fighting in the Pacific indicated that, after seeing Japanese prisoners, 42 percent of the Americans "felt all the more like killing them."[65] Probably because of extended contact, however, submariners often developed a rapport with prisoners. There is little doubt that experience with prisoners often broke down some of the hatred manifested toward the Japanese. When the *Seahorse* reached Pearl Harbor on 1 November 1944, some of the crew protested when Marines led Seiza Mitsuma off the submarine blindfolded and shackled. They also took up a collection to provide him with clothing, candy, and cigarettes during his captivity.[66]

The crew of the *Tambor* felt similarly upset when Gus was hauled off the submarine by Marines at gunpoint, blindfolded and handcuffed. At his departure the crew had given him a pair of dungarees, a Brooklyn Dodgers sweatshirt, and a navy cap. The prisoner in turn had made a point of shaking each crewman's hand and bowing when they reached port. His fate would remain unknown.[67]

In a few instances prisoners left a letter that, when translated, proved to express gratitude for the kindness they had received on board. At times prisoners professed a changed attitude not only toward their captors but about war in general. The prisoner known as Charlie on the *Flying Fish* wrote a note to the skipper, thanking him for his kindness and saying that "he would give his life to the cause of peace forevermore."[68]

There were instances, too, of submariners maintaining contact with former prisoners after the war. In May 1945, while lifeguarding in the waters of Bungo-Suido Strait between the islands of Kyushu and Shikoku, the USS *Atule* recovered a Japanese aviator after witnessing him being shot down by an American B-29. Paul Schratz later recalled that the aviator represented "an amazing intelligence catch," providing information on Japanese magnetic anomaly detectors used for tracking submerged submarines.[69] When the prisoner initially refused to give his name, the crew nicknamed him Bungo after his place of capture. In reality the prisoner was twenty-two-year-old Lieutenant Masayoshi Kojima. Suffering from burns, he was treated with petroleum jelly and bandages on board the *Atule* before being turned over to Marines at Midway a month later.

Once repatriated to Japan in January 1946, Kojima kept in touch with the pharmacist's mate who had treated his wounds on the *Atule*. The daughter of the *Atule*'s skipper, Jason Mauer, also later tracked him down while teaching in Japan.[70] Despite the almost universal fear among Japanese prisoners that they would be ostracized by their families and society after the war, it appears that almost all were quickly integrated. Kojima became a rear admiral in the postwar Japanese Navy, and in 1990 he attended a convention of *Atule* veterans in the United States. These attempts to maintain contact suggest that, at least in some cases, such cross-cultural encounters were valued on both sides.

12

Submarines and Bombers

The moral and ethical dilemmas of World War II are encapsulated in the Allied bombing campaigns carried out against Germany and Japan. Over 99 percent of Japan's civilian casualties were the result of air raids; by the end of the war, air attacks had killed 600,000 civilians.[1] One of General Douglas MacArthur's aides, Bonner Fellers, described the bombing of Japan as "one of the most ruthless and barbaric killings of non-combatants in all of history."[2] At least some submariners were equally appalled. Tom Paine, an officer with the USS *Pompon*, declared, "[T]here is no humanity in destroying cities."[3] James Calvert, who from the bridge of the USS *Atule* once observed a huge armada of B-29s on its way to bomb Japan, expressed similar feelings: "What had these civilians, as individuals, done to deserve such a fate?"[4]

Compared to the air war, the submarine war is often depicted as a relatively "clean" fight. Naval historian Peter Padfield, for instance, describes area bombing, the targeting of entire cities, as "unnecessary, unscientific and foolish," in contrast to the restrained submarine war.[5] As the preceding pages have illustrated, however, the submarine war was often more brutal than represented. Indeed, the air and submarine campaigns paralleled and intersected one another in a number of ways.

In the European theater, when Admiral Dönitz instructed his U-boat crews to forgo aiding survivors, he evoked Allied air attacks: "Be harsh, having in mind that the enemy takes no regard of women and children in his bombing attacks on German cities."[6] The U-boat commander Heinz Eck, convicted for the *Peleus* massacre, allegedly told his crew, "If we are influenced by too much sympathy we must also think of our wives and children who die as the victims of air attack at home."[7] By the same token, it is claimed that U.S. submarine commander Mush Morton justified his shooting of survivors from the *Buyo Maru* by citing the precedent of area bombing. At least he could claim to be killing soldiers rather than civilians.[8]

The Allied bombing campaign and the submarine war followed similar trajectories. In the early stages of the war, unrestricted warfare sprang partly from feelings of impotence. Sir Arthur Harris, Britain's chief of Bomber Command, described aerial bombing as "our only means of getting at the enemy in a way that would hurt at all."[9] Particularly after the German air raid on Coventry in November 1940, there was little hesitation to strike back at German population centers.

The shift in strategy is illustrated by the air campaign against German U-boat bases. The British had initially tried to destroy German submarine pens, but had found that they were unable to inflict significant damage even using 2,000-pound bombs. The targets thus broadened from the submarine bases to the towns surrounding them. In the early months of 1943 the urban areas of Lorient, Saint Nazaire, and Brest were largely destroyed by Allied bombing.[10]

Even more powerfully than the German air raid on Coventry had prompted British retaliation, the attack on Pearl Harbor inspired Americans with a desire to strike back. With much of America's battle fleet destroyed, unleashing the country's submarines on Japanese merchant shipping became the quickest way to retaliate. Although the Doolittle raid in April 1942 shocked the Japanese as intended, the limited damage inflicted meant there was little point in repeating the exercise. Tokyo would not be bombed again by American aircraft until November 1944.[11]

The early air raids on Japan focused on military and industrial targets, but the results proved disappointing so, like the British in Europe, the Americans resorted to area bombing on a massive scale. As Michael Gordin puts it, the American military experienced a "gradual downward creep" of moral standards that continually broadened definitions of legitimate targets.[12] After the capture of bases on Saipan, Guam, and Tinian in the Mariana Islands, which brought Japan's home islands within striking distance of the new B-29 Superfortress bombers, the U.S. bombing campaign commenced in earnest. Whereas Doolittle's B-25 Mitchell bombers had carried bomb loads of 2,000 pounds, the new B-29s could carry nearly ten times this payload. By 1944 more effective incendiary bombs using napalm had also been developed.[13] Faced with the need to justify a huge expenditure on bombers, and a desire to counter Japan's propaganda that it was winning the war, the United States began incendiary strikes on Japanese cities. The mixture of manufacturing and residential districts in urban Japan served to justify area bombing and ensured that firebombing had horrific consequences.

In a massive raid on Tokyo the night of 9–10 March 1945, 334 B-29s bombed the city from the relatively low altitude of 7,000 feet for two hours. It proved the most deadly single mission of the war. Fanned by strong winds, fires swept a densely populated area of fifteen square miles, destroying 267,000 buildings and killing an estimated 88,000 people. Eventually the Twentieth Air Force bombed sixty-six cities in Japan, and at the height of the attacks, on 10 July 1945, 2,000 aircraft were involved.[14] General Curtis LeMay described his policy as "Bomb and burn 'em until they quit."[15]

The Tokyo fires of March 1945 could be seen 150 miles away, and smoke enveloped the aircraft as they flew over the city.[16] High-altitude bombing, however, generally gave air crews little indication of the destruction being wrought and only in rare instances did the men in the air sense the grisly reality of the ground. Victims were often killed unintentionally and indiscriminately; those killed in the air raids on Tokyo, for example, included some 200 Allied prisoners of war.[17]

Like the air war, the submarine war gradually escalated with technological developments, more equipment, and the availability of more trained men. In the early years of the war, unreliable torpedoes largely hamstrung the effectiveness of the submarine service. Improvements in torpedoes, as well as innovations in radar and construction, made the submarine service increasingly deadly. Once war production reached full throttle, attacks arguably assumed a logic that had as much to do with resources as moral purpose.[18]

Submarines, carrying thousands of gallons of fuel and tons of explosive warheads, were no less killing machines than bombers. Each torpedo carried 565 pounds of Torpex, so that the standard load of twenty-four torpedoes amounted to 13,560 pounds of high explosive.[19] As in the case of bomber crews, submariners conducting torpedo attacks were often insulated from the full consequences of their actions. More often than not, submarines attacking convoys were forced to immediately dive in anticipation of fierce depth charge counterattacks. Submarine crews generally had little sense of whom or what the ships they sank carried and they, like bombers, claimed many unintended victims.

U.S. submarines were responsible for inadvertently killing an estimated 10,000 Allied prisoners of war.[20] Over 800 Australian POWs were killed after the USS *Sturgeon* sank the *Montevideo Maru* off the north coast of Luzon on 1 July 1942. The same year the USS *Grouper* inadvertently killed British POWs when it torpedoed the *Lisbon Maru* in the East China Sea near Shanghai. When the USS *Snook* sank the *Arisan Maru,* only 5 of the 1,800 American prisoners on board survived. Similarly, the sinking of the *Shinyo Maru* by the USS *Paddle* resulted in the death of all but 82 of the 750 U.S. prisoners on board. When the HMS *Tradewind* sank the *Junyo Maru* on 18 September 1944, most of the nearly 6,000 American, British, and Dutch prisoners on board were lost.[21] So desperate had the situation become that U.S. submariners were eventually instructed to search for Allied survivors in the vicinity of any Japan-bound ships they sank.[22]

Given the scramble for worthwhile targets late in the war, it is probably no coincidence that during 1945 two submarine skippers made tragic mistakes resulting in their court-martial. In January the war's only documented case of an American submarine sinking a U.S. ship occurred when the USS *Guardfish* mistook the salvage tug *Extractor* for a Japanese I-class submarine. A court-martial found the skippers of both vessels guilty of negligence.[23]

Greater loss of life, albeit enemy lives, resulted on 1 April 1945 when the USS *Queenfish* sank the 11,600-ton *Awa Maru*. The sinking of a target this size would normally have been a matter for jubilation, but it transpired that the ship, traveling from Singapore after delivering Red Cross supplies for Allied prisoners of war, had been guaranteed safe passage by the U.S. government. The *Queenfish* skipper, Charles Loughlin, had missed communications decreeing the ship's safe conduct, and in foggy conditions mistook it for a destroyer. He fired a spread of four torpedoes, all of which connected with the target.

It would be some hours before Loughlin realized his mistake. When the *Queenfish* approached the site of the sinking the crew found about twenty-five survivors in the water. Most of these pushed away proffered lifebuoys, but one man shouted for attention and agreed to be hauled on board the submarine. He hit his head on the hull in the process, and spent some hours unconscious before he could be interrogated. Loughlin then discovered his grave error. In the flurry of diplomatic exchanges that followed, the United States even offered to replace the lost ship.

Charles Lockwood later described the sinking of the *Awa Maru* as "the biggest error in the history of American submarine operations."[24] He especially worried that the incident might trigger "barbarous reprisals" against any submariners taken prisoner. When the *Queenfish* returned to port, Loughlin was relieved of command and then court-martialed by quite possibly the highest-ranking naval court of the war—the former skipper of the *Pompano*, Lewis Parks, served as the most junior officer. Since Loughlin had picked up a survivor, he could hardly deny sinking the *Awa Maru*. Although convicted of negligence in obeying orders, in light of his previous war service, he received only a letter of admonition. Ironically, the members of the court received a harsher letter of reprimand from high command for not punishing Loughlin more severely.[25]

At least one other U.S. submarine narrowly missed sinking a hospital ship. On the USS *Razorback* skipper Charles Brown lined up on a large transport in the East China Sea; only after unleashing five torpedoes did Brown spot a huge red cross on the ship's hull. For the first time in his career, Brown prayed that none of the torpedoes had hit their target.[26] Although many submariners believed that Japanese hospital ships were used for shipping war matériel and confessed to itchy trigger fingers, most determined to "play by the rules."[27] Having observed an illuminated hospital ship in the Java Sea, British skipper Alistair Mars called it "a pleasant reminder that if man is to remain civilized he must have rules even in war."[28]

Both bomber crews and submariners, with the highest casualty rates in the military, were largely preoccupied with their own survival rather than moral issues. In Europe the losses were staggering. The U.S. Eighth Air Force based in Britain lost almost 4,300 bombers and over 17,000 men. The U.S. Army Air Force lost over 120,000 men during the war, many in training accidents.[29] With the loss of so many friends and comrades, it is little wonder that men frequently became hardened to violence toward the enemy, whether combatants or civilians. The British veteran Ian Easton recalled: "Our reactions to the atom bomb were absolute delight. We regarded the Japanese as expendable. They had fought a filthy war, murdered our captured pilots, and we had no feeling for them."[30] Similar sentiments were expressed in the submarine service. Frank Golay from the USS *Puffer* no doubt reflected the views of many when he wrote, "Let's drop a few more atomic persuaders and get this war over—and get us home."[31]

Although the numbers involved were smaller, U.S. submariners suffered an even higher fatality rate than aviators and a casualty rate six times that of other naval forces.[32] With the loss of fifty-two boats during the war, about one in five of the Americans making war patrols died. Nearly everyone in the submarine service lost close friends, and some lost blood relatives. Slade Cutter's best friend from the *Pompano*, Dave Connole, died on his first patrol in command of the USS *Trigger*. Corwin Mendenhall lost his Academy classmates Butch Allen and George Brown on the USS *Sculpin*. George Pierce, commander of the USS *Tunny*, lost his older brother, killed commanding the *Argonaut*.[33] Even as the war wound down the losses continued, with seven submarines destroyed in 1945. Frank Golay believed that many of the losses resulted from "the scarcity of targets combined with the young skippers eager to make a record."[34]

From the enemy's point of view, those serving on bombers and submarines were more culpable than other combatants. Captured airmen were subjected to special abuse; in Germany some were marched through towns where women spat at them while children hurled rocks.[35] In Japan their treatment was far more appalling. One of the reasons Japan refused to ratify the Geneva Convention was the belief that it would effectively extend the range of Allied bombers; airmen might risk crashing in Japanese territory in the knowledge that they would be treated as prisoners rather than war criminals.[36] In one case captured aircrew from a B-29 were subjected to vivisection without anesthetic in a Kyushu hospital. Even after the surrender, sixteen B-29 aircrew members at Fukuoda were hacked to death by their Japanese guards.[37]

Dale Russell, a torpedoman on the *Flying Fish,* feared similar reprisals. "After the way we submariners had ravaged their shipping lanes, not only these past weeks, but all through the war years, the anger we had actuated in the enemy would have no bounds. My belief was that the Japanese would probably invent methods of unique torture just for us."[38]

Like aviators, prisoners from submarines were indeed treated more harshly than other captives. The nine men who survived after the USS *Tang* was sunk by a boomeranging torpedo were slapped, kicked, rifle-butted and burned with cigarettes by the Japanese sailors who recovered them. At the port of Takao on Formosa, they were paraded through the town on a flatbed truck before being taken to a secret naval intelligence prison at Ofuna south of Yokohama.

Officially known as the Navy Yokosuka Guard Unit Ueki Detachment, the prison was unofficially called the Torture Farm. The *Tang* crewmen were kept here along with other submarine survivors, pilots, and some technicians. As "special" prisoners they were accused of making war on civilians.[39] One of the *Tang* crewmen, Clay Decker, recalled being told that they were considered war criminals because 90 percent of the crews on merchant ships were civilians.

They were informed that they would receive only half of the rations issued to other POWs, and the Red Cross was not notified of their capture, leaving their families in limbo about their fates.[40] To make room for an increasing number of captured pilots, after nearly five months at Ofuna the *Tang* survivors were transferred to another camp near Omori on the outskirts of Tokyo, where their labor included clearing away the wreckage from Allied air raids.[41]

A number of survivors from the USS *Sculpin* also ended up at Ofuna, arriving on 5 December 1943. After the *Sculpin* crewmen scuttled their submarine, sailors on the destroyer *Yamagumo* shot at survivors in the water before picking up forty-one of the eighty-four men. At Truk, two of the wounded *Sculpin* survivors had amputations without anesthetic while being interrogated. When the survivors were shipped from Truk on the carrier *Chuyo,* it was sunk by the *Sculpin*'s sister submarine, the USS *Sailfish.* The twenty-one *Sculpin* prisoners who reached Ofuna were further interrogated and eventually put to work as slave labor in the copper mines of Ashio.[42]

Like the aerial bombing of cities, the submarine campaign represented the conceptualization of war against an entire society. The increasingly mechanized nature of modern warfare meant that it made sense to attack an enemy's industry and workforce.[43] It was a proposition accepted at least in part by civilians themselves; the Japanese word for the home front, *jugo,* literally translates as "behind the gun."[44]

Whereas during the First World War civilians represented about one in twenty of those killed, the ratio for the Second World War became one in two.[45] Destruction was no longer confined to battlefields and battle zones, but could be delivered indiscriminately. After the firebombing of Tokyo in March 1945, General Curtis LeMay, head of XXI Bomber Command in the Pacific, proclaimed, "There are no innocent civilians."[46] Not quite so bluntly, Admiral Chester Nimitz wrote, "In modern total war, there is no effective distinction between contraband and non-contraband."[47] By extension, there was no distinction between merchant seamen and fishermen; both were supplying the enemy. Admiral Ernest King, chief of Naval Operations, and General H. H. "Hap" Arnold, chief of the Army Air Force, both pursued a policy of "strangulation," through sea blockade and aerial bombardment respectively, that starved civilians as well as soldiers.[48]

Why was total war against Japan prosecuted so ruthlessly? John Dower argues in *War without Mercy* that the element of "race" meant that both sides fought the Pacific war with a heightened brutality.[49] There were other elements apart from race, though, that fueled an accelerating callousness toward the Japanese. One was a growing awareness of Japanese atrocities. Initially fearing reprisals, the U.S. government had stifled stories of Japanese war crimes after the fall of Bataan in 1942. Atrocities committed by Japanese submariners had also been initially suppressed, partly out of fear of how this might affect the morale of merchant seamen. By the beginning of 1944, however, the scale of Japanese war crimes in the Philippines was known, and the story of the Bataan "Death March" had been published in American newspapers.[50]

Contact with victims of the Japanese could harden the resolve of submariners to prosecute the war to their utmost. Landon Davis Jr. sensed a change in attitude after the USS *Pampanito* recovered British and Australian prisoners left at sea after American submarines had sunk their transports. The POWs' stories of mistreatment in captivity inspired "a great hate for the Japs." According to Davis, "[T]here wasn't one of us who wouldn't go out of our way now to take a good hard sock at those Japs, whereas before we were sort of noncommittal about it, even though were fighting the war very seriously."[51]

Both the air and submarine wars reached their extremes in the latter part of the war, when arguably victory was at hand. A. C. Grayling, among others, claims that the bombing of German and Japanese cities reached its height once the war had essentially been won. Grayling argues that increased opportunity rather than necessity drove the bombing campaigns. While aircraft and munitions were increasing on the one hand, enemy resistance was dissipating on the other. To use Grayling's analogy, the situation was like a runaway truck without brakes, gathering speed as it rolls downhill.[52]

In a similar way the submarine war accelerated as more and

more submarines became operational, even while Japan's ability to conduct antisubmarine warfare diminished. Some military leaders believed that neither invasion nor atomic bombs were necessary to win the war—conventional aircraft bombing and submarine naval blockade were already having a devastating effect.[53]

The other side of this argument, however, is that a war of attrition was necessary to precipitate Japan's surrender and forestall a land invasion that would have caused catastrophic losses on both sides. The mass civilian suicides that accompanied the American invasion of Saipan reinforced grim predictions about the consequences of invading the home islands.[54] A big difference existed between Japan facing imminent defeat and the Japanese government accepting unconditional surrender.[55] As the war became more one-sided, it also became more desperate. The Americans suffered their highest number of combat deaths for one month in March 1945, with 20,325 killed in action—the same month as the firebombing of Tokyo.[56] For at least some in the Japanese military, the use of atomic bombs allowed them to face surrender, since it could be interpreted as a technological rather than as a spiritual defeat.[57]

Japan's adoption of suicide attacks further convinced many in the Allied camp that total annihilation afforded the only path to victory. Kamikaze air attacks, beginning during the battle of Leyte Gulf in October 1944, escalated so that by the end of the Okinawa campaign Japanese aviators flew over 2,500 suicide missions. The battle of Okinawa, 350 miles from the Japanese mainland, claimed nearly 40,000 American casualties, with over 100,000 dead on the Japanese side.[58]

In such a war of attrition, mass destruction appeared a not irrational approach. According to the United States Strategic Bombing Survey, bombing did more than anything else to convince Japanese civilians of the futility of continuing the war.[59] Submarine attacks on small craft off Japan's coastlines reinforced the same message. With the Japanese Navy reduced to relying on converted fishing boats and similar craft for escorts, the former German naval attaché to Japan, Vice Admiral Paul H. Weneker, ranked American submarine attacks on merchant shipping as more important than bombing in bringing Japan to its knees.[60]

Despite similarities between the air and submarine war, there were crucial differences in the way that submariners and bombers responded to the exigencies of total war. The aircrews that attacked German and Japanese cities acted on specific orders from higher command; there was little room for personal morality. Air Marshal Arthur Harris of Britain's Bomber Command believed that those with "sensitive minds" had no place in leading a bombing force.[61] American general Curtis LeMay took a similar view, stating, "[A]ll war is immoral and if you let that bother you, you're not a good soldier."[62] Even so, bomber crews were almost inevitably given to believe that they were attacking military or industrial targets. Perhaps the main concession to conscience was that aircraft began dropping leaflets before bombing missions, warning the local population to flee.[63]

In contrast to the command structure that ordered bombing raids, decisions in the submarine service were largely made by skippers acting on their own initiative. Indeed, one of the things submarine commanders prized most was a degree of autonomy. Admiral Charles Lockwood, as commander of the Pacific submarine fleet, believed that the skipper on the spot was best positioned to make day-to-day decisions rather than following the dictates of someone at a distant desk.[64] As a result, at least when it came to mounting gun attacks on small craft, individual commanders exercised enormous discretion.

Conclusion

Writing of Allied bomber attacks on Hamburg, Keith Lowe suggests that the Second World War might in some senses be framed as a battle between the urge to total destruction and the attempt to keep such extreme instincts in check.[1] The submarine gun war exemplifies a similar battle between competing impulses. Contrary to the often clinical representations of the submarine war in the Pacific, submariners prosecuted the war with an often callous indifference to human life. In a postwar interview, Charles Loughlin, skipper of the USS *Queenfish,* conceded that "some of our submarines did some pretty bad things during World War II."[2] But, to borrow John Dower's phrase, it was not entirely a war without mercy.

Many submariners felt the elation of combat even as they experienced fear of death, not infrequently describing attacks in aesthetic terms.[3] When the USS *Seahorse* attacked a small schooner with its five-inch and 40 mm guns in April 1945, the patrol report noted, "Our tracers made a beautiful sight ricocheting into the dark sky after sunset."[4] Similarly, when the USS *Blenny* sank a junk with one five-inch shell, the patrol report described the hit as making "a beautiful explosion of illuminated grain about 200 feet in air."[5] After the USS *Puffer* set off a series of explosions by firing its five-inch gun at barges loaded with aviation gasoline off the coast of Bali in July 1945, Commander Carl R. Dwyer described the scene as "magnificent." Dwyer enthused that it was the "most amazing sight" he witnessed during the war.[6]

In part, submariners were enthralled by their weapons' firepower. When the USS *Segundo* made contact with a four-masted sailing vessel off the coast of Korea, the crew initially tried to sink it with a torpedo. After the torpedo missed, the *Segundo* crew opened up with the 40 mm guns from only about 300 yards, quickly leaving the vessel a sinking wreck. Clearly pleased by their deadly accuracy, the writer of the patrol report exclaimed, "These guns are superb and wicked."[7] When the *Segundo* got into a gunfight with two patrol vessels a week later, the guns were again praised as doing "a beautiful job."[8]

The "beauty" of attacks referred not only to the sheer visual spectacle but, at least implicitly, to the destruction of the enemy. Roy Davenport, commander of the USS *Haddock,* recalled a coordinated attack made on a convoy with the USS *Segundo* and USS *Razorback* on 6–7 December 1944: "It was a truly beautiful three hours of action with ships blowing up simultaneously all around the horizon. To have had the pleasure of seeing this entire convoy destroyed was something we'd always hoped to see."[9]

Some submariners expressed regret at the loss of life when they torpedoed a ship, but most often it became a matter for celebration. As explained by Dale Russell, a torpedoman on the USS *Flying Fish,* "[T]here was little or no thought of the people who had been on the vessel."[10] Contrary to the reckoning of battles between land forces, which emphasized body counts, naval accounting focused on ships destroyed rather than loss of life.[11] Landon L. Davis Jr. of the USS *Pampanito* noted: "It is quite seldom in the submarine navy that we come in contact with the actual so-called horrors and disagreeable side of war. We go merrily along and sink a ship and then go under the waves and never see the result of the thing."[12] The soundmen might hear the gruesome noises of a ship breaking up and occasionally even the screams of its crew, but most submariners kept the reality of death at a distance. Lewis Parks, recalling his time on the *Parche* as a wolf pack commander, noted the macabre incongruity: a series of devastating attacks killing thousands of enemy sailors was followed by the crew eating celebratory cream puffs.[13]

Attitudes could change, however, when crews came into close contact with the survivors. After the USS *Balao* sank a trawler with gunfire on the morning of 18 March 1945, nine men were spotted in the water with the capsized vessel. The patrol report confessed, "There is little joy in seeing one's enemies freezing to death."[14] Dale Russell of the *Flying Fish* recalled that after sinking a ship in fog, he and his crewmates were able to hear the desperate and eerie cries of those left in the water fighting for their lives. "From this night on, this portion of the war would be burned into our hearts and minds."[15] Slade Cutter also contrasted the difference between sinking a ship by torpedo and by gun action. Although in the former kind of attack one knew intellectually that hundreds of people were being killed, "you're firing a torpedo and you don't see it and you don't think of it."[16] He would be haunted, though, by the small craft he sank with gunfire.

Even a hardened warrior like Gene Fluckey experienced at least one instance of empathy for his victims. After bombarding a lumber mill at Shibetoro in Nemuro Strait, he observed an elderly man trying to save his life's work from the resulting fire. Having failed in his efforts, the man stared out to the submarine and threw his arms up in defeat and grief. Fluckey later observed, "I could almost feel his tears running down my cheeks, or were they mine? War is such hell."[17]

Surviving documents suggest relatively little direction from above about the way submariners should conduct themselves in dealing with small craft. U.S. policy makers assumed there would be little if any neutral shipping involved in a war with Japan. Perhaps in part because unrestricted warfare was never legalized, there were few limits put on its execution.[18] Apart from occasional remarks in division and squadron commanders' endorsements of war patrol reports, there is little indication that they promulgated hard-and-fast rules of engagement. The tone of a submarine war patrol was most deeply stamped by the character of its officers, especially its skipper. Even more than other warships, a submarine was imprinted by its commander's personality.[19]

During the course of the war only 465 men commanded a U.S. submarine on patrols.[20] Even this modest figure is inflated, since many commanders were quickly relieved of command or self-selected for other duties. Some of those who excelled during peacetime proved to be psychologically unprepared for war. Indeed, it seemed impossible to predict which men would do well under combat conditions, but most observers agreed that successful skippers possessed a rare combination of qualities. Perhaps most of all, according to William Kinsella, they finely balanced aggression with sound judgment.[21] As Charles Lockwood put it, skippers often walked a fine line between commendation and court-martial.[22]

Background and breeding often reinforced the confidence and independence of submarine commanders. All but a handful were graduates of the Naval Academy at Annapolis, an institution intended to mold gentlemen as well as sailors. In the 1930s the Academy curriculum still included dancing, although cadets had to make do with wooden chairs for partners. Many submarine officers came from privileged backgrounds; over half a dozen submarine officers were the sons of admirals (Chester Nimitz Jr., Manning and Thomas Kimmel, Edward Spruance, John S. McCain Jr., Joseph R. DeFrees Jr., John B. Griggs III, Roger Paine), and many more came from illustrious military families. Edward Beach's father, for example, had graduated with the Academy class of 1888, and later became a professor of international law there. Charles Loughlin's father was an army colonel killed during World War I. The father of Eric Lloyd Barr Jr. had won a Navy Cross as a submariner during World War I, while the father of Sam Loomis Jr. at one time commanded Destroyer Division 38 of the Asiatic Fleet. Others were the sons of academics and politicians: Richard O'Kane's father taught entomology at the University of New Hampshire, and Bob Brown, a young officer lost with the USS *Scorpion,* was the son of a Georgia congressman.[23]

The fact that 75 of the 465 World War II submarine commanders were eventually promoted to flag rank is some indication of their abilities and success.[24] Inclined toward self-reliance, submarine officers were fond of comparing themselves to corsairs and Civil War cavalry officers, who also exercised their own kind of bold independence.[25] As Paul Schratz put it, "Nothing equals the unforgettable romance of independent command."[26] Part of the service ethos was a belief that the individual still mattered, and that submarines afforded greater autonomy than could be had anywhere else in the military.[27]

With the privilege of command, though, came enormous responsibility. More than in most other military situations, the success and even survival of a submarine depended on the skill and judgment of one man. Current Doctrine Submarines, promulgated in 1944, emphasized "freedom to exercise initiative" as essential to effective submarine operations, but warned that no other form of warfare was "more susceptible to failure through mistakes, indecision, or hesitation on the part of the individual commanding officer."[28]

Under such crushing responsibility, some skippers, such as Gordon B. Rainer on the *Dolphin*, suffered breakdowns on patrol; others, such as Theodore Charles Aylward on the *Searaven*, developed debilitating physical symptoms under the psychological strain. On the USS *Pintado*, skipper William Lawrence suffered nightmares, sometimes waking up his officers with an unearthly scream. Thomas Burton Klakring dreamed incessantly of being captured by the Japanese.[29]

"Fatigue" was the usual euphemism for those suffering what decades later became labeled post-traumatic stress disorder.[30] After the USS *Sculpin* was repeatedly depth charged, skipper Lucius Chappell recorded the effects on his crew as "sleeplessness, chronic headaches, general lassitude, loss of appetite, marked decrease in mental alertness, emotional instability, and increasing nervousness."[31] In order to help stave off such symptoms, sedatives were often administered to the submarine's crew.

On the USS *Seahorse*, Slade Cutter had to relieve his executive officer, Lieutenant John Currie, after numerous depth charge attacks made Currie's hands shake so badly he was unable to plot their course as navigator. Cutter had his own struggles at sea, where he tried to keep himself alert with endless cups of coffee and Benzedrine, followed by attempts to rest with the aid of sleeping pills and Old Crow whisky.[32] Like their crews, commanders experienced a fear of death, but felt even more compelled to mask it. In a postwar interview, James Blanchard conceded he was "scared as hell" but had to be careful not to show it to the crew.[33]

Many submariners became more or less resigned to the idea that they would not survive the war. Clay Decker, an officer on the *Tang*, recalled: "Every night you laid your head on your pillow, you were aware that the piece of iron that's a submarine could end up being a tomb."[34] But most of the submariners were young, and with youth also came optimism and a sense of immortality. As Slade Cutter put it, "That's the beauty of being young. You stick your head in a buzz-saw and hope for the best."[35] After being nearly killed by a bullet in a surface gun attack, Paul Schratz convinced himself that "the Japs had their chance and blew it."[36] Thereafter he faced danger with relative equanimity.

The naval writer Fred T. Jane once claimed, "A crude desire to kill the enemy seems ever to have been a valuable asset."[37] Richard O'Kane, who as executive officer of the *Wahoo* and skipper of the *Tang* became one of World War II's most successful submarine officers, exemplified this maxim. Murray Frazee, executive officer on the *Tang*, claimed O'Kane remained ever eager to "sink more ships, kill more Japs."[38] Writer Alex Kershaw points out that the words "Jap" and "Nip" were never capitalized in O'Kane's patrol reports; more often the Japanese were simply "debris."[39] He was, in the words of Ned Beach, on a "mission of vengeance."[40] O'Kane experienced a survivor's guilt in later life for not going down with his boat, but never for killing Japanese.[41]

Most skippers, though, according to Lawson Ramage, required a psychological adjustment to kill people. "[I]t is something to get to the point where you can kill somebody, which isn't natural to you. As a matter of fact, it appalls you, even the thought of such a thing and you then find yourself getting to the point where you have to do it—this is a tremendous hurdle."[42]

Although there was often little time to consider the consequences of their actions while on patrol, men on leave sometimes pondered the moral dimension of the submarine war. While recuperating on the Hawaiian island of Maui, James Calvert, an officer of the USS *Jack*, vividly recalled some of the disturbing images from his last patrol and the "relentless search for semi-defenseless merchant ships to kill." His spirits were buoyed only by a fellow naval officer, who told him, "[D]on't ever forget that the Japanese asked for this war."[43]

For William Hazzard, commander of the USS *Blenny,* sinking a tanker off Cam Rahn Bay brought home some of the horror of war. He could see men fleeing along the burning catwalks of the tanker as the ship sank. A more disturbing incident came later, when a survivor apparently suffering a skull fracture tried to climb on board the submarine. Hazzard refused to take the man, partly fearing the impact on the *Blenny* crew's morale if the men started to see their victims as people rather than targets.[44]

While this is no doubt an oversimplification, the evidence points toward two personality types among commanders. One type relished combat and the opportunity to obliterate the Japanese. The other type of commander accepted the need to destroy enemy craft but tried to avoid unnecessary killing. There were those like Mush Morton and William Germershausen, who appeared to revel in close-quarter actions, with no qualms about the destruction of the enemy, whether combatants or fishermen. Germershausen, skipper of the USS *Spadefish,* professed having acquired "romantic notions" from stories about privateers and the like, and he had the quartermaster fashion a battle flag to be flown from the *Spadefish's* bridge when the submarine went into gun actions.[45] In the Sea of Japan, Germershausen was incensed when his wolf pack commander, Earl Hydemann, refused permission to sink more small vessels; according to one account, he physically confronted Hydemann over the issue when they were back at Pearl Harbor. Later the *Spadefish* crew looked for ways of more efficiently destroying small craft, receiving training from Marines on the use of flamethrowers.[46]

With his neatly combed blond hair and open face, Eugene Fluckey might have been mistaken for an Iowa farm boy or a Baptist minister, but as commander of the USS *Barb,* Fluckey relentlessly pursued the destruction of the enemy. Both the devastating efficiency of submarine gun actions and the difficulty sometimes encountered sinking wooden craft are suggested by the USS *Barb's* attack during the afternoon of 26 July 1945. After sighting a trawler on the horizon, the *Barb* moved to within 400 yards before opening up with its 20 mm gun as well as .50-caliber and .30-caliber machine guns. Although the craft caught fire and stopped dead in the water, the hull proved tougher than expected. Having trained with Marines at Midway on the use of rifle grenades, the crew next tried to sink the vessel by firing grenades at close range. Finally, after taking a couple of prisoners, the *Barb* finished off the trawler by ramming it at slow speed, caving in its side.[47]

While some submariners looked for more efficient ways of destroying small craft, there were others, like Slade Cutter and Paul Schratz, who found attacking fishing boats repellant and unlikely to seriously contribute to the war effort. Most skippers shaded in between these extremes. They were willing to destroy unarmed craft, but did so out of a sense of duty rather than preference. They recognized that in a war of attrition, the object was not only to kill enemy soldiers but to break the will of the enemy to continue fighting.[48] At the same time, many submarine commanders took actions to try to minimize the loss of life, especially of non-Japanese.

At times, too, the initiative to adopt more humane measures came not from the skipper but from his officers. Much of the activity of the USS *Treader*, operating in the Yellow Sea during 1945, involved sinking junks of around 300 tons. The submarine's chief engineer, William Robert Anderson, noticed that it was not uncommon for women and children to be on board the junks. He recommended that the occupants be given a chance to abandon the vessels before they were sunk by shooting at their waterlines.[49]

The early-twentieth-century British admiral Sir John Fisher once proclaimed, "Moderation in war is imbecility."[50] A. P. V. Rogers claims that during World War II the principle of proportionality—that is, ensuring that damage to civilians was not out of proportion to the potential military advantage—simply did not exist for the most part.[51] But many submarine commanders did make this calculation in an attempt to avoid unnecessary suffering to noncombatants. Perhaps the majority of submariners tried to balance military efficiency with a measure of humanitarianism.[52]

Appendix
Submarine Gun Attacks in the Pacific, 1942–1945

United States				
Vessel type	1942	1943	1944	1945
Auxiliary minesweeper			4	1
Barge	1	2		22
Cargo ship	6	16	16	7
Coaster		1	2	24
Escort			3	4
Fishing vessel				1
Frigate			2	
Gun boat			1	
Junk		1	1	113
Landing craft/barge	4	1	1	2
Lugger			3	44
Minelayer		1		
Miscellaneous	1		1	7
Motorboat				1
Oiler	1	3	1	3
Passenger-cargo ship		3		
Patrol vessel		4	14	9
Picket		1		21
Prau/native boat			1	3
Sailing vessel			2	15
Sampan	25	48	62	54

Vessel type	1942	1943	1944	1945
Schooner	1	16	14	109
Sea truck			16	82
Small craft		1	2	50
Sub chaser	2	6	2	14
Trawler	9	16	51	45
Tug			1	10
Yacht	1	1	1	
Total	51	121	201	641
Total subs making attacks	17	37	83	91
Britain				
Auxiliary			1	
Barge			2	5
Cargo ship			3	
Coaster			75	95
Escort			1	
Fishing vessel			1	
Hulk				1
Junk			121	177
Landing craft			7	26
Lighter			13	23
Lugger			2	5
Merchant vessel	1		5	
Minesweeper				2
Motor gunboat				1
Motor launch			2	
Oiler			1	3
Patrol vessel			2	1
Q ship				1
Sampan			5	1
Schooner			32	12
Small craft			7	15

Vessel type	1942	1943	1944	1945
Sub chaser		1	2	4
Submarine				1
Sub tender				1
Torpedo boat				2
Transport				1
Trawler			1	4
Tug			10	12
Total	1	1	293	393
Total subs making attacks	1	1	31	36
The Netherlands				
Cargo ship			1	
Coaster	1		5	2
Fishing vessel				1
Junk			4	
Landing craft			1	
Merchant vessel		1		
Oiler			1	1
Prau			2	5
Small craft				1
Total	1	1	14	10
Total subs making attacks	1	1	5	6

Notes: In the absence of standard definitions by submariners, the categories used offer only a rough guide to the types of vessels attacked. The figures provided include only attacks claimed to be successful. In a small number of cases more than one submarine simultaneously attacked the same target. The figures also include a small number of craft destroyed by burning or demolition.

Sources: Compiled from John D. Alden, *U.S. Submarine Attacks during World War II (Including Allied Submarine Attacks in the Pacific Theatre)* (Annapolis, MD: Naval Institute Press, 1989); John D. Alden and Craig R. McDonald, *United States and Allied Submarine Successes in the Pacific and Far East during World War II* (Jefferson, NC: McFarland, 2009).

Notes

Abbreviations

CBC   Clay Blair Collection, American Heritage Center, University of Wyoming, Laramie

LC   Library of Congress, Manuscript Division, Washington, DC

NARA   U.S. National Archives and Record Administration, College Park, MD

SFM   Submarine Force Museum, Groton, CT

SM   Submarine Memorabilia, WWII Submarine War Patrol Reports, reproduced on DVD, discs 1–28

UBSM   USS *Bowfin* Submarine Museum, Pearl Harbor, HI

Introduction

1. I. J. Galantin, *Take Her Deep! A Submarine against Japan in World War II* (1987; repr., London: Unwin Hyman, 1988), 47.

2. George Grider, with Lydel Sims, *War Fish* (London: Cassell, 1959), 12–13.

3. Robert Gannon, *Hellions of the Deep: The Development of American Torpedoes in World War II* (University Park: Pennsylvania State University Press, 1996), 198; Mark P. Parillo, *The Japanese Merchant Marine in World War II* (Annapolis, MD: U.S. Naval Institute Press, 1993), 207.

4. William Tuohy, *The Bravest Man: Richard O'Kane and the Amazing Submarine Adventures of the USS* Tang (2001; repr., New York: Ballantine Books, 2006), 269–70.

5. Calvin Moon Interview, 21, Rutgers Oral History Archives of World War II, http://fas-history.rutgers.edu/oralhistory/Interviews/moon-calvin .html (accessed 2 September 2005).

6. C. Kenneth Ruiz, with John Bruning, *The Luck of the Draw: The Memoir of a World War II Submariner* (St. Paul, MN: Zenith, 2005), 238.

7. Geoffrey Till, "The Battle of the Atlantic as History," in *The Battle of the Atlantic, 1939–1945: The 50th Anniversary International Naval Conference,* ed. Stephen Howarth and Derek Law (London: Greenhill Books, 1994), 587.

8. Harley Cope and Walter Karig, *Battle Submerged: Submarine Fighters of World War II* (New York: Norton, 1951), 215; Clay Blair Jr., *Hitler's U-Boat War: The Hunters, 1939–1942* (1996; repr., New York: Modern Library, 2000), 21; Gordon Williamson, *Grey Wolf: U-Boat Crewmen of World War II* (Oxford: Osprey, 2001), 53, 55; Peter Padfield, *War beneath the Sea: Submarine Conflict, 1939–1945* (London: Pimlico, 1995), 64–65; 303–4; Clay Blair Jr., *Hitler's U-Boat War: The Hunted, 1942–1945* (1998; repr., London: Cassell, 2001), 316.

9. Joel Ira Holwitt, *"Execute against Japan": The U.S. Decision to Conduct Unrestricted Submarine Warfare* (College Station: Texas A&M University Press, 2009), 67–69; Anthony Newpower, *Iron Men and Tin Fish: The Race to Build a Better Torpedo during World War II* (Westport, CT: Praeger Security International, 2006), 97–98.

10. See, for example, Commander Submarine Force, Pacific Fleet, Current Doctrine Submarines, February 1944, 6, Naval Historical Center, Washington, DC, http://www.history.navy.mil/library/online/sub_doctrine.htm (accessed 13 June 2008); Dale Russell, *Hell Above, Deep Water Below* (Tillamook, OR: Bayocean Enterprises, 1995), 10; Norman Friedman, *US Naval Weapons: Every Gun, Missile, Mine and Torpedo Used by the US Navy from 1883 to the Present Day* (Annapolis, MD: U.S. Naval Institute Press, 1983), 54–55.

11. Quoted in Mike Ostlund, *Find 'Em, Chase 'Em, Sink 'Em: The Mysterious Loss of the WWII Submarine USS* Gudgeon (Guildford, CT: Lyons, 2006), 318.

12. Charles Lockwood, *Sink 'Em All: Submarine Warfare in the Pacific* (1951; repr., New York: Bantam Books, 1984), 141; Commander Submarine Force, Pacific Fleet, Current Doctrine Submarines, February 1944, 71–72.

13. Michael Wilson, *A Submariners' War: The Indian Ocean, 1939–45* (Stroud, UK: Tempus, 2000), 105–6; Charles Eliott Loughlin, *The Reminiscences of Rear Admiral Charles Elliot Loughlin, U.S. Navy (Retired)* (Annapolis, MD: U.S. Naval Institute Press, 1982), 115; Theodore Roscoe, *United States Submarine Operations in World War II* (Annapolis, MD: U.S. Naval Institute Press, 1949), 422–23; Clay Blair Jr., *Silent Victory: The U.S. Submarine War against Japan* (1975; repr., Annapolis, MD: U.S. Naval Institute Press, 2001), 764; Flint Whitlock and Ron Smith, *The Depths of Courage: American Submariners at War with Japan, 1941–1945* (New York: Berkley Caliber, 2007), 225–26; Jonathan J. McCullough, *A Tale of Two Subs: An Untold Story of World War II, Two Sister Ships, and Extraordinary Heroism* (New York: Grand Central, 2008), 232, 241–45; Corwin Mendenhall, *Submarine Diary: The Silent Stalking of Japan* (Annapolis, MD: U.S. Naval Institute Press, 1991), 288–89.

14. Quoted in Gannon, *Hellions of the Deep,* 45.

15. Holger H. Herwig, "Innovation Ignored: The Submarine Problem;

Germany, Britain, and the United States, 1919–1939," in *Military Innovation in the Interwar Period,* ed. Williamson Murray and Allan R. Millett (Cambridge: Cambridge University Press, 1996), 260. See also, for example, Buford Rowland and William B. Boyd, *U.S. Navy Bureau of Ordnance in World War II* (Washington, DC: Bureau of Ordnance Department of the Navy, 1953), 90, 96, 109.

16. Roscoe, *Submarine Operations,* 111–12; Charles Rush, "One-Boat Wolfpack," *Naval History* 22 (February 2008): 24–26; Lockwood, *Sink 'Em All,* 50; David C. Evans, ed., *The Japanese Navy in World War II: In the Words of Former Japanese Naval Officers* (1969; repr., Annapolis, MD: U.S. Naval Institute Press, 1986), 397.

17. History of USS *Pompano,* disc 4, SM.

18. Creed Burlingame Interview (taped), box 96, CBC.

19. Quoted in Tuohy, *The Bravest Man,* 151–52. See also Paul Chapman, *Submarine* Torbay (London: Robert Hale, 1989), 21.

20. Holwitt, *"Execute against Japan,"* 80.

21. Norvell G. Ward, *The Reminiscences of Norvell G. Ward* (Annapolis, MD: U.S. Naval Institute Press, 1996), 110–11; Rowland, *Bureau of Ordnance,* 394; Milan Vego, *Operational Warfare at Sea: Theory and Practice* (London: Routledge, 2009), 14.

22. William T. Kinsella Interview (taped), box 98, CBC; Maurice H. Rindskopf, in *Submarine Stories: Recollections from the Diesel Boats,* ed. Paul Stillwell (Annapolis, MD: U.S. Naval Institute Press, 2007), 109.

23. See Carl Boyd, *American Command of the Sea through Carriers, Codes and the Silent Service: World War II and Beyond* (Newport News, VA: Mariners' Museum, 1995), 36; James Calvert, *Silent Running: My Years on a World War II Attack Submarine* (New York: John Wiley and Sons, 1995), 109.

24. Ward, *Reminiscences,* 154; Stephen L. Moore, Spadefish: *On Patrol with a Top-Scoring World War II Submarine* (Dallas: Atriad, 2006), 38; Holwitt, *"Execute against Japan,"* 80; Lockwood, *Sink 'Em All,* 42.

25. Lawson P. Ramage, in Stillwell, *Submarine Stories,* 165–69; Tuohy, *The Bravest Man,* 294–95; Cope and Karig, *Battle Submerged,* 118.

26. Quoted in Craig R. McDonald, *The USS* Puffer *in World War II: A History of the Submarine and Its Wartime Crew* (Jefferson, NC: McFarland, 2008), 127. See also John D. Alden, *The Fleet Submarine in the U.S. Navy: A Design and Construction History* (London: Arms and Armour, 1979), 93.

27. See Rowland, *Bureau of Ordnance,* 258; Cope and Karig, *Battle Submerged,* 217–18; Newpower, *Iron Men and Tin Fish,* 98.

28. Charles Lockwood to Vice Admiral R. S. Edwards, 25 November 1942, Papers of Charles A. Lockwood, Correspondence, 1940–42, box 12, folder 65, LC; Holwitt, *"Execute against Japan,"* 73.

29. Alden, *Fleet Submarine,* 93.

30. Rowland, *Bureau of Ordnance,* 258, 262; Friedman, *US Naval Weapons,* 54, 56; Moore, Spadefish, 37; Alden, *Fleet Submarine,* 94; USS *Bergall* Deck Guns, http://www.bergall.org/320 (accessed 6 July 2007). The designation 25-caliber represented the length of the barrel, with one caliber equal to the shell diameter of 5 inches; thus the barrel length was 125 inches.

31. See Norman Polmar, *The American Submarine* (Annapolis, MD: Nautical and Aviation Publishing Company of America, 1981), 64; Alden, *Fleet Submarine,* 94; Paul Kemp, *A Pictorial History of the Sea War, 1939–1945* (London: Arms and Armour, 1995), 83; Moore, Spadefish, 397; Friedman, *US Naval Weapons,* 54.

1. Pearl Harbor

1. Roscoe, *Submarine Operations,* 9–10; Whitlock and Smith, *Depths of Courage,* 11; Gannon, *Hellions of the Deep,* 197.

2. Janet M. Manson, *Diplomatic Ramifications of Unrestricted Submarine Warfare, 1939–1941* (Westport, CT: Greenwood, 1990), 1, 5, 160; W. T. Mallison Jr., *Studies in the Law of Naval Warfare: Submarines in General and Limited Wars* (Washington, DC: Government Printing Office, 1968), 90.

3. Jean-Marie Henckaerts, "The Development of International Humanitarian Law and the Continued Relevance of Custom," in *The Legitimate Use of Military Force: The Just War Tradition and the Customary Laws of Armed Conflict,* ed. Howard M. Hensel (Aldershot, UK: Ashgate, 2008), 117; Blair, *The Hunters, 1939–1942,* 7; Gary M. Anderson and Adam Gifford Jr., "Privateering and the Private Production of Naval Power," *Cato Journal* 11 (Spring/Summer 1991): 103–5; Gary M. Anderson and Adam Gifford Jr., "Order Out of Anarchy: The International Law of War," *Cato Journal* 15 (Spring/Summer 1995): 28; Paul E. Fontenoy, *Submarines: An Illustrated History of Their Impact* (Santa Barbara: ABC-Clio, 2007), 15.

4. Chuck Lawliss, *The Submarine Book: An Illustrated History of the Attack Submarine* (Shrewsbury, UK: Airlife, 2000), 68–69; V. E. Tarrant, *The U-Boat Offensive, 1914–1945* (London: Arms and Armour, 1989), 12.

5. Fontenoy, *Submarines,* 15–16.

6. Ronald H. Spector, *At War at Sea: Sailors and Naval Combat in the Twentieth Century* (New York: Viking, 2001), 115.

7. Quoted in Richard Dean Burns, "Regulating Submarine Warfare, 1921–41: A Case Study in Arms Control and Limited War," *Military Affairs* 35 (April 1971): 59.

8. See Ingrid Detter De Lupis, *The Law of War* (Cambridge: Cambridge University Press, 1987), 267; Adam Roberts and Richard Guelff, eds., *Documents on the Laws of War* (1982; repr., Oxford: Clarendon, 1989), 147–50; Emily O. Goldman, *Sunken Treaties: Naval Arms Control between the Wars*

(University Park: Pennsylvania State University Press, 1994), 293–94, 317; Geoffrey Best, *Humanity in Warfare* (New York: Columbia University Press, 1983), 259.

9. Blair, *The Hunters, 1939–1942,* 66–67, 425; Friedrich Ruge, *Sea Warfare, 1939–1945: A German Viewpoint* (London: Cassell, 1957), 45–46; Lawliss, *Submarine Book,* 88; Howarth and Law, *Battle of the Atlantic,* 60; Andrew Williams, *The Battle of the Atlantic* (London: BBC, 2002), 16; Padfield, *War beneath the Sea,* 4–7, 55, 59; J. Rohwer and G. Hummerchen, *Chronology of the War at Sea, 1939–1945: The Naval History of World War Two* (1972; repr., London: Greenhill Books, 1992), 1.

10. Padfield, *War beneath the Sea,* 56; Bernard Edwards, *The Grey Widow-Maker: Twenty-four Disasters at Sea* (London: Robert Hale, 1990), 81–89; Dan Van Der Vat, *Stealth at Sea: The History of the Submarine* (London: Orion, 1995), 190.

11. Lawliss, *Submarine Book,* 88; Ruge, *Sea Warfare,* 48; Mallison, *Law of Naval Warfare,* 115; Padfield, *War beneath the Sea,* 65; Williams, *Battle of the Atlantic,* 59; Manson, *Diplomatic Ramifications,* 97; Burns, "Submarine Warfare," 60.

12. Wilson, *Submariners' War,* 18; Newpower, *Iron Men and Tin Fish,* 56; Fontenoy, *Submarines,* 31.

13. Roberts and Guelff, *Laws of War,* 149–50.

14. Quoted in Padfield, *War beneath the Sea,* 65; Williams, *Battle of the Atlantic,* 211.

15. Quoted in Blair, *The Hunted, 1942–1945,* 65. For accounts of the incident, see also Padfield, *War beneath the Sea,* 294–96; Ruge, *Sea Warfare,* 232; Williamson, *Grey Wolf,* 5, 52; Tony Bridgland, *Waves of Hate: Naval Atrocities of the Second World War* (Annapolis, MD: U.S. Naval Institute Press, 2002), 63–90; Wilson, *Submariners' War,* 128.

16. Tuohy, *The Bravest Man,* 42; Bruce Henderson, *Down to the Sea: An Epic Story of Naval Disaster and Heroism in World War II* (New York: Harper Collins, 2007), 16; Whitlock and Smith, *Depths of Courage,* 10; Lawliss, *Submarine Book,* 98–99; Polmar, *American Submarine,* 57.

17. Ronald H. Spector, *Eagle against the Sun: The American War with Japan* (New York: Vintage Books, 1985), 153; Robert Fyne, *The Hollywood Propaganda of World War II* (London: Scarecrow, 1997), 152; Gordon Daniels, "The Great Tokyo Air Raid, 9–10 March 1945," in *Modern Japan: Aspects of History, Literature and Society,* ed. W. G. Beasley (Tokyo: Charles E. Tuttle, 1976), 121.

18. Quoted in Herwig, "Innovation Ignored," 256. See also Manson, *Diplomatic Ramifications,* 34; Holwitt, *"Execute against Japan,"* 83, 124.

19. See Holwitt, *"Execute against Japan,"* especially 2, 79, 160, 169, 183; Spector, *At War at Sea,* 287.

20. Kinsella interview; Richard Voge, quoted in Holwitt, *"Execute against Japan,"* 82.

21. See the Reminiscences of James Fife, Interviews Conducted 1961–62, 196, 242, Oral History Research Office, Columbia University, New York.

22. Bruce A. Elleman and S. C. M. Paine, eds., *Naval Coalition Warfare: From the Napoleonic War to Operation Iraqi Freedom* (London: Routledge, 2008), 115–16; Vego, *Operational Warfare,* 14–15, 211; Max Hastings, *Retribution: The Battle for Japan, 1944–45* (New York: Knopf, 2008), 268.

23. Spector, *Eagle against the Sun,* 85; William Bruce Johnson, *The Pacific Campaign in World War II: From Pearl Harbor to Guadalcanal* (London: Routledge, 2006), 55; Roscoe, *Submarine Operations,* 5–6; Steven L. Carruthers, *Japanese Submarine Raiders, 1942: A Maritime Mystery* (Narrabeen, New South Wales: Casper, 2006), 57; Shigeru Fukudome, "The Hawaii Operation," in Evans, *Japanese Navy,* 32.

24. Mochitsura Hashimoto, *Sunk: The Story of the Japanese Submarine Fleet, 1942–1945,* trans. E. H. M. Colegrave (London: Hamilton, 1955), 12; David Jenkins, *Battle Surface: Japan's Submarine War against Australia, 1942–44* (Sydney: Random House, 1992), 32; Sadao Asada, *From Mahan to Pearl Harbor: The Imperial Japanese Navy and the United States* (Annapolis, MD: U.S. Naval Institute Press, 2006), 180; Michael A. Palmer, *Command at Sea: Naval Command and Control since the Sixteenth Century* (Cambridge, MA: Harvard University Press, 2005), 256.

25. Dallas Woodbury Isom, *Midway Inquest: Why the Japanese Lost the Battle of Midway* (Bloomington: Indiana University Press, 2007), 252; Fontenoy, *Submarines,* 38; Interrogation of Vice-Admiral Paul H. Weneker, *United States Strategic Bombing Survey (Pacific),* Interrogations of Japanese Officials, Naval Analysis Division, http://ibiblio.org/hyperwar/AAF/USSBS/IJO/IJO-70.html (accessed 11 April 2008).

26. Hashimoto, *Sunk,* 61–64; Arthur Hezlet, *The Submarine and Sea Power* (London: Peter Davies, 1967), 199.

27. Masataka Chihaya, "The Withdrawal from Kiska," in Evans, *Japanese Navy,* 253–54; Lockwood, *Sink 'Em All,* 340.

28. David Stevens, *A Critical Vulnerability: The Impact of the Submarine Threat on Australia's Maritime Defence, 1915–1954* (Canberra: Sea Power Centre, 2005), 172; Mark Felton, *Slaughter at Sea: The Story of Japan's Naval War Crimes* (Annapolis, MD: U.S. Naval Institute Press, 2007), 138; Holwitt, *"Execute against Japan,"* 139, 215; Robert Greenhalgh Albion and Jennie Barnes Pope, *Sea Lanes in Wartime: The American Experience, 1775–1945* (n.p.: Archon Books, 1968), 301.

29. Stevens, *A Critical Vulnerability,* 173, 231; Newpower, *Iron Men and Tin Fish,* 114.

30. Carruthers, *Japanese Submarine Raiders,* 193; Stevens, *A Critical Vulnerability,* 185–86, 191, 201, 209.

31. Carruthers, *Japanese Submarine Raiders,* 201; Stevens, *A Critical Vulnerability,* 332.

32. Felton, *Slaughter at Sea,* 155–56; Lockwood, *Sink 'Em All,* 226; Stevens, *A Critical Vulnerability,* 278.

33. Jenkins, *Battle Surface,* 7, 32, 255, 289–91; Bernard Edwards, *Blood and Bushido: Japanese Atrocities at Sea, 1941–1945* (Worcester, UK: Self Publishing Association, 1991), 42; Blair, *The Hunted, 1942–1945,* 231–32; Hastings, *Retribution,* 338, 426; Oz at War, http://www.ozatwar.com (accessed 13 June 2008); Jean Hood, ed., *Submarine: An Anthology of First-hand Accounts of War under the Sea, 1939–1945* (London: Conway, 2007), 358; Spector, *Eagle against the Sun,* 481.

34. Quoted in Henderson, *Down to the Sea,* 19.

35. Quoted in Hood, *Submarine,* 230.

36. Quentin Russell Seiler, foreword to Ostlund, *Find 'Em,* xiii.

37. Lawson P. Ramage, *Reminiscences of Vice Admiral Lawson P. Ramage* (Annapolis, MD: U.S. Naval Institute Press, 1975), 59.

38. Whitlock and Smith, *Depths of Courage,* 6, 8, 11.

39. Quoted in ibid., 160–61.

40. Edward L. Beach Sr., with Edward L. Beach Jr., *From Annapolis to Scapa Flow: The Autobiography of Edward K. Beach Sr.* (Annapolis, MD: U.S. Naval Institute Press, 2003), 291–92.

41. Calvert, *Silent Running,* 39.

42. Quoted in Blair, *Silent Victory,* 106, 352.

43. Quoted in Ostlund, *Find 'Em,* 55.

44. USS *Bluegill* (SS-242), http://home.flash.net/~stromain/BlueGill/ (accessed 9 July 2007).

45. Russell, *Hell Above,* 121.

46. Quoted in Padfield, *War beneath the Sea,* 400.

47. Quoted in Tuohy, *The Bravest Man,* 259.

48. Quoted in Whitlock and Smith, *Depths of Courage,* 288.

49. Hosey Mays, in Stillwell, *Submarine Stories,* 160; Moore, Spadefish, 284.

50. Jaye Garrison Interview (transcript), 9 May 1992, Oral History Collection, UBSM.

2. Trouble with Trawlers

1. Quoted in Stillwell, *Submarine Stories,* 4. See also Carl LaVO, *Slade Cutter: Submarine Warrior* (Annapolis, MD: U.S. Naval Institute Press, 2003), 79.

2. Lewis Parks Interview (taped), boxes 98 and 99, CBC.

3. LaVO, *Slade Cutter,* 81, 86; USS *Pompano* First War Patrol Report, disc 4, SM; Roscoe, *Submarine Operations,* 93–94.

4. Slade Cutter, quoted in Stillwell, *Submarine Stories,* 1, 3, 6–7; USS

Pompano Second War Patrol Report, 22–24 May 1942, UBSM; LaVO, *Slade Cutter,* 79, 90.

5. Quoted in LaVO, *Slade Cutter,* 40.

6. Parks interview. For other characterizations of Cutter, see Blair, *Silent Victory,* 677; Don Keith, *Final Patrol: True Stories of World War II Submarines* (New York: NAL Caliber, 2006), 245–48; Stillwell, *Submarine Stories,* 1; "Submariner Gets Support to Make Admiral," *Naval History* 18 (August 2004): 62; Ward, *Reminiscences,* 89.

7. Dave Bouslog, *Maru Killer: The War Patrols of the USS* Seahorse (Sarasota, FL: Seahorse Books, 1996), 32–33, 39–41.

8. Rowland, *Bureau of Ordnance,* 53, 59–60; Commander Submarine Force, Pacific Fleet, Current Doctrine Submarines, February 1944, 72.

9. USS *Seahorse* Second War Patrol Report, 29 October 1943, Target Data, UBSM.

10. Friedman, *US Naval Weapons,* 55; Rowland, *Bureau of Ordnance,* 235; Don Keith, *In the Course of Duty: The Heroic Mission of the USS* Batfish (New York: NAL Caliber, 2005), 34; Tony DiGuilian, "Definitions and Information about Naval Guns," http://www.navweapons.com/ (accessed 1 August 2007); USS *Bergall,* Deck Guns.

11. Quoted in LaVO, *Slade Cutter,* 126.

12. Quoted in ibid., 127.

13. Bouslog, *Maru Killer,* 41–43.

14. Slade Cutter, *The Reminiscences of Captain Slade D. Cutter* (Annapolis, MD: U.S. Naval Institute Press, 1985), 72–74; LaVO, *Slade Cutter,* 136.

15. USS *Pollack* Second War Patrol Report, 10–11 March 1942, disc 4, SM.

16. USS *Pollack* First War Patrol Report, Endorsement, disc 4, SM; Graeme Cook, *Silent Marauders* (London: Hart-Davis, MacGibbon, 1976), 53–55; F. W. Lipscomb, *The British Submarine* (London: Adam and Charles Black, 1954), 100.

17. USS *Pollack* Second War Patrol Report, Endorsement.

18. Ibid.

19. USS *Pollack* Third War Patrol Report, Endorsement, disc 4, SM.

20. Tuohy, *The Bravest Man,* 215.

21. Compiled from John D. Alden, *U.S. Submarine Attacks during World War II (Including Allied Submarine Attacks in the Pacific Theatre)* (Annapolis, MD: U.S. Naval Institute Press, 1989); John D. Alden and Craig R. McDonald, *United States and Allied Submarine Successes in the Pacific and Far East during World War II* (Jefferson, NC: McFarland, 2009). See appendix. Note that these statistics refer only to gun attacks claimed as successful in sinking or damaging craft.

22. John G. Butcher, *The Closing of the Frontier: A History of the Marine Fisheries of Southeast Asia, c. 1850–2000* (Leiden: KITLV, 2004), 169.

23. Quoted in Tuohy, *The Bravest Man*, 150.

24. Charles Lockwood and Hans Christian Adamson, *Hellcats of the Sea* (New York: Greenberg, 1955), 195.

25. Galantin, *Take Her Deep!* 45–46.

26. Quoted in USS *Thresher* (SS-200), History, http://www.broseker.net/babroseker/history.htm (accessed 30 July 2007).

27. USS *Tinosa* Seventh War Patrol Report, 18 June 1944, UBSM.

28. Paul R. Schratz, *Submarine Commander: A Story of World War II and Korea* (Lexington: University Press of Kentucky, 1988), 116; USS *Sterlet* Second War Patrol Report, 9 October 1944, UBSM.

29. Burlingame interview; Roy M. Davenport, *Clean Sweep* (New York: Vantage Books, 1986), 1.

30. See Parks interview; James D. Hornfischer, *The Last Stand of the Tin Can Sailors: The Extraordinary World War II Story of the U.S. Navy's Finest Hour* (2004; repr., New York: Bantam Books, 2005), 176; Rowland, *Bureau of Ordnance*, 53, 55.

31. Quoted in Robert J. Casey, *Battle Below: The War of the Submarines* (Indianapolis: Bobbs-Merrill, 1945), 304.

32. USS *Silversides* First War Patrol Report, 10 May 1942, UBSM; Burlingame interview; Keith, *Final Patrol*, 76; Tuohy, *The Bravest Man*, 56; Larry Kimmett and Margaret Regis, *U.S. Submarines in World War II: An Illustrated History* (Seattle: Navigator, 1996), 56; Casey, *Battle Below*, 301–5; McDonald, *USS* Puffer, 87.

33. Parks interview.

34. Slade Cutter, in Stillwell, *Submarine Stories*, 6; LaVO, *Slade Cutter*, 97, 104–6; USS *Pompano* Third War Patrol Report, 4–5 September 1942, disc 4, SM.

35. Based on cases compiled by Charles R. Hinman. See On Eternal Patrol, http://wwwoneternalpatrol.com (accessed 17 January 2007).

36. Rick Cline, *Final Dive: The Gallant and Tragic Career of the WWII Submarine USS* Snook (Placentia, CA: R. A. Cline, 2001), 66–68.

37. USS *Croaker* Second War Patrol Report, Endorsement, disc 15, SM.

38. Ramage, *Reminiscences*, 103–4.

39. Galantin, *Take Her Deep!* 182. See also Garrison interview.

40. Quoted in Casey, *Battle Below*, 335.

41. Mallison, *Law of Naval Warfare*, 4; Victor Rudenno, *Gallipoli: Attack from the Sea* (Sydney: University of New South Wales Press, 2008), 38–39; Paul Halpern, "The Naval Coalition against the Central Powers, 1914–1918," in Elleman and Paine, eds., *Naval Coalition Warfare*, 102.

42. See Williams, *Battle of the Atlantic*, 175; Jenkins, *Battle Surface*, 218; George J. Billy and Christine M. Billy, *Merchant Mariners at War: An Oral History of World War II* (Gainesville: University Press of Florida, 2008), 140, 142, 147.

43. Tarrant, *U-Boat Offensive,* 100.

44. Padfield, *War beneath the Sea,* 69; Howarth and Law, *Battle of the Atlantic,* 189; Williams, *Battle of the Atlantic,* 172; Blair, *The Hunters, 1939–1942,* 145, 260; Peter C. Smith, *Naval Warfare in the English Channel, 1939–1945* (Barnsley, UK: Pen and Sword, 2007), 84–85; Lipscomb, *British Submarine,* 223; Keith Lowe, *Inferno: The Fiery Destruction of Hamburg, 1943* (New York: Scribner, 2007), 289.

45. Quoted in Bridgland, *Waves of Hate,* 153; see also 146–52.

46. Henry T. Chen, *Taiwanese Distant-Water Fisheries in Southeast Asia, 1936–1977* (St. John's, Newfoundland: International Maritime Economic History Association, 2009), 8, 23.

47. USS *Guardfish* First War Patrol Report, 22 August 1942, disc 11, SM.

48. Ward, *Reminiscences,* 162.

49. McDonald, *USS* Puffer, 61; Mendenhall, *Submarine Diary,* 205–6.

50. Harry J. Benda, James K. Irikura, and Koichi Kishi, *Japanese Military Administration in Indonesia: Selected Documents,* Translation Series 6 (New Haven, CT: Yale University Southeast Asia Studies, 1965), 23, 34.

51. Mendenhall, *Submarine Diary,* 258.

52. Hansgeng Jentschura, Dieter Jung, and Peter Milker, *Warships of the Imperial Japanese Navy, 1869–1945,* trans. Anthony Preston and J. D. Brown (London: Arms and Armour, 1977), 196.

53. USS *Archerfish* Fourth War Patrol Report, 13 August 1944, http://www.ussarcherfish.com/warptrl/patr014.htm (accessed 4 July 2007).

54. USS *Thresher* (SS-200), History.

55. George Edwin Bogaars Interview (transcript), 8 December 1983, accession no. 000379, National Archives of Singapore; Doug Hurst, *The Fourth Ally: The Dutch Forces in Australia during World War II* (Canberra: Doug Hurst, 2001), 17; Chen, *Taiwanese Distant-Water Fisheries,* 8.

56. Roscoe, *Submarine Operations,* 111; Spector, *Eagle against the Sun,* 154; Robert J. McLaughlin and Sally E. Parry, *We'll Always Have the Movies: American Cinema during World War II* (Lexington: University Press of Kentucky, 2006), 71; Lockwood, *Sink 'Em All,* 81.

57. IJN *Akagi Maru:* Tabular Record of Movement, Combined Fleet, http://www.combinedfleet.com (accessed 12 March 2008).

58. USS *Finback* Fifth War Patrol Report, Enemy A/S Measures, disc 13, SM.

59. Galantin, *Take Her Deep!* 45, 85–86.

60. USS *Pompano* Sixth War Patrol Report, Enemy A/S Measures, disc 4, SM.

61. William Godfrey Jr. Interview, Rutgers Oral History Archives, 17.

62. USS *Batfish* Second War Patrol Report, 20–21 March, http://www.ussbatfish.com (accessed 5 July 2007).

63. USS *Gunnel* Fourth War Patrol Report, with commentary by executive officer Lloyd R. Vasey, http://www.jmlavelle.com/gunnel/patr014.htm (accessed 7 November 2007).

64. USS *Finback* Second War Patrol Report, 3 November 1942, disc 13, SM.

65. USS *Redfin* Fourth War Patrol Report, 19 September 1944, UBSM.

66. USS *Batfish* Second War Patrol Report, 23 March 1944.

67. Butcher, *Closing of the Frontier,* 169.

68. Quoted in *Sydney Morning Herald,* 5 August 1942, 7.

69. Ibid.; Jenkins, *Battle Surface,* 263–64. See also Patricia Miles, "After the Battle of Terrigal: Merchant Navy Losses off the New South Wales Coast in World War II," 7, Maritime Heritage Online, http://maritime.heritage.nsw .gov.au/ (accessed 11 June 2008).

3. *Wahoo*

1. U.S. Navy press release, On Eternal Patrol; USS *Bowfin*–News, http:// www.bowfin.org/website/news (accessed 17 January 2007); The Submarine USS *Wahoo* (SS-238), http://www.mackinnon.org/wahoo-home.html (accessed 17 January 2007).

2. Morton, quoted in Associated Press interview, Dudley Morton Papers, UBSM; Tuohy, *The Bravest Man,* 3; Padfield, *War beneath the Sea,* 339; Grider and Sims, *War Fish,* 44; Lockwood and Adamson, *Hellcats of the Sea,* 7; Thomas Parrish, *The Submarine: A History* (London: Viking Penguin, 2004), 389; James F. DeRose, *Unrestricted Warfare: How a New Breed of Officers Led the Submarine Force to Victory in World War II* (New York: John Wiley and Sons, 2000), 56; Keith Wheeler, *War under the Pacific* (Alexandria, VA: Time-Life Books, 1980), 64; Holwitt, *"Execute against Japan,"* 163.

3. Roscoe, *Submarine Operations,* 205.

4. Quoted in Legends of the Deep, http://www.warfish.com (accessed 23 March 2007).

5. Grider and Sims, *War Fish,* 51.

6. Holwitt, *"Execute against Japan,"* 80; DeRose, *Unrestricted Warfare,* 55; Burlingame interview.

7. DeRose, *Unrestricted Warfare,* 62.

8. USS *Wahoo* Second War Patrol Report, 14 December 1942, in J. T. McDaniel, ed., *U.S.S.* Wahoo *(SS-238) American Submarine War Patrol Reports* (Riverdale, GA: Riverdale Books, 2003), 32.

9. Ibid., 32, 43–44; DeRose, *Unrestricted Warfare,* 62; Forest J. Sterling, *Wake of the* Wahoo (Philadelphia: Chilton, 1960), 44.

10. Reminiscences of James Fife, 362–63.

11. DeRose, *Unrestricted Warfare,* 105; Blair, *Silent Victory,* 538.

12. Richard O'Kane, Wahoo: *The Patrols of America's Most Famous World War II Submarine* (Novato, CA: Presidio, 1987), 199.

13. DeRose, *Unrestricted Warfare*, 69; UBSM exhibit.

14. See Tuohy, *The Bravest Man*, 38; Werner Gruhl, *Imperial Japan's World War Two, 1931–1945* (New Brunswick, NJ: Transaction, 2007), 49; Blair, *The Hunted, 1942–1945*, 158–59; Spector, *Eagle against the Sun*, 222; Newpower, *Iron Men and Tin Fish*, 140–41.

15. Quoted in DeRose, *Unrestricted Warfare*, 92.

16. Photo, Morton Papers.

17. *Time*, 22 February 1943, 24.

18. Morton Papers.

19. USS *Wahoo* Third War Patrol Report, 26 January 1943, in McDaniel, *U.S.S.* Wahoo, 50.

20. Lockwood, *Sink 'Em All*, 65.

21. Tuohy, *The Bravest Man*, 398–99.

22. USS *Wahoo* Third War Patrol Report, 26 January 1943, 50–51.

23. Quoted in David Jones and Peter Nunan, *U.S. Subs Down Under: Brisbane, 1942–1945* (Annapolis, MD: U.S. Naval Institute Press, 2005), 98; Clary, in Legends of the Deep.

24. Quoted in Tuohy, *The Bravest Man*, 399.

25. Ibid., 398–99.

26. See McDonald, *USS Puffer*, 48; Hastings, *Retribution*, 292.

27. Quoted in Holwitt, "*Execute against Japan*," 81.

28. DeRose, *Unrestricted Warfare*, 65–66, 77, 94, 287.

29. Quoted in Hastings, *Retribution*, 172.

30. Quoted in Bridgland, *Waves of Hate*, 136. See also Boyd, *American Command*, 22; Ruge, *Sea Warfare*, 233; Gruhl, *Imperial Japan's World War Two*, 186.

31. See Jones and Nunan, *U.S. Subs Down Under*, 98; DeRose, *Unrestricted Warfare*, 81; Padfield, *War beneath the Sea*, 343; Spector, *Eagle against the Sun*, 127–28; Felton, *Slaughter at Sea*, 54.

32. Quoted in Tuohy, *The Bravest Man*, 399.

33. Newspaper clipping, *Wahoo* Boat Book, SFM.

34. DeRose, *Unrestricted Warfare*, 72; Tuohy, *The Bravest Man*, 5.

35. Quoted in Tuohy, *The Bravest Man*, 400.

36. Holwitt, "*Execute against Japan*," 173–74.

37. USS *Wahoo* Fourth War Patrol Report, 21 March 1943, in McDaniel, *U.S.S.* Wahoo, 71.

38. Quoted in Legends of the Deep.

39. USS *Wahoo* Fourth War Patrol Report, 25 March 1943, in McDaniel, *U.S.S.* Wahoo, 75.

40. Quoted in Legends of the Deep.

4. Atrocities

1. Chapman, *Submarine* Torbay, 62.

2. See Leo Braudy, *From Chivalry to Terrorism: War and the Changing Nature of Masculinity* (New York: Vintage Books, 2005), 42–43.

3. Quoted in Chapman, *Submarine* Torbay, 67.

4. Quoted in Bridgland, *Waves of Hate*, 99.

5. Padfield, *War beneath the Sea*, 145–49.

6. Galantin, *Take Her Deep!* 49. See also Chapman, *Submarine* Torbay, 161, 163; Edward Young, *One of Our Submarines* (Hertfordshire, UK: Wordsworth Editions, 1997), 302; Mendenhall, *Submarine Diary*, 154.

7. Padfield, *War beneath the Sea*, 379–82; Blair, *The Hunted, 1942–1945*, 530–33; Michael Gunton, *Dive! Dive! Dive! Submarines at War* (London: Constable, 2003), 57–58; Dönitz, quoted in James Owen, *Nuremberg: Evil on Trial* (London: Headline Review, 2006), 240; Bridgland, *Waves of Hate*, 108–12.

8. Manson, *Diplomatic Ramifications*, 6.

9. Admiral Doenitz, *Memoirs: Ten Years and Twenty Days* (London: Weidenfeld and Nicolson, 1958), 263. See also Owen, *Nuremberg*, 238.

10. Williams, *Battle of the Atlantic*, 209–10; Blair, *The Hunters, 1939–1942*, 565.

11. Nimitz's statement, 11 May 1946, in Mallison, *Law of Naval Warfare*, appendix B, 192; Owen, *Nuremberg*, 237, 241.

12. Quoted in Owen, *Nuremberg*, 319; Blair, *The Hunted, 1942–1945*, 704.

13. Williams, *Battle of the Atlantic*, 286; Blair, *The Hunted, 1942–1945*, 609, 704; Manson, *Diplomatic Ramifications*, 180; Burns, "Submarine Warfare," 61.

14. Felton, *Slaughter at Sea*, 7.

15. Stephen Howarth, *Fighting Ships of the Rising Sun: The Drama of the Imperial Japanese Navy, 1895–1945* (New York: Atheneum, 1983), 325.

16. Quoted in Mallison, *Law of Naval Warfare*, 142; Wilson, *Submariners' War*, 91. Those ships whose survivors were attacked included the *Donerail, Langkoeas, Scotia, British Chivalry, Sutlej, Ascot, Daisy Moller, Nancy Moller, Tjisalak, Jean Nicolet, Richard Hoovey, John A. Johnson,* and *Mamutu*.

17. James F. Dunnigan and Albert A. Nofi, *Victory at Sea: World War II in the Pacific* (New York: William Morrow, 1995), 295; Jenkins, *Battle Surface*, 82; Yuki Tanaka, *Hidden Horrors: Japanese War Crimes in World War II* (Boulder, CO: Westview, 1996), 194; Gunton, *Dive!* 59; Ulrich Straus, *The Anguish of Surrender: Japanese POWs of World War II* (Seattle: University of Washington Press, 2003), 36; Felton, *Slaughter at Sea*, 72, 162; Arthur Page, *Between Victor and Vanquished: An Australian Interrogator in the War against Japan* (Canberra: Australian Military History Publications, 2008), 120, 125–26.

18. Jenkins, *Battle Surface*, 278–79; Gruhl, *Imperial Japan's World War Two*, 103; Edwards, *Blood and Bushido*, 70–76.

19. *Weekend Australian*, 29–30 March 2008, 3.

20. Felton, *Slaughter at Sea*, 98.

21. Edwards, *Blood and Bushido*, 92–117, 120–50; Jenkins, *Battle Surface*, 284; Gruhl, *Imperial Japan's World War Two*, 103.

22. Billy and Billy, *Merchant Mariners at War*, 2, 126.

23. Harold L. Clark Statement, Statements by Survivors SS *John A. Johnson* Following Torpedoing by Japanese Submarine, November 1944, ARC id 296781, NARA, http://arcweb.archives.gov/arac/servlet/arc (accessed 29 June 2007).

24. Survivor Statements, ARC id 296781, 296779, 296792, NARA; Edwards, *Blood and Bushido*, 234–43.

25. Yomiuri Shimbun, *From Marco Polo Bridge to Pearl Harbor: Who Was Responsible?* ed. James E. Auer (Tokyo: Yomiuri Shimbun, 2006), 212.

26. Jenkins, *Battle Surface*, 284; Padfield, *War beneath the Sea*, 435, 465; T. O. Paine, *The Transpacific Voyage of His Imperial Japanese Majesty's Submarine I-400 (Tom Paine's Journal, July–December 1945)* (Los Angeles: T. O. Paine, 1984), 8; Edwards, *Blood and Bushido*, 181–202, 218–33; Gunton, *Dive!* 59; Mallison, *Law of Naval Warfare*, 142; Bridgland, *Waves of Hate*, 138–45; Evan Thomas, *Sea of Thunder: Four Commanders and the Last Great Naval Campaign, 1941–1945* (New York: Simon and Schuster, 2006), 585; Wilson, *Submariners' War*, 92–97; Roger Bell, Sean Brawley, and Chris Dixon, *Conflict in the Pacific, 1937–1951* (Cambridge: Cambridge University Press, 2005), 204.

27. Jenkins, *Battle Surface*, 284; Edwards, *Blood and Bushido*, 247; Felton, *Slaughter at Sea*, 102, 111–12, 142, 144.

28. See, for example, Tim Maga, *Judgment at Tokyo: The Japanese War Crimes Trials* (Lexington: University Press of Kentucky, 2001), 98–100.

29. Quoted in Carruthers, *Japanese Submarine Raiders*, 191.

30. Michael Sturma, *Death at a Distance: The Loss of the Legendary USS Harder* (Annapolis, MD: U.S. Naval Institute Press, 2006), 168.

31. Mendenhall, *Submarine Diary*, 144–45.

32. Philip Nichols Interview (taped), box 99, CBC; USS *Bergall* Third War Patrol Report, 27 January 1945, http://www.bergall.org/320 (accessed 6 July 2007).

33. Attack on *Taiei Maru*, (Blue 440), 1942–45, RG 313, NARA.

34. Statement by Commander J. W. Blanchard, *Albacore* Boat Book, SFM.

35. Ibid.. See also James Blanchard Interview (taped), box 98, CBC; Blair, *Silent Victory*, 658.

36. William Hazzard Interview (taped), box 97, CBC.

37. Bouslog, *Maru Killer*, 148–49.

38. Alastair Mars, *H.M.S. Thule Intercepts* (London: Elek Books, 1956), 169.

39. Ibid., 195.

40. See Tony Waters, *When Killing Is a Crime* (Boulder, CO: Lynne Rienner, 2007), 73–74.

41. Quoted in Thomas, *Sea of Thunder,* 108.

5. Sampans and Schooners

1. Paul R. Schratz, *The Reminiscences of Captain Paul Richard Schratz* (Annapolis, MD: U.S. Naval Institute Press, 1996), 61.

2. USS *Scorpion* First War Patrol Report, 20–22 April 1943, UBSM.

3. Schratz, *Reminiscences,* 60–62, 74. See also USS *Scorpion* First War Patrol Report, 29–30 April 1943; Paul R. Schratz, in Stillwell, *Submarine Stories,* 128–30.

4. USS *Finback* Sixth War Patrol Report, 19 August 1943, disc 13, SM.

5. See appendix.

6. See Burlingame interview; G. R. C. Worchester, *The Junks and Sampans of the Yangtze* (Shanghai: Department of the Inspectorate General of Customs, 1947), 51.

7. See, for example, Moore, Spadefish, 253–54; Schratz, *Reminiscences,* 85; USS *Seawolf* (SS-197), http://www.csp.navy.mil/ww2boats/seawolf.htm (accessed 12 February 2004).

8. Quoted in Cline, *Final Dive,* 22.

9. Galantin, *Take Her Deep!* 46.

10. Mendenhall, *Submarine Diary,* 144.

11. Quoted in McCullough, *A Tale of Two Subs,* 203; Hood, *Submarine,* 55.

12. USS *Sculpin* Seventh War Patrol Report, 19 June 1943, UBSM.

13. Galantin, *Take Her Deep!* 48.

14. McCullough, *A Tale of Two Subs,* 205.

15. See appendix; David Norton, Written Accounts of *Bowfin* War Patrols, UBSM.

16. Norton, *Bowfin* War Patrols; Martin Sheridan, *Overdue and Presumed Lost: The Story of the USS* Bullhead (1947; repr., Annapolis, MD: U.S. Naval Institute Press, 2004), 45–46.

17. USS *Bowfin* Second War Patrol Report, 9 November 1943, UBSM.

18. Blair, *Silent Victory,* 488–89; Edwin P. Hoyt, Bowfin: *The Story of One of America's Fabled Fleet Submarines in World War II* (New York: Van Nostrand Reinhold, 1983), 44, 60, 210; Kimmett and Regis, *U.S. Submarines,* 78.

19. USS *Bowfin* Third War Patrol Report, 16 January 1944, UBSM.

20. Ruiz and Bruning, *Luck of the Draw,* 213; USS *Pollack* Seventh War Patrol Report, 11 June 1943, UBSM.

21. Roscoe P. Thompson, interview with author, 9 October 2002, Bunbury, Western Australia.

22. Parillo, *Japanese Merchant Marine,* 174–76; Yomiuri, *From Marco Polo Bridge,* 143–45; Isom, *Midway Inquest,* 264; Johnson, *Pacific Campaign,* 282.

23. Submarines, Seventh Fleet Bulletin no. 15, 30 July 1943, Blue 443/2, RG 313, NARA.

24. Parillo, *Japanese Merchant Marine,* 98; Edwin T. Layton with Roger Pineau and John Costello, *"And I Was There": Pearl Harbor and Midway— Breaking the Secrets* (1985; repr., Annapolis, MD: U.S. Naval Institute Press, 2006), 471–72; McCullough, *A Tale of Two Subs,* 162–63.

25. See Ramage, *Reminiscences,* 172; Spector, *Eagle against the Sun,* 453; Boyd, *American Command,* 21, 38–40; Rohwer and Hummerchen, *War at Sea,* 185, 190, 204, 210, 214, 253.

26. John Coye Interview (taped), box 97, CBC.

27. Parillo, *Japanese Merchant Marine,* 90.

28. See Gannon, *Hellions of the Deep,* 71, 145, 199.

29. Parillo, *Japanese Merchant Marine,* 89; Kinsella interview; Beatrice Trefalt, "Fanaticism, Japanese Soldiers and the Pacific War, 1937–45," in *Fanaticism and Conflict in the Modern Age,* ed. Matthew Hughes and Gaynor Johnson (London: Frank Cass, 2005), 43; Galantin, *Take Her Deep!* 180; John Ellis, *Brute Force: Allied Strategy and Tactics in the Second World War* (London: Andre Deutsch, 1990), 470; Gannon, *Hellions of the Deep,* 195.

30. Fontenoy, *Submarines,* 34; H. P. Willmott, *The Battle of Leyte Gulf: The Last Fleet Action* (Bloomington: Indiana University Press, 2005), 234; Robert Schultz and James Shell, *We Were Pirates: A Torpedoman's Pacific War* (Annapolis, MD: U.S. Naval Institute Press, 2009), 162; *United States Strategic Bombing Survey: Summary Report (Pacific War)* (Washington, DC: Government Printing Office, 1946), 11.

31. Atsushi Oi, in Evans, *Japanese Navy,* 386.

32. Peter N. Davies, "A Guide to the Emergence of Japan's Modern Shipping Industries," in *International Merchant Shipping in the Nineteenth and Twentieth Centuries: The Comparative Dimension,* ed. Lewis R. Fischer and Even Lange (St. John's, Newfoundland: International Maritime Economic History Association, 2008), 113; Tomohei Chida and Peter N. Davies, *The Japanese Shipping and Shipbuilding Industries: A History of Their Modern Growth* (London: Athlone, 1990), 53, 56; Lawliss, *Submarine Book,* 104; Parillo, *Japanese Merchant Shipping,* 169, 171.

33. USS *Ray* Seventh War Patrol Report, 23 May 1945, UBSM.

34. See Lawliss, *Submarine Book,* 104; Tuohy, *The Bravest Man,* 28; Arnold S. Lott, *Most Dangerous Sea: A History of Mine Warfare, and an Account of U.S. Navy Mine Warfare Operations in World War II and Korea* (Annapolis, MD: U.S. Naval Institute Press, 1959), 217; Parillo, *Japanese Merchant Marine,* 194.

35. Eugene Fluckey, *Thunder Below! The USS* Barb *Revolutionizes Submarine Warfare in World War II* (Urbana: University of Illinois Press, 1992), 200.

36. Quoted in ibid., 211.

6. Pickets and the Picayune

1. Hastings, *Retribution,* 269; LaVO, *Slade Cutter,* 173; Newpower, *Iron Men and Tin Fish,* 188.

2. Ramage, *Reminiscences,* 173–74.

3. Hastings, *Retribution,* 42; Holwitt, *"Execute against Japan,"* 165–66.

4. Calvert, *Silent Running,* 115; Tomiji Koyanagi and Atsushi Oi, in Evans, *Japanese Navy,* 363, 407; Willmott, *Battle of Leyte Gulf,* 11.

5. Yomiuri, *From Marco Polo Bridge,* 235; David C. Earhart, *Certain Victory: Images of World War II in the Japanese Media* (New York: M. E. Sharpe, 2008), 399.

6. See Gannon, *Hellions of the Deep,* 194; Padfield, *War beneath the Sea,* 436; Kimmett and Regis, *U.S. Submarines,* 106; Tuohy, *The Bravest Man,* 349; Willmott, *Battle of Leyte Gulf,* 234.

7. Moore, Spadefish, 219.

8. USS *Hake* Fourth War Patrol Report, 27 March 1944, Attack Data, disc 17, SM.

9. USS *Finback* Seventh War Patrol Report, 30–31 January 1944, Attack Data, disc 13, SM.

10. Calvert, *Silent Running,* 159–62.

11. *Strategic Bombing Survey: Summary,* 15.

12. USS *Halibut* Ninth War Patrol Report, Endorsements, 3 May 1944, UBSM; Galantin, *Take Her Deep!* 180–81.

13. USS *Tunny* Sixth War Patrol Report, Endorsement, disc 20, SM.

14. Endorsement by M. Comstock, USS *Sunfish* Seventh War Patrol Report, http://www.geocities.com.Heartland/Hills/2364 (accessed 23 July 2007).

15. USS *Sunfish* Seventh War Patrol Report, 7 July 1944.

16. Ibid.

17. Correspondence and press clippings, *Sunfish* Boat Book, SFM.

18. *Sunfish* (SS-281), http://uboat.net/allies/warships/ship/3027.html (accessed 12 March 2008).

19. USS *Sunfish* Seventh War Patrol Report, 7 July 1944.

20. Parillo, *Japanese Merchant Marine,* 182–83.

21. USS *Gunnel* Sixth War Patrol Report, 18 August 1944, http://www.jmlavelle.com/gunnel/patr016.htm (accessed 7 November 2007).

22. Friedman, *US Naval Weapons,* 76–77; Alden, *Fleet Submarine,* 94; Mars, *H.M.S.* Thule, 185; USS *Croaker* Second War Patrol Report, 17 October 1944, disc 15, SM.

23. Guy O'Neil, Commentary on *Gunnel*'s Sixth War Patrol; Report of Special Mission, USS *Hake* Seventh War Patrol Report, disc 17, SM.

24. See, for example, Cline, *Final Dive,* 150.

25. Fluckey, *Thunder Below!* 169.

26. USS *Finback* Eighth War Patrol Report, 19 April 1944, Attack Data, disc 13, SM.

27. USS *Batfish* Third War Patrol Report, 1 July 1944, Attack Data, http:// www.ussbatfish.com (accessed 5 July 2007).

28. USS *Batfish* Third War Patrol Report, Remarks.

29. USS *Bergall* First War Patrol Report, 2 November 1944, disc 23, SM.

30. Ibid.

31. Hazzard interview; Leon Huffman Interview (taped), box 97, CBC.

32. USS *Bergall* First War Patrol Report, Endorsements.

33. USS *Hake* Third War Patrol Report, Endorsement, disc 17, SM.

34. USS *Hake* Third War Patrol Report, 13 February 1944, Attack Data.

35. USS *Segundo* Second War Patrol Report, 6 December 1944, http:// www.segundo398.org/ (accessed 18 July 2007).

36. Russell, *Hell Above,* 49.

37. USS *Hawkbill* Second War Patrol Report, 29 December 1944, disc 24, SM.

38. Mendenhall, *Submarine Diary,* 264–65.

39. Cline, *Final Dive,* 25–26.

40. Quoted in McDonald, *USS* Puffer, 134, 140.

41. USS *Sunfish* Ninth War Patrol Report, 5 December 1944, http://www .geocities.com.Heartland/Hills/2364 (accessed 23 July 2007).

42. Ibid.

43. Hornfischer, *Tin Can Sailors,* 405–6.

44. Thomas, *Sea of Thunder,* 3–4, 142; Yomiuri, *From Marco Polo Bridge,* 236; Stevens, *A Critical Vulnerability,* 262.

45. Galantin, *Take Her Deep!* 212.

46. R. W. Christie, "*Bluegill* on Patrol: A Story of Cutlasses, Gunfire and Depth-Bombs," *Blue Book,* July 1946, 97–99. See also Ramage, *Reminiscences,* 179; Galantin, *Take Her Deep!* 226.

47. Gannon, *Hellions of the Deep,* 195.

48. Parillo, *Japanese Merchant Marine,* 150.

49. USS *Balao* Sixth War Patrol Report, Attack Data, disc 20, SM.

50. USS *Hawkbill* Second War Patrol Report, 29 December 1944.

51. Ramage, *Reminiscences,* 140–41.

52. Supplementary Report to USS *Tambor* Twelfth War Patrol Report, disc 8, SM; Alden, *Fleet Submarine,* 94; Rohwer and Hummerchen, *War at Sea,* 315.

53. USS *Ronquil* Second War Patrol Report, 17 November 1944, UBSM; USS *Ronquil* (SS-396), http://ussronquil.com/History/history.htm (accessed 17 July 2007); Rohwer and Hummerchen, *War at Sea,* 315; World War II Forums, http://www.ww2f.com/167717-post499.html (accessed 9 September 2008).

54. Quoted in Schultz and Shell, *We Were Pirates,* 178. See also USS *Tambor* Twelfth War Patrol Report, 16 and 18 November 1944; Moore, Spadefish, 243–44.

55. Anthony Miers to Rear-Admiral Pott, British Embassy, Washington, DC, 11 November 1943, 1/5, Papers of Rear-Admiral Sir Anthony Miers, Churchill Archives Center, Cambridge.

56. Russell, *Hell Above,* 86.

57. See Alden, *Fleet Submarine,* 94; USS *Bergall,* Deck Guns; Russell, *Hell Above,* 95; Friedman, *US Naval Weapons,* 78; Rowland, *Bureau of Ordnance,* 219, 221, 234; USS *Icefish* Fifth War Patrol Report, Prologue, http://www.ussicefish.com/ (accessed 13 July 2007).

58. Supplementary Report to USS *Tambor* Twelfth War Patrol Report, disc 8, SM.

59. Cline, *Final Dive,* 119, 158.

60. Ron Smith, *Torpedoman* (n.p., 1993), 190. See also Whitlock and Smith, *Depths of Courage,* 263.

61. Quoted in Rick Cline, *Submarine* Grayback: *The Life and Death of the WWII Sub, USS* Grayback (Placentia, CA: R. A. Cline, 1999), 164, 211.

62. Lockwood, *Sink 'Em All,* 270.

63. Report of Short Range Practice, 20 November 1944, Blue 443/2, RG 313, NARA.

64. USS *Finback* Eighth War Patrol Report, Attack Data.

65. Rowland, *Bureau of Ordnance,* 262, 287; Lockwood, *Sink 'Em All,* 244.

66. Lockwood, *Sink 'Em All,* 245.

67. Ibid., 154, 260; Blair, *Silent Victory,* 787–89, 825.

68. Fluckey, *Thunder Below!* 408; Gannon, *Hellions of the Deep,* 147–48, 200–201.

69. Lockwood, *Sink 'Em All,* 269. See also Alden, *Fleet Submarine,* 94; Rohwer and Hummerchen, *War at Sea,* 332.

70. Lockwood, *Sink 'Em All,* 268, 270.

71. See, for example, Supplementary Report to USS *Tambor* Twelfth War Patrol Report; Ken Henry and Don Keith, *Gallant Lady: A Biography of the USS* Archerfish (New York: Tom Doherty Associates, 2004), 65.

72. Moore, Spadefish, 37.

73. USS *Ronquil* Second War Patrol Report, 17 November 1944.

74. USS *Tambor* Twelfth War Patrol Report, 16 November 1944, Target Data.

75. Quoted in Casey, *Battle Below,* 335–36.

7. Straits of Malacca

1. Anthony Miers to Admiral Barry, 11 November 1943, Miers Papers.

2. Miers Report, 25 January 1944, Miers Papers.

3. Report enclosed in Miers to Admiral H. Pott, 4 March 1944, Miers Papers.

4. Innes McCartney, *British Submarines, 1939–45* (Oxford: Osprey, 2006), 23; Cook, *Silent Marauders*, 113, 115–17.

5. Mark C. Jones, "Experiment at Dundee: The Royal Navy's 9th Submarine Flotilla and Multinational Naval Cooperation during World War II," *Journal of Military History* 72 (October 2008): 1195; Newpower, *Iron Men and Tin Fish*, 109.

6. Colin Smith, *Singapore Burning: Heroism and Surrender in World War II* (London: Viking, 2005), 230–31; Hurst, *The Fourth Ally*, 16, 21, 45; Wilson, *Submariners' War*, 63–64.

7. Nichols interview; Bobette Gugliotta, *Pigboat 39: An American Sub Goes to War* (Lexington: University Press of Kentucky, 1984), 137–38, 141.

8. Hurst, *The Fourth Ally*, 69, 80, 122, 125; Ian Trenowden, *Malayan Operations Most Secret–Force 136* (1978; repr., Singapore: Heinemann, 1983), 62, 74.

9. Wilson, *Submariners' War*, 76–77.

10. Lipscomb, *British Submarine*, 205, 208, 224; Wilson, *Submariners' War*, 109.

11. Cook, *Silent Marauders*, 117; McCartney, *British Submarines*, 38, 41; Lipscomb, *British Submarine*, 225, 233; Wilson, *Submariners' War*, 119.

12. Lipscomb, *British Submarine*, 235, 243; Wilson, *Submariners' War*, 119; Lynne Cairns, *Fremantle's Secret Fleets: Allied Submarines Based in Western Australia during World War II* (Fremantle: Western Australian Maritime Museum, 1995), 9, 50; Hezlet, *The Submarine*, 201, 221; W. J. Holmes, *Undersea Victory: The Influence of Submarine Operations in the War in the Pacific* (New York: Doubleday, 1966), 352–53, 452; McCartney, *British Submarines*, 43.

13. Ralph Christie Interview (taped), box 97, CBC.

14. Young, *One of Our Submarines*, 305.

15. Miers to Barry, 11 November 1943; Barry to Miers, 12 January 1944, Miers Papers.

16. Chapman, *Submarine* Torbay, 17; Young, *One of Our Submarines*, 304; Fontenoy, *Submarines*, 28.

17. Lipscomb, *British Submarine*, 23, 39; Wilson, *Submariners' War*, 160.

18. Mars, *H.M.S.* Thule, 13.

19. Quoted in Julian Thompson, *The Imperial War Museum Book of the War at Sea* (London: Sidgwick and Jackson, 1996), 211–12.

20. Lipscomb, *British Submarine*, 234.

21. Wilson, *Submariners' War*, 119.

22. Padfield, *War beneath the Sea*, 434; Wilson, *Submariners' War*, 113–14; Edward Young, *Undersea Patrol* (New York: McGraw-Hill, 1952), 184. Compare to Vego, *Operational Warfare*, 221.

23. Wilson, *Submariners' War*, 158; Choon Hon Foong, ed., *The Price of Peace: True Accounts of the Japanese Occupation of Singapore*, trans. Clara Show (Singapore: Asiapac Books, 1997), 1, 24, 27, 29.

24. Ionides to Christie, 15 December 1943, Papers of Ralph W. Christie, Correspondence 1941–45, LC.

25. Hezlet, *The Submarine*, 201; Padfield, *War beneath the Sea*, 436; Cook, *Silent Marauders*, 118.

26. Young, *One of Our Submarines*, 222–23. See also David Brown, ed., *The British Pacific and East Indies Fleets: 'The Forgotten Fleets' 50th Anniversary* (Liverpool: Brodie, 1995), 62.

27. Wilson, *Submariners' War*, 143; McCartney, *British Submarines*, 41.

28. Rohwer and Hummerchen, *War at Sea*, 284; HMS *Tantivy*, U-boat .net, http://www.uboat.net (accessed 23 June 2008); McCartney, *British Submarines*, 42.

29. Wilson, *Submariners' War*, 150.

30. Lipscomb, *British Submarine*, 234.

31. Manson, *Diplomatic Ramifications*, 155.

32. Lipscomb, *British Submarine*, 234.

33. Young, *One of Our Submarines*, 263.

34. Ivon A. Donnelly, *Chinese Junks and Other Native Craft* (1924; repr., Singapore: Graham Brash, 1988), 9–12; Worchester, *Junks and Sampans*, 69–70; Sam Willis, *Fighting at Sea in the Eighteenth Century: The Art of Sailing Warfare* (Woodbridge, UK: Boydell, 2008), 154; Richard Crompton-Hall, *The Underwater War, 1939–1945* (Poole, UK: Blandford, 1982), 51.

35. Parks interview.

36. Parillo, *Japanese Merchant Marine*, 192.

37. Shimura Tomihisa, quoted in Frank Gibney, ed., *Senso: The Japanese Remember the Pacific War,* trans. Beth Cary (London: M. E. Sharpe, 1995), 144–45.

38. Mars, *H.M.S. Thule*, 66.

39. Wilson, *Submariners' War*, 141.

40. USS *Blenny* Fourth War Patrol Report, Remarks, disc 23, SM.

41. Young, *One of Our Submarines*, 209.

42. Gruhl, *Imperial Japan's World War Two*, 91–92.

43. Mars, *H.M.S. Thule*, 66–67, 82, 94.

44. George Woodward, quoted in Hood, *Submarine*, 35.

45. Mars, *H.M.S. Thule*, 78–80.

46. Ibid., 81; Young, *One of Our Submarines*, 285.

47. Quoted in *Times* (London), 7 May 1988, 1, 24.

48. Nichols interview.

49. Quoted in *Times* (London), 7 May 1988, 1, 24.

50. Lipscomb, *British Submarine*, 241; Wilson, *Submariners' War*, 146–48.

51. George Woodward, quoted in Hood, *Submarine*, 36.

52. Mars, *H.M.S. Thule*, 83, 86–87.

53. Ibid., 76.

54. Young, *One of Our Submarines*, 274–76.

55. Ibid., 307–10.

56. Wilson, *Submariners' War,* 143–45.

57. McCartney, *British Submarines,* 42–43; Brown, *British Pacific,* 19.

8. Boarding Parties

1. LaVO, *Slade Cutter,* 105.

2. Mendenhall, *Submarine Diary,* 164–65.

3. See Gerry Simpson, *Law, War and Crime: War Crimes Trials and the Reinvention of Criminal Law* (Cambridge: Polity, 2007), 161, 172–74; Rubin, *Piracy,* 28, 316.

4. Rudenno, *Gallipoli,* 157.

5. Schultz and Shell, *We Were Pirates,* 168; R. Kefauver, Gun Action on 18 April 1944, A16(1), box 9 (old box 4184), Commander Submarine Force in US Pacific Fleet, RG 313, NARA.

6. Quoted in Moore, Spadefish, 286.

7. Quoted in ibid., 287.

8. Alan Powell, *War by Stealth: Australians and the Allied Intelligence Bureau, 1942–1945* (Melbourne: Melbourne University Press, 1996), 170; Colin Burgess, *Freedom or Death: Australia's Greatest Escape Stories from Two World Wars* (Sydney: Allen and Unwin, 1994), 63–76.

9. See Sturma, *Death at a Distance,* 69–83, 105–12.

10. See A. B. Feuer, *Commando! The M/Z Units' Secret War against Japan* (Westport, CT: Praeger, 1996), 17–18; Rowan E. Waddy, "An Adventure in Sarawak, Borneo," n.d., 16, Charles Darwin University, Darwin; Jack Wong Sue, *Blood on Borneo* (Perth: WA Skindivers, 2001), 56.

11. Cecil Anderson Interview, 24 August 1990, Oral History Unit, OH2365/3, Battye Library of West Australian History, Perth; Politician Project, series A3269, control E7/A, National Archives of Australia, Melbourne; Christie, *"Bluegill* on Patrol," 97–99.

12. G. B. Courtney, *Silent Feet: The History of "Z" Special Operations, 1942–1945* (Melbourne: R. J. and S. P. Austin, 1993), 139; Feuer, *Commando!* 41.

13. Anderson interview; Rowan E. Waddy, "A Submarine Adventure in South China Sea, 1945," 1992, 6, Charles Darwin University, Darwin.

14. Feuer, *Commando!* 56; Powell, *War by Stealth,* 178.

15. Politician Project, series A3269, control E7/A.

16. Fluckey, *Thunder Below!* 217, 228, 231–32.

17. Tuohy, *The Bravest Man,* 376–77.

18. USS *Tirante* First War Patrol Report, 6 April 1945, disc 28, SM.

19. Edward G. McGrath, "A First Class Pirate," clipping in *Tirante* Boat Book, SFM.

20. USS *Tirante* Second War Patrol Report, 22 June 1945, UBSM.

21. USS *Tirante* Second War Patrol Report, 24 June 1945.

22. Ibid.

23. Quoted in John D. Alden, "Away the Boarding Party," *U.S. Naval Proceedings,* January 1965, 70.

24. USS *Batfish* Sixth War Patrol Report, 23 January 1945, Attack Data, http://www.ussbatfish.com (accessed 5 July 2007).

25. McDonald, *USS* Puffer, 99, 202–3.

26. USS *Balao* Ninth War Patrol Report, 24 May 1945, disc 20, SM.

27. USS *Segundo* Fifth War Patrol Report, 21 May 1945, http://www .segundo398.org/ (accessed 18 July 2007).

28. USS *Segundo* Fifth War Patrol Report, 7 June 1945.

29. USS *Icefish* Fifth War Patrol Report, 5 August 1945.

30. USS *Hawkbill* Fifth War Patrol Report, Directives, disc 24, SM.

31. USS *Blenny* Fourth War Patrol Report, 27 July, 2–3 August, 6 August 1945; C. M. Turnbull, *A History of Singapore, 1819–1988* (1977; repr., Oxford: Oxford University Press, 1997), 199.

32. USS *Hawkbill* Fifth War Patrol Report, 17 July 1945.

33. Lockwood, *Sink 'Em All,* 258–59.

34. USS *Hawkbill* Fifth War Patrol Report, 20 July 1945.

35. USS *Cod* Seventh War Patrol Report, Endorsement, UBSM.

36. USS *Cod* Seventh War Patrol Report, 3 August 1945; Alden, "Away the Boarding Party," 70, 74.

37. Hazzard interview; USS *Blenny* Fourth War Patrol Report, 3 August 1945.

9. Mopping Up

1. Hazzard interview.

2. Quoted in Whitlock and Smith, *Depths of Courage,* 363.

3. USS *Blenny* Fourth War Patrol Report, 1 August 1945.

4. USS *Blenny* (SS-324), http://www.webenet.net/~ftoon/memory/f _memory.html (accessed 4 July 2007).

5. USS *Blenny* Fourth War Patrol Report, 24 July, 2–3 August 1945.

6. USS *Blenny* Fourth War Patrol Report, 4, 8, and 10 August 1945.

7. Chida and Davies, *Japanese Shipping,* 58; *Strategic Bombing Survey: Summary,* 11.

8. Calvert, *Silent Running,* 226.

9. Russell, *Hell Above,* 94.

10. USS *Hawkbill* Fifth War Patrol Report, 12 July 1945. See also Alden, *Fleet Submarines,* 94; Rohwer and Hummerchen, *War at Sea,* 332, Russell, *Hell Above,* 181–82.

11. Galantin, *Take Her Deep!* 258.

12. Mendenhall, *Submarine Diary,* 264.

13. Hezlet, *The Submarine,* 223; Whitlock and Smith, *Depths of Courage,* 2; McDonald, *USS* Puffer, 175.

14. Lockwood and Adamson, *Hellcats of the Sea,* 57.

15. USS *Seahorse* Seventh and Eighth War Patrol Report, Endorsements, disc 21, SM.

16. Thomas Metz, quoted in McDonald, *USS* Puffer, 191.

17. USS *Tunny* Eighth War Patrol Report, 4 April 1945, Attack Data, disc 20, SM.

18. USS *Blenny* Third War Patrol Report, 30 May 1945, disc 23, SM.

19. USS *Icefish* Fourth War Patrol Report, 28 June 1945, http://www.ussicefish.com/ (accessed 13 July 2007).

20. Ward, *Reminiscences,* 218.

21. Calvert, *Silent Running,* 234.

22. Hastings, *Retribution,* 279; *Strategic Bombing Survey: Summary,* 14; Hezlet, *The Submarine,* 222–23; Willmott, *Battle of Leyte Gulf,* 233.

23. USS *Seahorse* Seventh War Patrol Report, Endorsement. See also, for example, Pacific Fleet Confidential Letter 18CL-44, 13 May 1944, Blue 443/2, RG 313, NARA.

24. CINCPOA Standard Operating Procedure SOP-1, 15 September 1944, Blue 443/2, RG 313, NARA.

25. *Strategic Bombing Survey: Summary,* 11, 19; Rowland, *Bureau of Ordnance,* 167, 170.

26. Thomas R. H. Havens, *Valley of Darkness: The Japanese People and World War Two* (Lanham, MD: University Press of America, 1986), 49–50, 80; Samuel Hideo Yamashita, *Leaves from an Autumn of Emergencies: Selections from the Wartime Diaries of Ordinary Japanese* (Honolulu: University of Hawaii Press, 2003), 85, 98; Hastings, *Retribution,* 43.

27. Thomas, *Sea of Thunder,* 336–37; Rowland, *Bureau of Ordnance,* 170; *Strategic Bombing Survey: Summary,* 16.

28. Remco Raben, "Indonesian *Rōmusha* and Coolies under Naval Administration," in *Asian Labor in the Wartime Japanese Empire: Unknown Histories,* ed. Paul H. Kratoska (London: M. E. Sharpe, 2005), 201.

29. USS *Barb* Twelfth War Patrol Report, 26 July 1945, UBSM; Fluckey, *Thunder Below!* 401–2.

30. Hashimoto, *Sunk,* 18–19, 29–32; Jenkins, *Battle Surface,* 243, 247–48, 250–51, 266; Tuohy, *The Bravest Man,* 349; Carruthers, *Japanese Submarine Raiders,* 24; Earhart, *Certain Victory,* 256; Cairns, *Fremantle's Secret Fleets,* 35.

31. Kimmett and Regis, *U.S. Submarines,* 50; Lockwood, *Sink 'Em All,* 119.

32. Galantin, *Take Her Deep!* 180, 202.

33. Report of Night Bombardment Practice, 27 November 1944, Blue 443/2, RG 313, NARA.

34. USS *Tang* Second War Patrol Report, 24 April 1944, disc 21, SM. See also Bouslog, *Maru Killer,* 70–71; Tuohy, *The Bravest Man,* 218; USS *Tang* Second War Patrol Report, 30 April 1944, Endorsement.

35. Cook, *Silent Marauders,* 122.

36. USS *Puffer* Seventh War Patrol Report, 26 March 1945, disc 18, SM. See also USS *Puffer* (SS-268) Ships History, http://www.usspuffer.org/ (accessed 13 July 2007); McDonald, *USS* Puffer, 203.

37. Christie, "*Bluegill* on Patrol," 97–99; Tony Banham, *The Sinking of the Lisbon Maru: Britain's Forgotten Wartime Tragedy* (Hong Kong: Hong Kong University Press, 2006), 193; USS *Blenny* Third War Patrol Report, Attack Data; Lockwood, *Sink 'Em All,* 305–6.

38. USS *Batfish* Seventh War Patrol Report, 24 July 1945, Attack Data, http://www.ussbatfish.com (accessed 5 July 2007).

39. Fluckey, *Thunder Below!* 346–48.

40. USS *Hawkbill* Fifth War Patrol Report, Attack Data.

41. Quoted in LaVO, *Slade Cutter,* 192.

42. History of the USS *Bashaw,* Division of Naval History, http://www.geocities.com/bashawss241/ww2record.htm?20073 (accessed 3 July 2007).

43. USS *Blenny* Third War Patrol Report, Endorsement.

44. USS *Blenny* Fourth War Patrol Report, 27 July 1945.

45. Stillwell, *Submarine Stories,* 181.

46. USS *Baya* Fifth War Patrol Report, 29–30 June 1945, http://www.ussbaya.com (accessed 6 July 2007).

47. Alden, "Away the Boarding Party," 69.

48. USS *Bergall* Fifth War Patrol Report, 30 May 1945, UBSM.

49. See Schratz, *Reminiscences,* 64; Lockwood Papers, box 18, folder 128, LC.

50. USS *Ray* Seventh War Patrol Report, Endorsement.

51. Alden, "Away the Boarding Party," 71.

52. Ibid.

53. Whitlock and Smith, *Depths of Courage,* 352–53.

54. Lockwood and Adamson, *Hellcats of the Sea,* 151; Kimmett and Regis, *U.S. Submarines,* 126; Walter Beyer Interview (transcript), 9 May 1992, Oral History Collection, UBSM.

55. Lockwood, *Sink 'Em All,* 279; Ward, *Reminiscences,* 215; Moore, Spadefish, 247, 311; William Germershausen Interview (taped), box 97, CBC.

56. Germershausen interview; Moore, Spadefish, 38, 245–46.

57. Alexander K. Tyree Interview (transcript), 28 September 1996, Oral History Collection, UBSM.

58. Ramage, *Reminiscences,* 190–91.

59. Lockwood and Adamson, *Hellcats of the Sea,* 108–9, 114, 294.

60. Beyer interview.

61. Lockwood and Adamson, *Hellcats of the Sea,* 311.

62. Ibid., 152–53. See also Moore, Spadefish, 334.

63. Tyree interview.

64. Lockwood and Adamson, *Hellcats of the Sea,* 290.

65. Russell, *Hell Above,* 103, 149–50.

66. Ibid., 150–52.

67. Julian T. Burke Jr., quoted in Stillwell, *Submarine Stories,* 189.

68. Moore, Spadefish, 312; USS *Tunny* Ninth War Patrol Report, Endorsement, disc 20, SM.

69. Quoted in Moore, Spadefish, 357.

70. Germershausen interview; Moore, Spadefish, 342–71.

71. Russell, *Hell Above,* 159–60, 165; Hezlet, *The Submarine,* 223.

72. USS *Hawkbill* Fifth War Patrol Report, 20 July 1945.

73. USS *Puffer* Eighth War Patrol Report, 5 July 1945, http://www.usspuffer .org/ (accessed 13 July 2007); see also USS *Puffer* (SS-268) Ships History.

74. USS *Puffer* Eighth War Patrol Report, 5 July 1945.

75. McDonald, *USS* Puffer, 239–40.

76. Fluckey, *Thunder Below!* 313, 361–63.

77. USS *Balao* Tenth War Patrol Report, 14 August 1945, disc 20, SM.

10. Survivors

1. Quoted in Williams, *Battle of the Atlantic,* 211.

2. Padfield, *War beneath the Sea,* 95.

3. See, for example, Billy and Billy, *Merchant Mariners at War,* 25, 76.

4. C. B. A. Behrens, *Merchant Shipping and the Demands of War* (London: Her Majesty's Stationery Office, 1955), 154–55, 172, 181; Williams, *Battle of the Atlantic,* 225, 286; Holwitt, *"Execute against Japan,"* 167, 181; Tony Lane, "The Human Economy of the British Merchant Navy," in Howarth and Law, *Battle of the Atlantic,* 50; Macdonald Critchley, *Shipwreck-Survivors: A Medical Study* (London: J. and A. Churchill, 1943), 48–52; Hastings, *Retribution,* 267; Lockwood, *Sink 'Em All,* 333.

5. Charles Andrews Interview (taped), box 96, CBC.

6. Quoted in Manson, *Diplomatic Ramifications,* 181. See also, for example, Doenitz, *Memoirs,* 256; Mallison, *Law of Naval Warfare,* 11.

7. Burns, "Submarine Warfare," 61.

8. Lockwood, *Sink 'Em All,* 202; Keith, *Final Patrol,* 203–10; USS *Pampanito,* San Francisco, taped tour and integrated oral history, 15 August 2002; Hastings, *Retribution,* 277; Charles Loughlin Interview (taped), box 98, CBC; Loughlin, *Reminiscences,* 97; Fluckey, *Thunder Below!* 124, 146.

9. Moore, Spadefish, 196; Cairns, *Fremantle's Secret Fleets,* 62.

10. Ward, *Reminiscences,* 147–48.

11. Fluckey, *Thunder Below!* 124; quoted in Lockwood, *Sink 'Em All,* 204.

12. Michael Sturma, *The USS Flier: Death and Survival on a World War II Submarine* (Lexington: University Press of Kentucky, 2008), 100, 125; Cairns, *Fremantle's Secret Fleets*, 62.

13. Lockwood, *Sink 'Em All*, 107.

14. See Jim Christley, *US Submarines, 1941–45* (New York: Osprey, 2006), 42; Tuohy, *The Bravest Man*, 227; Polmar, *American Submarine*, 72; Lockwood, *Sink 'Em All*, 282–83; Blair, *Silent Victory*, 866.

15. Hastings, *Retribution*, 37, 111.

16. Blair, *Silent Victory*, 756–57; Wilson, *Submariners' War*, 76; Lockwood, *Sink 'Em All*, 248.

17. Bill Gleason, "Diary of a War Patrol—USS *Gurnard* (SS-254)," *Polaris*, June 1985, http:// www.subvetpaul.com/SAGA_6_85.htm (accessed 1 July 2005).

18. William Anderson Interview (taped), box 96, CBC.

19. USS *Bluefish* Ninth War Patrol Report, Remarks, UBSM.

20. Kinsella interview.

21. USS *Hake* Third War Patrol Report, 13 February 1944, Attack Data.

22. USS *Hawkbill* Fourth War Patrol Report, 29–30 March 1945, Endorsements, disc 24, SM; USS *Hawkbill* communication reported in USS *Bergall* Fifth War Patrol Report, 29 May 1945.

23. Joyce C. Lebra, *Japan's Greater East Asia Co-prosperity Sphere in World War II: Selected Readings and Documents* (London: Oxford University Press, 1975), xiii–xiv, 160; Nicholas Tarling, *A Sudden Rampage: The Japanese Occupation of Southeast Asia, 1941–1945* (Honolulu: University of Hawaii Press, 2001), 124, 219, 254; Bell, Brawley, and Dixon, *Conflict in the Pacific*, 115; Hastings, *Retribution*, 14; Harry J. Benda, *The Crescent and the Rising Moon: Indonesian Islam under the Japanese Occupation, 1942-1945* (The Hague: W. van Hoeve, 1958), 120, 122, 170.

24. Quoted in McLaughlin and Parry, *We'll Always Have the Movies*, 123.

25. Russell, *Hell Above*, 165–66.

26. Havens, *Valley of Darkness*, 92, 104; Lebra, *Co-prosperity Sphere*, 109–10; Earhart, *Certain Victory*, 49–50; Saburo Ienaga, *Japan's Last War: World War II and the Japanese, 1931-1945* (Canberra: Australian National University Press, 1979), 158; Cheah Boon Kheng, "Memory and Hating and Moral Judgement: Oral and Written Accounts of the Japanese Occupation of Malaya," in *War and Memory in Malaysia and Singapore*, ed. P. Lim Pui Huen and Diana Wong (Singapore: Institute of Southeast Asian Studies, 2000), 54; Turnbull, *History of Singapore*, 194; Felton, *Slaughter at Sea*, 185.

27. USS *Segundo* Fourth War Patrol Report, 29 May 1945, http://www .segundo398.org/ (accessed 18 July 2007).

28. USS *Tirante* First War Patrol Report, 6 April 1945.

29. USS *Tirante* Second War Patrol Report, 22 June 1945.

30. Pacific Fleet Confidential Letter 43CL-44, 4 December 1944, Blue 443/2 [78], RG 313, NARA.

31. Fluckey, *Thunder Below!* 374.

32. Thomas, *Sea of Thunder,* 63; Hastings, *Retribution,* 194.

33. Lebra, *Co-prosperity Sphere,* 160; Tarling, *A Sudden Rampage,* 202, 260; Philip A. Seaton, *Japan's Contested War Memories: The "Memory Rifts" in Historical Consciousness of World War II* (London: Routledge, 2007), 60; Huen and Wong, *War and Memory,* 15–16, 139; Foong, *Price of Peace,* 9, 80.

34. Turnbull, *History of Singapore,* 190, 198; Benda, Irikura, and Kishi, *Japanese Military Administration,* 180; Huen and Wong, *War and Memory,* 152–53; Felton, *Slaughter at Sea,* 86.

35. USS *Balao* Eighth War Patrol Report, 19 March 1945, disc 20, SM.

36. Kinsella interview.

37. USS *Ray* Seventh War Patrol Report, 24 May 1945.

38. Ibid.

39. Kinsella interview.

40. Alden, "Away the Boarding Party," 73.

41. Quoted in Moore, Spadefish, 224.

42. Ibid., 224–25.

43. See Parillo, *Japanese Merchant Marine,* 81.

44. USS *Blenny* Third War Patrol Report, 30 May 1945, Attack Data.

45. USS *Blenny* Fourth War Patrol Report, 8 August 1945.

46. USS *Blenny* Fourth War Patrol Report, 10 August 1945.

47. Lockwood, *Sink 'Em All,* 44–45.

48. Lockwood to W. J. Suits, 14 November 1942, box 12, folder 65, Lockwood Papers, LC.

49. See David Koh Wee Hock, ed., *Legacies of World War II in South and East Asia* (Singapore: Institute of Southeast Asian Studies, 2007), 75.

50. Ostlund, *Find 'Em,* 245–47.

51. USS *Puffer* Second War Patrol Report, quoted in McDonald, *USS Puffer,* 96–97.

52. Quoted in Hood, *Submarine,* 397.

53. Mars, *H.M.S.* Thule, 78, 88, 92.

54. USS *Bashaw* Fifth War Patrol Report, 21 February 1945, UBSM.

55. USS *Flasher* Sixth War Patrol Report, 21 February 1945, UBSM.

56. Quoted in Alden, "Away the Boarding Party," 71.

57. Ibid., 72.

58. USS *Bugara* Third War Patrol Report, Endorsement, UBSM; Holmes, *Undersea Victory,* 468–69.

59. USS *Icefish* Fifth War Patrol Report, 7 and 11 August 1945, Health, Food and Habitability.

60. USS *Croaker* Sixth War Patrol Report, 11 August 1945, disc 15, SM.

61. Young, *One of Our Submarines,* 286–88.

11. Japanese Prisoners

1. *Destination Tokyo,* dir. Delmer Daves (Warner Brothers, 1943). See also Lawrence H. Suid, *Guts and Glory: The Making of the American Military Image in Film* (Lexington: University Press of Kentucky, 2002), 80, 82; Fyne, *Hollywood Propaganda,* 70, 179.

2. Quoted in Ienaga, *Japan's Last War,* 49.

3. Tarling, *A Sudden Rampage,* 253.

4. Straus, *Anguish of Surrender,* 3; Johnson, *Pacific Campaign,* 305.

5. Lockwood, *Sink 'Em All,* 55.

6. Quoted in Mallison, *Law of Naval Warfare,* 136. See also Manson, *Diplomatic Ramifications,* 181.

7. USS *Haddo* Seventh War Patrol Report, 21 September 1944, UBSM.

8. Quoted in Ostlund, *Find 'Em,* 300.

9. See Moore, Spadefish, 251.

10. Reprinted in Legends of the Deep. See also Trefalt, "Fanaticism," 43–44.

11. USS *Balao* Eighth War Patrol Report, 18 March 1945.

12. See Pacific Fleet Confidential Letter 43CL-44, 4 December 1944, [78], RG313, NARA; Russell, *Hell Above,* 129.

13. Russell, *Hell Above,* 131.

14. Quoted in Bouslog, *Maru Killer,* 153–54. See also James B. O'Meara, in Stillwell, *Submarine Stories,* 174–76.

15. Ellis, *Brute Force,* 493.

16. USS *Tunny* Fifth War Patrol Report, 1 April 1944, disc 20, SM.

17. USS *Tirante* First War Patrol Report, 16 April 1945.

18. USS *Redfin* Fourth War Patrol Report, 19 September 1944.

19. Straus, *Anguish of Surrender,* 141; Johnson, *Pacific Campaign,* 217; Page, *Between Victor and Vanquished,* 129.

20. USS *Barb,* Testimony of Prisoner of War, Flag Files (Blue 440), 1942–45 [5–6], RG313, NARA.

21. See Page, *Between Victor and Vanquished,* 167.

22. Calvert, *Silent Running,* 161.

23. Fluckey, *Thunder Below!* 16, 374.

24. See, for example, Bob Haughney, in Hood, *Submarine,* 426.

25. USS *Barb* Twelfth War Patrol Report, 23 June 1945.

26. USS *Barb* Twelfth War Patrol Report, 26 July 1945.

27. USS *Bowfin* Sixth War Patrol Report, 4 September 1944.

28. Kinsella interview.

29. USS *Sunfish* Seventh War Patrol Report, 6 July 1944. See also, for example, USS *Tirante* First War Patrol Report, 30 March 1945.

30. Ramage, *Reminiscences,* 141–42.

31. USS *Blenny* Third War Patrol Report, 30 May 1945.

32. Hazzard interview.

33. USS *Tambor* Fourth War Patrol Report, 10 November 1942, Remarks, disc 8, SM; Schultz and Shell, *We Were Pirates,* 99.

34. See, for example, USS *Croaker* Sixth War Patrol Report, 11 August 1945.

35. See Pacific Fleet Confidential Letter 43CL-44, 4 December 1944.

36. Blanchard interview.

37. Tuohy, *The Bravest Man,* 265.

38. See, for example, USS *Balao* Eighth War Patrol Report, 20 March 1945; Tim Cook, "The Politics of Surrender: Canadian Soldiers and Killing of Prisoners in the Great War," *Journal of Military History* 70 (July 2006): 641.

39. USS *Trout* Tenth War Patrol Report, 25 August, 22 September 1943, UBSM. See also USS *Trout* Fourth War Patrol Report, 9 June 1942, UBSM; Parrish, *Submarine,* 376.

40. Bouslog, *Maru Killer,* 153–54. See also, for example, Trefalt, "Fanaticism," 43–44; Page, *Between Victor and Vanquished,* 129.

41. Quoted in Lockwood and Adamson, *Hellcats of the Sea,* 268.

42. Office of the Chief of Naval Operations, Treatment of Prisoners of War, 19 December 1942, 1 February 1943, [28], (Blue 443/2), RG 313, NARA.

43. Henry and Keith, *Gallant Lady,* 52.

44. Statement of Commander J. W. Blanchard, *Albacore* Boat Book, SFM.

45. LaVO, *Slade Cutter,* 105–6. See also USS *Pompano* Third War Patrol Report, 4 September 1942.

46. Moore, Spadefish, 106.

47. Russell, *Hell Above,* 131–33.

48. Julian T. Burke Jr., in Stillwell, *Submarine Stories,* 189.

49. Quoted in Moore, Spadefish, 287.

50. Schultz and Shell, *We Were Pirates,* 128–29.

51. Fluckey, *Thunder Below!* 16, 18.

52. Calvert, *Silent Running,* 161.

53. Ostlund, *Find 'Em,* 302–3, 310–11.

54. Pacific Fleet Confidential Letter 43CL-44, 4 December 1944; Lockwood, *Sink 'Em All,* 330.

55. USS *Balao* Eighth War Patrol Report, 18 March 1945.

56. Tuohy, *The Bravest Man,* 258–60, 263–65.

57. Quoted in Moore, Spadefish, 225.

58. USS *Wahoo* Sixth War Patrol Report, 20 August 1943. See also DeRose, *Unrestricted Warfare,* 128; Sterling, *Wake of the* Wahoo, 196–97.

59. Sterling, *Wake of the* Wahoo, 196–97, 199–200.

60. Hugh S. Mackenzie, in Hood, *Submarine*, 391.

61. See, for example, Nichols interview; James B. O'Meara, in Stillwell, *Submarine Stories*, 174–76; Slade Cutter, *Reminiscences*, 75–76; Tuohy, *The Bravest Man*, 259.

62. Bouslog, *Maru Killer*, 143–44.

63. Bob Haughney, in Hood, *Submarine*, 426.

64. James B. O'Meara, in Stillwell, *Submarine Stories*, 174–76.

65. Quoted in Spector, *Eagle against the Sun*, 410.

66. Bouslog, *Maru Killer*, 153–54.

67. Schultz and Shell, *We Were Pirates*, 132.

68. Julian T. Burke Jr., in Stillwell, *Submarine Stories*, 189.

69. Schratz, *Reminiscences*, 86.

70. Straus, *Anguish of Surrender*, 240–42; from the *Orlando Sentinel*, WWII USS *Atule* (SS-403), http://www.atule.com (accessed 5 July 2007).

12. Submarines and Bombers

1. Havens, *Valley of Darkness*, 177; Bell, Brawley, and Dixon, *Conflict in the Pacific*, 175.

2. Quoted in Hastings, *Retribution*, 316.

3. Paine, *Transpacific Voyage*, 10.

4. Calvert, *Silent Running*, 246.

5. Padfield, *War beneath the Sea*, 478. See also, for example, Tarrant, *U-Boat Offensive*, 132.

6. Quoted in Blair, *The Hunted, 1942–1945*, 65.

7. Quoted in Padfield, *War beneath the Sea*, 381.

8. Joel Ira Holwitt, "Mush Morton and the *Buyo Maru* Massacre," *United States Naval Institute Proceedings* 129 (July 2003): 81.

9. Quoted in Michael Walzer, "World War II: Why Was This War Different?" in *War and Moral Responsibility*, ed. Marshall Cohen, Thomas Nagel, and Thomas Scanlon (Princeton, NJ: Princeton University Press, 1974), 98. See also A. C. Grayling, *Among the Dead Cities: The History and Moral Legacy of the WWII Bombing of Civilians in Germany and Japan* (New York: Walker, 2006), 261; David Kinsella and Craig L. Carr, eds., *The Morality of War: A Reader* (Boulder, CO: Lynne Rienner, 2007), 256.

10. Jean Kessler, "U-Boat Bases in the Bay of Biscay," in Howarth and Law, *Battle of the Atlantic*, 263; Henry Probert, "Allied Land-Based Anti-submarine Warfare," in Howarth and Law, *Battle of the Atlantic*, 382; Blair, *The Hunted, 1942–1945*, 164.

11. Hastings, *Retribution*, 288.

12. Michael D. Gordin, *Five Days in August: How World War II Became a Nuclear War* (Princeton, NJ: Princeton University Press, 2007), 18.

13. Trenowden, *Malayan Operations,* 197; Spector, *Eagle against the Sun,* 488, 491.

14. Ienaga, *Japan's Last War,* 199; Daniels, "The Great Tokyo Air Raid," 119, 125–26; Grayling, *Among the Dead Cities,* 76–77; Spector, *Eagle against the Sun,* 503, 505; Yomiuri, *From Marco Polo Bridge,* 195–96; Gordin, *Five Days in August,* 21; *Strategic Bombing Survey: Summary,* 16; Havens, *Valley of Darkness,* 176, 185.

15. Quoted in Hastings, *Retribution,* 296.

16. Daniels, "The Great Tokyo Air Raid," 126.

17. Alex Kershaw, *Escape from the Deep: The Epic Story of a Legendary Submarine and Her Courageous Crew* (Philadelphia: Da Capo, 2008) 176.

18. See W. G. Sebald, *On the Natural History of Destruction,* trans. Anthea Bell (London: Penguin, 2003), 18.

19. Kershaw, *Escape from the Deep,* 20.

20. Hastings, *Retribution,* 276.

21. Felton, *Slaughter at Sea,* 7, 21; Banham, *Sinking of the Lisbon Maru,* 97, 112; Wilson, *Submariners' War,* 143.

22. Lockwood, *Sink 'Em All,* 224.

23. Tuohy, *The Bravest Man,* 372; Galantin, *Take Her Deep!* 258.

24. Lockwood, *Sink 'Em All,* 285–86.

25. Loughlin interview; Parks interview; Loughlin, *Reminiscences,* 124–31.

26. Keith, *Final Patrol,* 218.

27. See, for example, USS *Batfish* Third War Patrol Report, 12 June 1944; USS *Finback* Fourth War Patrol Report, Endorsement, disc 13, SM; Tuohy, *The Bravest Man,* 310; Kershaw, *Escape from the Deep,* 49.

28. Mars, *H.M.S. Thule,* 169.

29. Rob Morris, *Untold Valor: Forgotten Stories of American Bomber Crews over Europe in World War II* (Washington, DC: Potomac Books, 2006), xiv, 160.

30. Quoted in Thompson, *Imperial War Museum,* 259.

31. Quoted in McDonald, *USS* Puffer, 250.

32. Robert D. Kaplan, *Hog Pilots, Blue Water Grunts: The American Military in the Air, at Sea, and on the Ground* (New York: Random House, 2007), 144.

33. LaVO, *Slade Cutter,* 193; Mendenhall, *Submarine Diary,* 163; Lockwood and Adamson, *Hellcats of the Sea,* 65; Moore, Spadefish, 312.

34. Quoted in McDonald, *USS* Puffer, 251.

35. Morris, *Untold Valor,* 91.

36. Johnson, *Pacific Campaign,* 121.

37. Hastings, *Retribution,* 368, 521.

38. Russell, *Hell Above,* 162.

39. Whitlock and Smith, *Depths of Courage,* 334–35, 344, 358; McCullough, *A Tale of Two Subs,* 264; Kershaw, *Escape from the Deep,* 137–39, 142–43.

40. Kershaw, *Escape from the Deep*, 153.

41. Ibid., 171–76.

42. Felton, *Slaughter at Sea*, 77–78; Moore, Spadefish, 18.

43. See William Mulligan, "Review Article: Total War," *War in History* 15, no. 2 (2008): 212–13; Sahr Conway-Lanz, *Collateral Damage: Americans, Noncombatant Immunity, and Atrocity after World War II* (New York: Routledge, 2006), 11; Braudy, *Chivalry to Terrorism*, 459.

44. Earhart, *Certain Victory*, 147.

45. Braudy, *Chivalry to Terrorism*, 476. See also Lowe, *Inferno*, 45.

46. Quoted in Grayling, *Among the Dead Cities*, 142.

47. E. B. Potter and Chester W. Nimitz, eds., *The Great Sea War: The Story of Naval Action in World War II* (Englewood Cliffs, NJ: Prentice-Hall, 1960), 420.

48. Bell, Brawley, and Dixon, *Conflict in the Pacific*, 172; Holwitt, "*Execute against Japan*," 182.

49. John W. Dower, *War without Mercy: Race and Power in the Pacific War* (New York: Pantheon Books, 1986), especially 8–10.

50. Wilson, *Submariners' War*, 97; Spector, *Eagle against the Sun*, 398; Dunnigan and Nofi, *Victory at Sea*, 562; McLaughlin and Parry, *We'll Always Have the Movies*, 71. See also, for example, Gunton, *Dive!* 59; Holmes, *Undersea Victory*, 392.

51. Recollections of Lieutenant Commander Landon L. Davis Jr., Naval Historical Center, http://www.history.navy.mil/library/online/oral_history _davis.htm (accessed 13 June 2008).

52. Grayling, *Among the Dead Cities*, 21, 169, 263.

53. Albion and Pope, *Sea Lanes in Wartime*, 355.

54. Gordin, *Five Days in August*, 62–63.

55. Barton J. Bernstein, "Introducing the Interpretative Problems of Japan's 1945 Surrender," in *The End of the Pacific War: Reappraisals*, ed. Tsuyoshi Hasegawa (Stanford, CA: Stanford University Press, 2007), 9.

56. Richard B. Frank, "Ketsu Gō: Japanese Political and Military Strategy in 1945," in Hasegawa, *End of the Pacific War*, 78.

57. Schratz, *Reminiscences*, 100.

58. Kaplan, *Hog Pilots*, 73.

59. *Strategic Bombing Survey: Summary*, 20–21.

60. *Strategic Bombing Survey (Pacific)*, Interrogations of Japanese Officials.

61. Quoted in Grayling, *Among the Dead Cities*, 120.

62. Quoted in ibid., 171.

63. See Lowe, *Inferno*, 311; Spector, *Eagle against the Sun*, 505–6.

64. Joseph E. Enright, with James W. Ryan, *Shinano! The Sinking of Japan's Secret Supership* (London: Bodley Head, 1987), 11.

Conclusion

1. Lowe, *Inferno,* ix.

2. Loughlin, *Reminiscences,* 179.

3. See Geoffrey C. Ward and Ken Burns, *The War: An Intimate History, 1941–1945* (New York: Knopf, 2007), xv.

4. Quoted in Bouslog, *Maru Killer,* 171–172.

5. USS *Blenny* Fourth War Patrol Report, 4 August 1945.

6. USS *Puffer* Eighth War Patrol Report, 5 July 1945.

7. USS *Segundo* Fifth War Patrol Report, 3 June 1945.

8. USS *Segundo* Fifth War Patrol Report, 8–9 June 1945.

9. Davenport, *Clean Sweep,* 185.

10. Russell, *Hell Above,* 121–22. See also, for example, George Woodward, quoted in Hood, *Submarine,* 27.

11. Willmott, *Battle of Leyte Gulf,* 216.

12. Recollections of Landon L. Davis.

13. Parks interview.

14. USS *Balao* Eighth War Patrol Report, 18 March 1945.

15. Russell, *Hell Above,* 123.

16. Quoted in LaVO, *Slade Cutter,* 136.

17. Fluckey, *Thunder Below!* 399.

18. See Manson, *Diplomatic Ramifications,* 174; Holwitt, *"Execute against Japan,"* 169.

19. See, for example, Calvert, *Silent Running,* 167.

20. Tuohy, *The Bravest Man,* xv, 387; Keith, *Final Patrol,* 281.

21. Kinsella interview.

22. Lockwood and Adamson, *Hellcats of the Sea,* 83–84.

23. Beach and Beach, *From Annapolis to Scapa Flow,* 24, 27, 123; Loughlin, *Reminiscences,* 1; Newpower, *Iron Men and Tin Fish,* 183; Lockwood, *Sink 'Em All,* 166; LaVO, *Slade Cutter,* 15; Kershaw, *Escape from the Deep,* 18; Schratz, *Reminiscences,* 121.

24. LaVO, *Slade Cutter,* 244.

25. See, for example, Casey, *Battle Below,* 93.

26. Schratz, *Submarine Commander,* 313.

27. See, for example, Grider, *War Fish,* 214; Paine, *Transpacific Voyage,* 26.

28. Commander Submarine Force, Pacific Fleet, Current Doctrine Submarines, February 1944, 2. See also Spector, *Eagle against the Sun,* 482.

29. Whitlock and Smith, *Depths of Courage,* 90; Mendenhall, *Submarine Diary,* 196; Eugene McKinney Interview (taped), box 97, CBC.

30. Braudy, *Chivalry to Terrorism,* 394.

31. McCullough, *A Tale of Two Subs,* 109.

32. Bouslog, *Maru Killer,* 81; LaVO, *Slade Cutter,* 159.

33. Blanchard interview.

34. Quoted in Kershaw, *Escape from the Deep,* 113. See also, for example, Whitlock and Smith, *Depths of Courage,* 218.

35. Quoted in LaVO, *Slade Cutter,* 61.

36. Schratz, *Reminiscences,* 72.

37. Quoted in Howarth, *Fighting Ships,* 320.

38. Quoted in Kershaw, *Escape from the Deep,* 32.

39. Ibid., 50.

40. Quoted in ibid., 54.

41. Ibid., 216.

42. Ramage, *Reminiscences,* 62.

43. Calvert, *Silent Running,* 93–94.

44. Hazzard interview.

45. Quoted in Moore, Spadefish, 351.

46. Ibid., 371, 394–95, 397.

47. USS *Barb* Twelfth War Patrol Report, 26 July 1945.

48. See Cook, "The Politics of Surrender," 640.

49. Anderson interview.

50. Quoted in Avner Offer, "Morality and Admiralty: 'Jacky' Fisher, Economic Warfare and the Laws of War," in *Naval History, 1850-Present,* ed. Andrew Lambert (Aldershot, UK: Ashgate, 2007), 1:372.

51. A. P. V. Rogers, "The Principle of Proportionality," in Hensel, *Use of Military Force,* 189, 203.

52. See Mallison, *Law of Naval Warfare,* 16, 97.

Bibliography

Archival Sources

American Heritage Center, University of Wyoming, Laramie

Clay Blair Collection
    William Robert Anderson Interview (taped), box 96
    Charles Andrews Interview (taped), box 96
    James Blanchard Interview (taped), box 98
    Creed Burlingame Interview (taped), box 96
    Ralph Christie Interview (taped), box 97
    John Coye Interview (taped), box 97
    Robert Dornin Interview (taped), box 97
    William Germershausen Interview (taped), box 97
    William Hazzard Interview (taped), box 97
    Leon Huffman Interview (taped), box 97
    William T. Kinsella Interview (taped), box 98
    Charles Loughlin Interview (taped), box 98
    Eugene McKinney Interview (taped), box 97
    Philip Nichols Interview (taped), box 99
    Lewis Parks Interview (taped), boxes 98 and 99

Battye Library of West Australian History,
Oral History Unit, Perth

Cecil Anderson Interview, 24 August 1990, OH2365/3
Jack Sue Interview, 1990, OH2365/5

Charles Darwin University, Darwin

Rowan E. Waddy, "An Adventure in Sarawak, Borneo," n.d.

Rowan E. Waddy, "A Submarine Adventure in South China Sea, 1945," 1992
Rowan E. Waddy, Paper Presented at Hervey Bay, Queensland, to Commemorate Operation Rimau and 50th Anniversary of Formation of Z Special Unit, 12 July 1992
Rowan E. Waddy, "Special Operations—Submarines," n.d.

Churchill Archives Center, Cambridge

Papers of Rear-Admiral Sir Anthony Miers

Columbia University, Oral History Research Office, New York

Reminiscences of James Fife, Interviews Conducted 1961–62

Library of Congress, Manuscript Division, Washington, DC

Papers of Ralph W. Christie, Correspondence, 1941–45
Papers of Charles A. Lockwood, Correspondence, 1940–42

National Archives of Australia, Melbourne

Politician Project, series A3269, control symbol E7/A
War Crimes, series MP 742/1, control symbol 336/1/1939

National Archives of Singapore

George Edwin Bogaars Interview (transcript), 8 December 1983, accession no. 000379

Naval Historical Center, Washington DC

Commander Submarine Force, Pacific Fleet, Current Doctrine Submarines, February 1944, http://www.history.navy.mil/library/online/sub_doctrine.htm (accessed 13 June 2008)
Recollections of Lieutenant Commander Landon L. Davis Jr., http://www.history.navy.mil/library/online/oral_history_davis.htm (accessed 13 June 2008)

Submarine Force Museum, Groton, CT

Albacore Boat Book
Bowfin Boat Book
Pollack Boat Book
Sunfish Boat Book
Wahoo Boat Book

U.S. National Archives and Records Administration, College Park, MD

Ernest J. King to Franklin D. Roosevelt, 19 March 1942, FDR-MR: Papers as President, Franklin D. Roosevelt Library, http://arcweb.archives .gov/arc/servelet/arc (accessed 29 June 2007)
Records of Naval Operating Forces, Commander Submarine Force, Pacific Fleet, Confidential General Administrative Files, Flag Files (blue 439), 1944–46; (blue 440), 1942–45; (blue 443/part 2), 1942–45, Record Group 313
Statements by Survivors SS *John A. Johnson* Following Torpedoing by Japanese Submarine, November 1944, A16-3/QS1-Enemy Attacks— Action Reports, Merchant Vessels, Records of Naval Districts and Shore Establishments, 1784–1981, Record Group 181, NARA—Pacific Region, http://arcweb.archives.gov/arac/servlet/arc (accessed 29 June 2007)

USS Bowfin *Submarine Museum, Pearl Harbor, HI*

Miscellaneous War Patrol Reports
Dudley Morton Papers
David Norton, Written Accounts of *Bowfin* War Patrols
Oral History Collection
    John Bertrand Interview (transcript), 8 May 1992
    Walter Beyer Interview (transcript), 9 May 1992
    Jaye Garrison Interview (transcript), 9 May 1992
    Richard Taylor Interview (transcript), 1992
    Alexander K. Tyree Interview (transcript), 28 September 1996

Personal Interview

Roscoe P. Thompson, interview with author, 9 October 2002, Bunbury, Western Australia

Personal Papers

Roscoe P. Thompson Diary and Biographical Notes

USS *Pampanito,* San Francisco

Taped tour and integrated oral history, 15 August 2002

War Patrol Reports (U.S.)

This massive and essential source of historical evidence has until recently been accessible only through a small number of archives. Many of the war patrol reports cited in this study were found at the USS *Bowfin* Submarine Museum, Pearl Harbor. A small number of war patrol reports have been published as edited books. Through the company Submarine Memorabilia, copies of U.S. war patrol reports converted from microfilm to DVD are available for purchase. Increasingly, selected war patrol reports have also become available on the Internet. This study has made use of all of these sources; the source for individual war patrol reports is cited in the endnotes.

Books and Articles

Albion, Robert Greenhalgh, and Jennie Barnes Pope. *Sea Lanes in Wartime: The American Experience, 1775–1945.* N.p.: Archon Books, 1968.

Alden, John D. "Away the Boarding Party." *U.S. Naval Proceedings,* January 1965, 68–75.

———. *The Fleet Submarine in the U.S. Navy: A Design and Construction History.* London: Arms and Armour, 1979.

———. *U.S. Submarine Attacks during World War II (Including Allied Submarine Attacks in the Pacific Theatre).* Annapolis, MD: U.S. Naval Institute Press, 1989.

Alden, John D., and Craig R. McDonald. *United States and Allied Submarine Successes in the Pacific and Far East during World War II.* Jefferson, NC: McFarland, 2009.

Anderson, Gary M., and Adam Gifford Jr. "Order Out of Anarchy: The International Law of War." *Cato Journal* 15 (Spring/Summer 1995): 25–39.

———. "Privateering and the Private Production of Naval Power." *Cato Journal* 11 (Spring/Summer 1991): 99–123.

Asada, Sadao. *From Mahan to Pearl Harbor: The Imperial Japanese Navy and the United States.* Annapolis, MD: U.S. Naval Institute Press, 2006.

Banham, Tony. *The Sinking of the* Lisbon Maru: *Britain's Forgotten Wartime Tragedy.* Hong Kong: Hong Kong University Press, 2006.

Beach, Edward L. *Submarine!* Melbourne: William Heinemann, 1953.

Beach, Edward L., Sr., with Edward L. Beach Jr. *From Annapolis to Scapa Flow: The Autobiography of Edward L. Beach Sr.* Annapolis, MD: U.S. Naval Institute Press, 2003.

Behrens, C. B. A. *Merchant Shipping and the Demands of War.* London: Her Majesty's Stationery Office, 1955.

Bell, Roger, Sean Brawley, and Chris Dixon. *Conflict in the Pacific, 1937–1951.* Cambridge: Cambridge University Press, 2005.

Benda, Harry J. *The Crescent and the Rising Moon: Indonesian Islam under the Japanese Occupation, 1942–1945.* The Hague: W. van Hoeve, 1958.

Benda, Harry J., James K. Irikura, and Koichi Kishi. *Japanese Military Administration in Indonesia: Selected Documents.* Translation Series 6. New Haven, CT: Yale University Southeast Asia Studies, 1965.

Best, Geoffrey. *Humanity in Warfare.* New York: Columbia University Press, 1983.

Billy, George J., and Christine M. Billy. *Merchant Mariners at War: An Oral History of World War II.* Gainesville: University Press of Florida, 2008.

Blair, Clay Jr. *Hitler's U-Boat War: The Hunted, 1942–1945.* 1998. Reprint, London: Cassell, 2001.

———. *Hitler's U-Boat War: The Hunters, 1939–1942.* 1996. Reprint, New York: Modern Library, 2000.

———. *Silent Victory: The U.S. Submarine War against Japan.* 1975. Reprint, Annapolis, MD: U.S. Naval Institute Press, 2001.

Bouslog, Dave. *Maru Killer: The War Patrols of the USS* Seahorse. Sarasota, FL: Seahorse Books, 1996.

Boyd, Carl. *American Command of the Sea through Carriers, Codes and the Silent Service: World War II and Beyond.* Newport News, VA: Mariners' Museum, 1995.

Braudy, Leo. *From Chivalry to Terrorism: War and the Changing Nature of Masculinity.* New York: Vintage Books, 2005.

Brenchley, Fred, and Elizabeth Brenchley. *Stoker's Submarine.* Sydney: Harper Collins, 2001.

Bridgland, Tony. *Waves of Hate: Naval Atrocities of the Second World War.* Annapolis, MD: U.S. Naval Institute Press, 2002.

Brown, David, ed. *The British Pacific and East Indies Fleets: 'The Forgotten Fleets' 50th Anniversary.* Liverpool: Brodie, 1995.

Burgess, Colin. *Freedom or Death: Australia's Greatest Escape Stories from Two World Wars.* Sydney: Allen and Unwin, 1994.

Burns, Richard Dean. "Regulating Submarine Warfare, 1921–41: A Case Study in Arms Control and Limited War." *Military Affairs* 35 (April 1971): 56–63.

Butcher, John G. *The Closing of the Frontier: A History of the Marine Fisheries of Southeast Asia, c. 1850–2000.* Leiden: KITLV, 2004.

Cairns, Lynne. *Fremantle's Secret Fleets: Allied Submarines Based in Western Australia during World War II.* Fremantle: Western Australian Maritime Museum, 1995.

Calvert, James. *Silent Running: My Years on a World War II Attack Submarine*. New York: John Wiley and Sons, 1995.

Carruthers, Steven L. *Japanese Submarine Raiders, 1942: A Maritime Mystery*. Narrabeen, New South Wales: Casper, 2006.

Casey, Robert J. *Battle Below: The War of the Submarines*. Indianapolis: Bobbs-Merrill, 1945.

Chapman, Paul. *Submarine* Torbay. London: Robert Hale, 1989.

Chen, Henry T. *Taiwanese Distant-Water Fishing in Southeast Asia, 1936–1977*. St. John's, Newfoundland: International Maritime Economic History Association, 2009.

Chida, Tomohei, and Peter N. Davies, *The Japanese Shipping and Shipbuilding Industries: A History of Their Modern Growth*. London: Athlone, 1990.

Christie, R. W. "*Bluegill* on Patrol: A Story of Cutlasses, Gunfire and Depth-Bombs." *Blue Book*, July 1946, 97–99.

Christley, Jim. *US Submarines, 1941–45*. New York: Osprey, 2006.

Cline, Rick. *Final Dive: The Gallant and Tragic Career of the WWII Submarine USS* Snook. Placentia, CA: R. A. Cline, 2001.

———. *Submarine* Grayback: *The Life and Death of the WWII Sub, USS* Grayback. Placentia, CA: R. A. Cline, 1999.

Cohen, Marshall, Thomas Nagel, and Thomas Scanlon, eds. *War and Moral Responsibility*. Princeton, NJ: Princeton University Press, 1974.

Conway-Lanz, Sahr. *Collateral Damage: Americans, Noncombatant Immunity, and Atrocity after World War II*. New York: Routledge, 2006.

Cook, Graeme. *Silent Marauders*. London: Hart-Davis, MacGibbon, 1976.

Cook, Haruko Taya, and Theodore F. Cook. *Japan at War: An Oral History*. New York: New Press, 1992.

Cook, Tim. "The Politics of Surrender: Canadian Soldiers and Killing of Prisoners in the Great War." *Journal of Military History* 70 (July 2006): 637–65.

Cope, Harley, and Walter Karig. *Battle Submerged: Submarine Fighters of World War II*. New York: Norton, 1951.

Courtney, G. B. *Silent Feet: The History of "Z" Special Operations, 1942–1945*. Melbourne: R. J. and S. P. Austin, 1993.

Critchley, Macdonald. *Shipwreck-Survivors: A Medical Study*. London: J. and A. Churchill, 1943.

Crompton-Hall, Richard. *The Underwater War, 1939–1945*. Poole, UK: Blandford, 1982.

Cutter, Slade. *The Reminiscences of Captain Slade D. Cutter*. Annapolis, MD: U.S. Naval Institute Press, 1985.

Daniels, Gordon. "The Great Tokyo Air Raid, 9–10 March 1945." In *Modern Japan: Aspects of History, Literature and Society*, edited by W. G. Beasley, 113–31. Tokyo: Charles E. Tuttle, 1976.

Davenport, Roy M. *Clean Sweep*. New York: Vantage Books, 1986.

Davies, Peter N. "A Guide to the Emergence of Japan's Modern Shipping Industries." In *International Merchant Shipping in the Nineteenth and Twentieth Centuries: The Comparative Dimension*, edited by Lewis R. Fischer and Even Lange, 105–24. St. John's, Newfoundland: International Maritime Economic History Association, 2008.

De Lupis, Ingrid Detter. *The Law of War*. Cambridge: Cambridge University Press, 1987.

DeRose, James F. *Unrestricted Warfare: How a New Breed of Officers Led the Submarine Force to Victory in World War II*. New York: John Wiley and Sons, 2000.

DiGiulian, Tony. "Definitions and Information about Naval Guns." June 2007. http://www.navweapons.com/ (accessed 1 August 2007).

Doenitz, Admiral. *Memoirs: Ten Years and Twenty Days*. London: Weidenfeld and Nicolson, 1958.

Donnelly, Ivon A. *Chinese Junks and Other Native Craft*. 1924. Reprint, Singapore: Graham Brash, 1988.

Doughty, Martin. *Merchant Shipping and War: A Study in Defence Planning in Twentieth-Century Britain*. London: Royal Historical Society, 1982.

Dower, John W. *War without Mercy: Race and Power in the Pacific War*. New York: Pantheon Books, 1986.

Dunnigan, James F., and Albert A Nofi. *Victory at Sea: World War II in the Pacific*. New York: William Morrow, 1995.

Earhart, David C. *Certain Victory: Images of World War II in the Japanese Media*. New York: M. E. Sharpe, 2008.

Edwards, Bernard. *Blood and Bushido: Japanese Atrocities at Sea, 1941–1945*. Worcester: Self Publishing Association, 1991.

———. *The Grey Widow-Maker: Twenty-four Disasters at Sea*. London: Robert Hale, 1990.

Elleman, Bruce A., and S. C. M. Paine, eds. *Naval Coalition Warfare: From the Napoleonic War to Operation Iraqi Freedom*. London: Routledge, 2008.

Ellis, John. *Brute Force: Allied Strategy and Tactics in the Second World War*. London: Andre Deutsch, 1990.

Enright, Joseph E., with James W. Ryan. *Shinano! The Sinking of Japan's Secret Supership*. London: Bodley Head, 1987.

Evans, David C., ed. *The Japanese Navy in World War II: In the Words of Former Japanese Naval Officers*. 1969. Reprint, Annapolis, MD: U.S. Naval Institute Press, 1986.

Felton, Mark. *Slaughter at Sea: The Story of Japan's Naval War Crimes*. Annapolis, MD: U.S. Naval Institute Press, 2007.

Feuer, A. B. *Commando! The M/Z Units' Secret War against Japan*. West-port, CT: Praeger, 1996.

Fluckey, Eugene. *Thunder Below! The USS* Barb *Revolutionizes Submarine Warfare in World War II*. Urbana: University of Illinois Press, 1992.

Fontenoy, Paul E. *Submarines: An Illustrated History of Their Impact*. Santa Barbara, CA: ABC-Clio, 2007.

Foong, Choon Hon, ed. *The Price of Peace: True Accounts of the Japanese Occupation of Singapore*. Translated by Clara Show. Singapore: Asia-pac Books, 1997.

Friedman, Norman. *US Naval Weapons: Every Gun, Missile, Mine and Torpedo Used by the US Navy from 1883 to the Present Day*. Annapolis, MD: U.S. Naval Institute Press, 1983.

Fyne, Robert. *The Hollywood Propaganda of World War II*. London: Scare-crow, 1997.

Galantin, I. J. *Take Her Deep! A Submarine against Japan in World War II*. 1987. Reprint, London: Unwin Hyman, 1988.

Gannon, Robert. *Hellions of the Deep: The Development of American Tor-pedoes in World War II*. University Park: Pennsylvania State University Press, 1996.

Gibney, Frank, ed. *Senso: The Japanese Remember the Pacific War*. Trans-lated by Beth Cary. London: M. E. Sharpe, 1995.

Gleason, Bill. "Diary of a War Patrol—USS *Gurnard* (SS-254)." *Polaris*, June 1985. http://www.subvetpaul.com/SAGA_6_85.htm (accessed 1 July 2005).

Goldensohn, Leon. *The Nuremberg Interviews: An American Psychiatrist's Conversations with the Defendants and Witnesses*. Edited by Robert Gellately. New York: Vintage Books, 2005.

Goldman, Emily O. *Sunken Treaties: Naval Arms Control between the Wars*. University Park: Pennsylvania State University Press, 1994.

Gordin, Michael D. *Five Days in August: How World War II Became a Nuclear War*. Princeton, NJ: Princeton University Press, 2007.

Grayling, A. C. *Among the Dead Cities: The History and Moral Legacy of the WWII Bombing of Civilians in Germany and Japan*. New York: Walker, 2006.

Grider, George, with Lydel Sims. *War Fish*. London: Cassell, 1959.

Gruhl, Werner. *Imperial Japan's World War Two, 1931–1945*. New Bruns-wick, NJ: Transaction, 2007.

Gugliotta, Bobette. *Pigboat 39: An American Sub Goes to War*. Lexington: University Press of Kentucky, 1984.

Gunton, Michael. *Dive! Dive! Dive! Submarines at War*. London: Con-stable: 2003.

Hasegawa, Tsuyoshi, ed. *The End of the Pacific War: Reappraisals.* Stanford, CA: Stanford University Press, 2007.

Hashimoto, Mochitsura. *Sunk: The Story of the Japanese Submarine Fleet, 1942–1945.* Translated by E. H. M. Colegrave. London: Hamilton, 1955.

Hastings, Max. *Retribution: The Battle for Japan, 1944–45.* New York: Knopf, 2008.

Havens, Thomas R. H. *Valley of Darkness: The Japanese People and World War Two.* Lanham, MD: University Press of America, 1986.

Henderson, Bruce. *Down to the Sea: An Epic Story of Naval Disaster and Heroism in World War II.* New York: Harper Collins, 2007.

Henry, Ken, and Don Keith. *Gallant Lady: A Biography of the USS Archerfish.* New York: Tom Doherty Associates, 2004.

Hensel, Howard M., ed. *The Legitimate Use of Military Force: The Just War Tradition and the Customary Law of Armed Conflict.* Aldershot, UK: Ashgate, 2008.

Herwig, Holger H. "Innovation Ignored: The Submarine Problem; Germany, Britain, and the United States, 1919–1939." In *Military Innovation in the Interwar Period,* edited by Williamson Murray and Allan R. Millett, 227–64. Cambridge: Cambridge University Press, 1996.

Hezlet, Arthur. *The Submarine and Sea Power.* London: Peter Davies, 1967.

Hock, David Koh Wee, ed. *Legacies of World War II in South and East Asia.* Singapore: Institute of Southeast Asian Studies, 2007.

Holmes, W. J. *Undersea Victory: The Influence of Submarine Operations in the War in the Pacific.* New York: Doubleday, 1966.

Holwitt, Joel Ira. *"Execute against Japan": The U.S. Decision to Conduct Unrestricted Submarine Warfare.* College Station: Texas A&M University Press, 2009.

———. "Mush Morton and the *Buyo Maru* Massacre." *U.S. Naval Institute Proceedings,* July 2003, 80–81.

Hood, Jean, ed. *Submarine: An Anthology of First-hand Accounts of War under the Sea, 1939–1945.* London: Conway, 2007.

Hornfischer, James D. *The Last Stand of the Tin Can Sailors: The Extraordinary World War II Story of the U.S. Navy's Finest Hour.* 2004. Reprint, New York: Bantam Books, 2005.

Howarth, Stephen. *The Fighting Ships of the Rising Sun: The Drama of the Imperial Japanese Navy, 1895–1945.* New York: Atheneum, 1983.

Howarth, Stephen, and Derek Law, eds. *The Battle of the Atlantic, 1939–1945: The 50th Anniversary International Naval Conference.* London: Greenhill Books, 1994.

Hoyt, Edwin P. *Bowfin: The Story of One of America's Fabled Fleet Submarines in World War II.* New York: Van Nostrand Reinhold, 1983.

Huen, P. Lim Pui, and Diana Wong, eds. *War and Memory in Malaysia and Singapore*. Singapore: Institute of Southeast Asian Studies, 2000.

Hurst, Doug. *The Fourth Ally: The Dutch Forces in Australia during World War II*. Canberra: Doug Hurst, 2001.

Ienaga, Saburo. *Japan's Last War: World War II and the Japanese, 1931–1945*. Canberra: Australian National University Press, 1979.

Isom, Dallas Woodbury. *Midway Inquest: Why the Japanese Lost the Battle of Midway*. Bloomington: Indiana University Press, 2007.

Jenkins, David. *Battle Surface: Japan's Submarine War against Australia, 1942–44*. Sydney: Random House, 1992.

Jentschura, Hansgeng, Dieter Jung, and Peter Milker. *Warships of the Imperial Japanese Navy, 1869–1945*. Translated by Antony Preston and J. D. Brown. London: Arms and Armour, 1977.

Johnson, William Bruce. *The Pacific Campaign in World War II: From Pearl Harbor to Guadalcanal*. London: Routledge, 2006.

Jones, David, and Peter Nunan. *U.S. Subs Down Under: Brisbane, 1942–1945*. Annapolis, MD: U.S. Naval Institute Press, 2005.

Jones, Mark C. "Experiment at Dundee: The Royal Navy's 9th Submarine Flotilla and Multinational Naval Cooperation during World War II." *Journal of Military History* 72 (October 2008): 1179–1212.

Kaplan, Robert D. *Hog Pilots, Blue Water Grunts: The American Military in the Air, at Sea, and on the Ground*. New York: Random House, 2007.

Keith, Don. *Final Patrol: True Stories of World War II Submarines*. New York: NAL Caliber, 2006.

———. *In the Course of Duty: The Heroic Mission of the USS* Batfish. New York: NAL Caliber, 2005.

Kemp, Paul. *A Pictorial History of the Sea War, 1939–1945*. London: Arms and Armour, 1995.

Kershaw, Alex. *Escape from the Deep: The Epic Story of a Legendary Submarine and Her Courageous Crew*. Philadelphia: Da Capo, 2008.

Kimmett, Larry, and Margaret Regis. *U.S. Submarines in World War II: An Illustrated History*. Seattle: Navigator, 1996.

Kinsella, David, and Craig L. Carr, eds. *The Morality of War: A Reader*. Boulder, CO: Lynne Rienner, 2007.

LaVO, Carl. *Slade Cutter: Submarine Warrior*. Annapolis, MD: U.S. Naval Institute Press, 2003.

Lawliss, Chuck. *The Submarine Book: An Illustrated History of the Attack Submarine*. Shrewsbury, UK: Airlife, 2000.

Layton, Edwin T., with Roger Pineau and John Costello. *"And I Was There": Pearl Harbor and Midway—Breaking the Secrets*. 1985. Reprint, Annapolis, MD: U.S. Naval Institute Press, 2006.

Lebra, Joyce C. *Japan's Greater East Asia Co-prosperity Sphere in World*

War II: Selected Readings and Documents. London: Oxford University Press, 1975.

Lipscomb, F. W. *The British Submarine.* London: Adam and Charles Black, 1954.

Lockwood, Charles. *Sink 'Em All: Submarine Warfare in the Pacific.* 1951. Reprint, New York: Bantam Books, 1984.

Lockwood, Charles, and Hans Christian Adamson. *Hellcats of the Sea.* New York: Greenberg, 1955.

Lott, Arnold S. *Most Dangerous Sea: A History of Mine Warfare, and an Account of U.S. Navy Mine Warfare Operations in World War II and Korea.* Annapolis, MD: U.S. Naval Institute Press, 1959.

Loughlin, Charles Elliot. *The Reminiscences of Rear Admiral Charles Elliot Loughlin, U.S. Navy (Retired).* Annapolis, MD: U.S. Naval Institute Press, 1982.

Lowe, Keith. *Inferno: The Fiery Destruction of Hamburg, 1943.* New York: Scribner, 2007.

Maga, Tim. *Judgment at Tokyo: The Japanese War Crimes Trials.* Lexington: University Press of Kentucky, 2001.

Mallison, W. T., Jr. *Studies in the Law of Naval Warfare: Submarines in General and Limited Wars.* Washington, DC: Government Printing Office, 1968.

Manson, Janet M. *Diplomatic Ramifications of Unrestricted Submarine Warfare, 1939–1941.* Westport, CT: Greenwood, 1990.

Mars, Alastair. *H.M.S.* Thule *Intercepts.* London: Elek Books, 1956.

May, Larry. *War Crimes and Just War.* Cambridge: Cambridge University Press, 2007.

McCartney, Innes. *British Submarines, 1939–45.* Oxford: Osprey, 2006.

McCullough, Jonathan J. *A Tale of Two Subs: An Untold Story of World War II, Two Sister Ships, and Extraordinary Heroism.* New York: Grand Central, 2008.

McDaniel, J. T., ed. *U.S.S.* Wahoo *(SS-238) American Submarine War Patrol Reports.* Riverdale, GA: Riverdale Books, 2003.

McDonald, Craig R. *The USS* Puffer *in World War II: A History of the Submarine and Its Wartime Crew.* Jefferson, NC: McFarland, 2008.

McKee, Christopher. *Sober Men and True: Sailor Lives in the Royal Navy, 1900–1945.* Cambridge, MA: Harvard University Press, 2002.

McLaughlin, Robert L., and Sally E. Parry. *We'll Always Have the Movies: American Cinema during World War II.* Lexington: University Press of Kentucky, 2006.

Mendenhall, Corwin. *Submarine Diary: The Silent Stalking of Japan.* Annapolis, MD: U.S. Naval Institute Press, 1991.

Miles, Patricia. "After the Battle of Terrigal: Merchant Navy Losses off the

New South Wales Coast in World War II." Maritime Heritage Online. http://maritime.heritage.nsw.gov.au/ (accessed 11 June 2008).

Moore, Stephen L. Spadefish: *On Patrol with a Top-Scoring World War II Submarine.* Dallas: Atriad, 2006.

Morris, Rob. *Untold Valor: Forgotten Stories of American Bomber Crews over Europe in World War II.* Washington, DC: Potomac Books, 2006.

Mulligan, William. "Review Article: Total War." *War in History* 15, no. 2 (2008): 211–21.

Newpower, Anthony. *Iron Men and Tin Fish: The Race to Build a Better Torpedo during World War II.* Westport, CT: Praeger Security International, 2006.

Offer, Avner. "Morality and Admiralty: 'Jacky' Fisher, Economic Warfare and the Laws of War." In *Naval History, 1850–Present,* edited by Andrew Lambert, 1:371–90. Aldershot, UK: Ashgate, 2007.

O'Kane, Richard H. Wahoo: *The Patrols of America's Most Famous World War II Submarine.* Novato, CA Presidio, 1987.

Ostlund, Mike. Find 'Em, Chase 'Em, Sink 'Em: *The Mysterious Loss of the WWII Submarine USS* Gudgeon. Guildford, CT: Lyons, 2006.

Owen, James. *Nuremberg: Evil on Trial.* London: Headline Review, 2006.

Padfield, Peter. *War beneath the Sea: Submarine Conflict, 1939–1945.* London: Pimlico, 1995.

Page, Arthur. *Between Victor and Vanquished: An Australian Interrogator in the War against Japan.* Canberra: Australian Military History Publications, 2008.

Paine, T. O. *The Transpacific Voyage of His Imperial Japanese Majesty's Submarine* I-400 *(Tom Paine's Journal, July–December 1945).* Los Angeles: T. O. Paine, 1984.

Palmer, Michael A. *Command at Sea: Naval Command and Control since the Sixteenth Century.* Cambridge, MA: Harvard University Press, 2005.

Parillo, Mark P. *The Japanese Merchant Marine in World War II.* Annapolis, MD: U.S. Naval Institute Press, 1993.

Parrish, Thomas. *The Submarine: A History.* London: Viking Penguin, 2004.

Polmar, Norman. *The American Submarine.* Annapolis, MD: Nautical and Aviation Publishing Company of America, 1981.

Potter, E. B., and Chester W. Nimitz, eds. *The Great Sea War: The Story of Naval Action in World War II.* Englewood Cliffs, NJ: Prentice-Hall, 1960.

Powell, Alan. *War by Stealth: Australians and the Allied Intelligence Bureau, 1942–1945.* Melbourne: Melbourne University Press, 1996.

Raben, Remco. "Indonesian *Rōmusha* and Coolies under Naval Administration." In *Asian Labor in the Wartime Japanese Empire: Unknown Histories,* edited by Paul H. Kratoska, 197–212. London: M. E. Sharpe, 2005.

Ramage, Lawson P. *Reminiscences of Vice Admiral Lawson P. Ramage.* Annapolis, MD: U.S. Naval Institute Press, 1975.

Roberts, Adam, and Richard Guelff, eds. *Documents on the Laws of War.* 1982. Reprint, Oxford: Clarendon, 1989.

Rohwer, J., and G. Hummerchen. *Chronology of the War at Sea, 1939–1945: The Naval History of World War Two.* 1972. Reprint, London: Greenhill Books, 1992.

Roscoe, Theodore. *United States Submarine Operations in World War II.* Annapolis, MD: U.S. Naval Institute Press, 1949.

Rowland, Buford, and William B. Boyd. *U.S. Navy Bureau of Ordnance in World War II.* Washington, DC: Bureau of Ordnance Department of the Navy, 1953.

Rubin, Alfred P. *The Law of Piracy.* New York: Transnational, 1998.

Rudenno, Victor. *Gallipoli: Attack from the Sea.* Sydney: University of New South Wales Press, 2008.

Ruge, Friedrich. *Sea Warfare, 1939–1945: A German Viewpoint.* London: Cassell, 1957.

Ruiz, C. Kenneth, with John Bruning. *The Luck of the Draw: The Memoir of a World War II Submariner.* St. Paul, MN: Zenith, 2005.

Rush, Charles. "One-Boat Wolfpack." *Naval History* 22 (February 2008): 24–27.

Russell, Dale. *Hell Above, Deep Water Below.* Tillamook, OR: Bayocean Enterprises, 1995.

Schratz, Paul R. *The Reminiscences of Captain Paul Richard Schratz.* Annapolis, MD: U.S. Naval Institute Press, 1996.

———. *Submarine Commander: A Story of World War II and Korea.* Lexington: University Press of Kentucky, 1988.

Schultz, Robert, and James Shell. *We Were Pirates: A Torpedoman's Pacific War.* Annapolis, MD: U.S. Naval Institute Press, 2009.

Seaton, Philip A. *Japan's Contested War Memories: The "Memory Rifts" in Historical Consciousness of World War II.* London: Routledge, 2007.

Sebald, W. G. *On the Natural History of Destruction.* Translated by Anthea Bell. London: Penguin, 2003.

Sheridan, Martin. *Overdue and Presumed Lost: The Story of the USS Bullhead.* 1947. Reprint, Annapolis, MD: U.S. Naval Institute Press, 2004.

Simpson, Gerry. *Law, War and Crime: War Crimes Trials and the Reinvention of Criminal Law.* Cambridge: Polity, 2007.

Smith, Colin. *Singapore Burning: Heroism and Surrender in World War II.* London: Viking, 2005.

Smith, Peter C. *Naval Warfare in the English Channel, 1939–1945.* Barnsley, UK: Pen and Sword, 2007.

Smith, Ron. *Torpedoman.* N.p., 1993.

Spector, Ronald H. *At War at Sea: Sailors and Naval Combat in the Twentieth Century.* New York: Viking, 2001.

———. *Eagle against the Sun: The American War with Japan.* New York: Vintage Books, 1985.

Sterling, Forest J. *Wake of the* Wahoo. Philadelphia: Chilton, 1960.

Stevens, David. *A Critical Vulnerability: The Impact of the Submarine Threat on Australia's Maritime Defence, 1915–1954.* Canberra: Sea Power Centre, 2005.

Stillwell, Paul, ed. *Submarine Stories: Recollections from the Diesel Boats.* Annapolis, MD: U.S. Naval Institute Press, 2007.

Straus, Ulrich. *The Anguish of Surrender: Japanese POWs of World War II.* Seattle: University of Washington Press, 2003.

Sturma, Michael. "Atrocity, Conscience and Unrestricted Warfare: U.S. Submarines during the Second World War." *War in History* 16, no. 7 (2009): 447–68.

———. *Death at a Distance: The Loss of the Legendary USS Harder.* Annapolis, MD: U.S. Naval Institute Press, 2006.

———. *The USS Flier: Death and Survival on a World War II Submarine.* Lexington: University Press of Kentucky, 2008.

"Submariner Gets Support to Make Admiral." *Naval History* 18 (August 2004): 62–63.

Sue, Jack Wong. *Blood on Borneo.* Perth: WA Skindivers, 2001.

Suid, Lawrence H. *Guts and Glory: The Making of the American Military Image in Film.* Lexington, KY: University Press of Kentucky, 2002.

Tanaka, Yuki. *Hidden Horrors: Japanese War Crimes in World War II.* Boulder, CO: Westview, 1996.

Tarling, Nicholas. *A Sudden Rampage: The Japanese Occupation of Southeast Asia, 1941–1945.* Honolulu: University of Hawaii Press, 2001.

Tarrant, V. E. *The U-Boat Offensive, 1914–1945.* London: Arms and Armour, 1989.

Thomas, Evan. *Sea of Thunder: Four Commanders and the Last Great Naval Campaign, 1941–1945.* New York: Simon and Schuster, 2006.

Thompson, Julian. *The Imperial War Museum Book of the War at Sea.* London: Sidgwick and Jackson, 1996.

Trefalt, Beatrice. "Fanaticism, Japanese Soldiers and the Pacific War, 1937–45." In *Fanaticism and Conflict in the Modern Age,* edited by Matthew Hughes and Gaynor Johnson, 33–47. London: Frank Cass, 2005.

Trenowden, Ian. *Malayan Operations Most Secret–Force 136*. 1978. Reprint, Singapore: Heinemann, 1983.

Tuohy, William. *The Bravest Man: Richard O'Kane and the Amazing Submarine Adventures of the USS Tang*. 2001. Reprint, New York: Ballantine Books, 2006.

Turnbull, C. M. *A History of Singapore, 1819–1988*. 1977. Reprint, Oxford: Oxford University Press, 1997.

United States Strategic Bombing Survey (Pacific). Interrogations of Japanese Officials. Naval Analysis Division. http://ibiblio,org/hyperwar/AAF/USSBS/IJO/IJO-70.html (accessed 11 April 2008).

United States Strategic Bombing Survey: Summary Report (Pacific War). Washington, DC: Government Printing Office, 1946.

Van Der Vat, Dan. *Stealth at Sea: The History of the Submarine*. London: Orion, 1995.

Vego, Milan. *Operational Warfare at Sea: Theory and Practice*. London: Routledge, 2009.

Ward, Geoffrey C., and Ken Burns. *The War: An Intimate History, 1941–1945*. New York: Knopf, 2007.

Ward, Norvell G. *The Reminiscences of Norvell G. Ward*. Annapolis, MD: U.S. Naval Institute Press, 1996.

Waters, Tony. *When Killing Is a Crime*. Boulder, CO: Lynne Rienner, 2007.

Weir, Gary E., and Walter J. Boyne. *Rising Tide: The Untold Story of the Russian Submarines That Fought the Cold War*. New York: Basic Books, 2003.

Wheeler, Keith. *War under the Pacific*. Alexandria, VA: Time-Life Books, 1980.

Whitlock, Flint, and Ron Smith. *The Depths of Courage: American Submariners at War with Japan, 1941–1945*. New York: Berkley Caliber, 2007.

Williams, Andrew. *The Battle of the Atlantic*. London: BBC, 2002.

Williamson, Gordon. *Grey Wolf: U-Boat Crewmen of World War II*. Oxford: Osprey, 2001.

Willis, Sam. *Fighting at Sea in the Eighteenth Century: The Art of Sailing Warfare*. Woodbridge, UK: Boydell, 2008.

Willmott, H. P. *The Battle of Leyte Gulf: The Last Fleet Action*. Bloomington: Indiana University Press, 2005.

Wilson, Michael. *A Submariners' War: The Indian Ocean, 1939–45*. Stroud, UK: Tempus, 2000.

Worchester, G. R. C. *The Junks and Sampans of the Yangtze*. Shanghai: Department of the Inspectorate General of Customs, 1947.

Yamashita, Samuel Hideo. *Leaves from an Autumn of Emergencies: Selections from the Wartime Diaries of Ordinary Japanese*. Honolulu: University of Hawaii Press, 2003.

Yomiuri Shimbun. *From Marco Polo Bridge to Pearl Harbor: Who Was Responsible?* Edited by James E. Auer. Tokyo: Yomiuri Shimbun, 2006.
Young, Edward. *One of Our Submarines.* Hertfordshire, UK: Wordsworth Editions, 1997.
——. *Undersea Patrol.* New York: McGraw-Hill, 1952.

Film

Destination Tokyo. Directed by Delmer Daves. Warner Brothers, 1943.

Selected Internet Sources

Combined Fleet. http://www.combinedfleet.com (accessed 12 March 2008).
Legends of the Deep. http://www.warfish.com (accessed 23 March 2007).
Naval Historical Center. http://www.history.navy.mil (accessed 23 March 2007).
On Eternal Patrol. http://www.oneternalpatrol.com (accessed 17 January 2007).
Oz at War. http://www.ozatwar.com (accessed 13 June 2008).
Rutgers Oral History Archives of World War II. http://oralhistory.rutgers .edu/Interviews (accessed 2 September 2005).
The Submarine USS *Wahoo* (SS-238). http://www.mackinnon.org/wahoo -home.html (accessed 17 January 2007).
Uboat.net. http://www.uboat.net (accessed 23 June 2008).
USS *Archerfish.* http://www.ussarcherfish.com/ (accessed 4 July 2007).
USS *Batfish.* http://www.ussbatfish.com (accessed 5 July 2007).
USS *Baya.* http://www.ussbaya.com (accessed 6 July 2007).
USS *Bergall.* http://www.bergall.org/320 (accessed 6 July 2007).
USS *Blenny* (SS-324). http://www.webenet.net/~ftoon/memory/f_memory .html (accessed 4 July 2007).
USS *Bluegill* (SS-242). http://home.flash.net/~stromain/BlueGill/ (accessed 9 July 2007).
USS *Gunnel* (SS-253). http://www.jmlavelle.com/gunnel/ (accessed 7 November 2007).
USS *Icefish.* http://www.ussicefish.com/ (accessed 13 July 2007).
USS *Puffer.* http://www.usspuffer.org/ (accessed 13 July 2007).
USS *Ronquil* (SS-396). http://ussronquil.com/History/history.htm (accessed 17 July 2007).
USS *Seawolf* (SS-197). http://www.csp.navy.mil/ww2boats/seawolf.htm (accessed 12 February 2004).
USS *Segundo.* http://www.segundo398.org/ (accessed 18 July 2007).

USS *Sunfish*. http://www.geocities.com/Heartland/Hills/2364 (accessed 23 July 2007).

USS *Thresher* (SS-200), History. http://www.broseker.net/babroseker/history.htm (accessed 30 July 2007).

WWII USS *Atule* (SS-403). http://www.atule.com (accessed 5 July 2007).

Index

Abdullah, Said, 141
Abe, Katsuo, 21
Adam, Max, 141
Adamant (British depot ship), 92
Admiralty Islands, 58, 153
Aegean Sea, 50
Akagi Maru (Japanese auxiliary cruiser), 37
Albacore (U.S. submarine), 58, 152, 153
Aleutian Islands, 18
Alexandria, Egypt, 90, 92, 93
Allen, Butch, 164
Allen, Thomas F., Jr., 79
Allied Intelligence Bureau, 103
Ambon Island, Indonesia, 103, 140, 141
ammunition, 31, 46, 55, 63–64, 69, 75, 88, 95, 96, 114, 115, 119, 122, 140, 143, 145
   high-capacity, 27–28, 127
   passers, 23, 33
   VT-fused, 86–87
Andaman Islands, 98, 100
Anderson, Cecil H., 103, 104
Anderson, William Robert, 135, 177
Anderson, William St. George, 97–98
Andrews, Charles, 132
Angler (U.S. submarine), 133, 134
antisubmarine warfare, 20, 71, 168
Antung Maru No. 284 (Chinese junk), 106
Antung Maru No. 293 (Chinese junk), 106
Archerfish (U.S. submarine), 36–37, 153

Argonaut (U.S. submarine), 47, 125, 164
Ariisuni, Tatsunoke, 56
Arisan Maru (Japanese transport), 162
Arizona (U.S. battleship), 59
Arnold, H. H., 167
Ascot (British steamer), 54
Ashley, James, 122
Asiatic Fleet, 16, 173
Aspro (U.S. submarine)
Athenia (British liner), 13, 14
atomic bombs, 164, 168
atrocities, 47, 50–51, 53, 55, 57, 59, 97, 147, 167
Austin, Marshall, 104
Australia, 35, 42, 56, 133, 143, 152
   commandos and, 103–4
   submarine attacks off, 20, 39, 97
   submarine bases and, 51, 67, 91, 92–93
   See also specific cities
Awa Maru (Japanese liner), 163
Aylward, Theodore Charles, 174

Babick, John, 110
Baggett, Robert Eugene, 84
Balao (U.S. submarine), 83, 86, 108, 127–28, 138–39, 147, 155, 171
Bali, 126, 170
Balikpapan, Borneo, 68
Barb (U.S. submarine), 72, 78, 87, 104, 118, 120, 127, 133, 149–50, 155, 176–77
Barr, Eric Lloyd, Jr., 103, 173

Barry, Claud Barrington, 89
Bashaw (U.S. submarine), 120, 143
Bataan, Philippines, 167
Batfish (U.S. submarine), 38, 39, 78–79, 107, 120
Baya (U.S. submarine), 121
Beach, Edward, Jr., 22, 149
Bennett, Carter, 87
Bergall (U.S. submarine), 57, 79, 121, 134
Biddle, Francis, 52
Blair Logie (British ship), 13
Blanchard, James W., 58–59, 152, 153, 174
Blenny (U.S. submarine), 59, 110–11, 113–14, 116, 121, 140, 141, 151, 170, 176
Blower (U.S. submarine), 119
Blueback (U.S. submarine), 121
Bluefish (U.S. submarine), 135
Bluegill (U.S. submarine), 22, 103, 104, 119
boarding parties, 8, 99–100, 101–11, 132
Boarfish (U.S. submarine), 110, 114
Bonefish (U.S. submarine), 34, 125, 126
Bonin Islands, 83, 85, 87, 151, 153
Borneo, 65, 74, 83, 93, 103, 120, 138, 140, 144
Bosnia (British freighter), 13
Bougainville, Solomon Islands, 20, 26, 42, 133
Bowfin (U.S. submarine), 23, 67, 68, 69, 87, 124, 150
Boyle, Francis Dennis, 86
Brewer, John, 156
Brisbane, Australia, 42, 43, 47
British Chivalry (British tanker), 54
Broach, John C., 80
Brooks, Dell, 148
Brown, Charles, 163–64
Brown, George, 164
Brown, John, 3, 42
Brown, Robert, 173
Bugara (U.S. submarine), 143–44

Burlingame, Creed, 5, 32, 33
Burke, Julian T., Jr., 125, 154
Burma, 94, 95, 100
Burrfish (U.S. submarine), 84
Bushman, George A., 55
Buyo Maru (Japanese transport), 45–48, 50, 51, 160

Cabrilla (U.S. submarine), 89
Calcattera, Herbert A., 33, 153
California (U.S. battleship), 22, 25
Calvert, James, 22, 115, 155, 159, 175
Camp, Jack, 22
Capitaine (U.S. submarine), 121
Carney, Robert B., 47
Caroline Islands, 78, 119
Cassedy, Hiram, 134
Celebes, Indonesia, 117–18, 142
Centaur (Australian hospital ship), 54
Ceylon, 51, 90, 91, 92, 94
Chapman, Paul, 50
Chappell, Lucius, 66, 174
Charr (U.S. submarine), 86
Chew, Alec, 104
Chinese, 65, 110, 113, 136, 139–41, 142, 143, 145, 151
    Japanese treatment of, 71, 138, 144
    junks and, 81–82, 95–97, 102, 106, 107, 108, 114
Christie, Ralph W., 82, 92, 93, 94, 98, 103
Churchill, Winston, 12, 13
Chuyo (Japanese carrier), 166
Clark, Harold L., 65
Clary, John, 45, 48, 49, 147
Clausen, John, 102
Clausen, Walter B., 44
Clyde (British submarine), 93
Cobia (U.S. submarine), 110, 121
Cod (U.S. submarine), 109–11, 121, 134
code breakers, 7
Cole, Cyrus Churchill, 86
Colombo, Ceylon, 54, 56, 90, 92
Congressional Medal of Honor, 6, 51
Connaway, Fred, 4

Connole, David, 164
convoys, 14, 36, 71, 75, 162
Coucal (U.S. submarine rescue ship),
    115
Coventry, England, 160
Crawford, George C., 29, 30
Crevalle (U.S. submarine), 23, 124
Croaker (U.S. submarine), 33, 145
Cunningham, Andrew, 50
Currie, John, 174
Curtin, John, 54
Cutter, Slade, 26–29, 30, 120, 172, 174,
    175, 177
Cynthia Olson (U.S. merchant ship), 19

Dace (U.S. submarine), 134
Dalupiri, Philippines, 80
Darter (U.S. submarine), 134
Davenport, Roy, 171
Davis, Landon L., Jr., 167, 171
Decker, Clay, 165, 175
Declaration of London (1909), 12
Defrees, Joseph R., Jr., 66–67, 173
DeRose, James, 46
Destination Tokyo (film), 146, 153
Dolphin (U.S. submarine), 42, 174
Dönitz, Karl, 14, 15, 35, 52, 53, 159
Doolittle raid, 16, 37, 138, 146, 160
Dower, John, 167
Drum (U.S. submarine), 6, 28
Dun Sai (Japanese trawler), 75, 150
Dureenbee (Australian trawler), 39, 40
Dutch East Indies, 37, 73
Dwyer, Carl B., 126–27, 170
Dykers, Thomas M., 34

East China Sea, 27, 74, 112, 137, 162,
    163
East Indies, 19, 37, 71, 73
Easton, Ian, 164
Ebisu Maru (Japanese ship), 77
Ebisu Maru No. 5 (Japanese ship), 37
Eck, Heinz Wilhelm, 51–52, 54, 159
Emidio (U.S. tanker), 19
England (U.S. destroyer), 20

English, Robert, 48
Enterprise (U.S. carrier), 17
Erck, Charles Frederick, 75
Extractor (U.S. salvage tug), 162

Fais Island, Caroline Islands, 119
Fellers, Bonner, 159
Felton, Mark, 53
Fife, James, 43, 121
Finback (U.S. submarine), 23, 37, 38,
    65, 74, 75, 78, 86
Fisher, John, 177
Fisher, Richard, 99, 100
Flasher (U.S. submarine), 1, 120, 143
Flounder (U.S. submarine), 104
Fluckey, Eugene, 72, 104, 127, 133, 138,
    149–50, 155, 172, 176
Flying Fish (U.S. submarine), 22, 81,
    84, 115, 124, 125, 136, 148, 153,
    154, 157, 165, 171, 172
Foley, Robert, 133
Forbes, George W., Jr., 135
Formosa, 25, 31, 38, 73, 165, 138
Frazee, Murray, 175
Fremantle, Australia, 34, 51, 54, 67, 89,
    91, 92–93, 98, 102, 103, 113, 126,
    134, 142, 157
Frolich, Wilhelm, 13
Fuga, Philippines, 80
Fukuoda, Japan, 165
Fulp, James Douglas, Jr., 80
Fulton (U.S. submarine tender), 84
Fusa Maru (Japanese patrol craft), 84
Fyfe, John K., 79

Galantin, Ignatius, 1, 31, 37, 38, 51, 66,
    67, 115, 119
Gar (U.S. submarine), 7
Gato (U.S. submarine), 3, 133
Geneva Convention, 11, 146, 153, 165
Germany, 12, 13, 35, 138, 159, 165
Germershausen, William, 84, 102, 123,
    125–26, 176
Gilbert Islands, 118, 133
Glitra (British steamer), 12

Golay, Frank, 107, 164, 165
Gordin, Michael, 160
Grant, Cary, 146
Grayback (U.S. submarine), 86
Grayling (U.S. submarine), 16
Grayling, A. C., 167
Grayson (U.S. destroyer), 84
Greater East Asia Co-prosperity
    Sphere, 136
Greenling (U.S. submarine), 4
Grenadier (U.S. submarine), 4, 21
Grider, George, 1
Grieves, Billy, 21
Griffith, Walter Thomas, 67–68
Griggs, John B., III, 173
Grouper (U.S. submarine), 162
Guadalcanal, Solomon Islands, 18, 26,
    44, 69, 118
Guam, 74, 86, 115, 119, 122, 161
Guardfish (U.S. submarine), 36, 133, 162
Gudgeon (U.S. submarine), 22, 142,
    147, 155
Gulf of Boni, 99
Gulf of Siam, 108, 110, 121, 122, 126,
    135, 143
Gulf of Tonkin, 108, 126, 154
Gunnel (U.S. submarine), 38, 77–78
guns
    Bofors 40 mm, 85
    Browning automatic rifle, 38, 64
    .50-caliber machine guns, 11, 26,
        29, 30, 38, 65, 66, 75, 79, 85, 102,
        120, 177
    five-inch/25-caliber, 7, 8, 85, 86,
        115, 143, 186n30
    four-inch, 29, 37, 45, 46, 49, 58, 65,
        76, 77, 78, 79, 83
    four-inch/50-caliber, 7, 85
    Oerlikon 20 mm, 28, 77, 95
    .30-caliber machine guns, 4, 23, 33,
        38, 58, 76, 79, 80, 177
    three-inch, 3, 4, 7, 11, 29, 30, 32,
        33, 36, 38, 63, 64, 66, 75, 85, 95,
        115, 152
Gurnard (U.S. submarine), 132, 134

Hachian Maru (Japanese transport), 5
Haddo (U.S. submarine), 147
Haddock (U.S. submarine), 87, 88, 171
Hague Convention (1899), 11
Hainan, China, 107, 143
Haines, John Meade, 80
Hake (U.S. submarine), 74, 78, 80, 135
Halibut (U.S. submarine), 34, 38, 75,
    82, 119
Haller, Robert, 47
Halsey, William, Jr., 21, 59
Hamburg, Germany, 170
Hamid, Abdul, 142
Hammerhead (U.S. submarine), 83, 114
Hammond, Douglas Thompson, 89
Harbin, Michael, 32, 37
Hardegen, Reinhard, 131
Harder (U.S. submarine), 57, 103
Harris, Arthur, 160, 169
Hart, Thomas C., 3
Hartenstein, Werner, 15
Hashimoto, Mochitsura, 18
Hattori, Masanori, 56
Hawaii, 19, 20
Hawkbill (U.S. submarine), 81, 83, 104,
    108–9, 115, 120, 121, 126, 135
Hazzard, William, 59, 111, 113–14, 151,
    176
Hitler, Adolf, 52
Hogan, Thomas Wesley, 34, 88
Hokkaido, Japan, 120, 125, 150
Hokoku Maru (Japanese vessel), 140
Hokuyo Maru No. 105 (Japanese ship), 77
Hon Doi Island, 103
Hong Kong, 93, 108, 119, 144
Honolulu, 19, 55
Honshu, Japan, 36, 38, 63, 64, 84, 87,
    116, 125, 127
Hornet (U.S. carrier), 16
Hornfischer, James, 82
Huffman, Leon Joseph, 80
Hydemann, Earl, 176

I-3 (Japanese submarine), 19
I-8 (Japanese submarine), 56

I-12 (Japanese submarine), 20, 55
I-17 (Japanese submarine), 118
I-21 (Japanese submarine), 20, 118
I-24 (Japanese submarine), 17, 20, 118
I-26 (Japanese submarine), 19, 56
I-29 (Japanese submarine), 20
I-32 (Japanese submarine), 20
I-37 (Japanese submarine), 54, 55
I-165 (Japanese submarine), 118
I-175 (Japanese submarine), 39
I-177 (Japanese submarine), 54
Icefish (U.S. submarine), 108, 116,
    144–45
Indian Ocean, 19, 20, 26, 56, 90, 92
Indians, 96, 100, 136, 141, 145
Indochina, 68, 92, 103, 110, 120
Indonesians, 136, 141, 151, 156
Ionides, H. M. C., 94
Iron Chieftain (Australian ship), 57
Itshakawa, S., 152
Ives, Norman S., 29
Iwo Jima, 153

Jack (U.S. submarine), 22, 75, 115, 116,
    150, 155
JANAC (Joint Army-Navy Assessment
    Committee), 2
Jane, Fred T., 175
Japan, 74, 82, 83, 93, 114, 123, 167, 172
    attacks in waters off, 32, 33, 36, 115
    boat builders in, 36
    bombing of, 16, 53, 160–61, 165
    Chinese and, 138
    imports of, 71, 73, 116, 122, 139
    Korea and, 136
    map of, 112
    prisoners and, 146, 150, 152, 158,
        162, 165
    rationing and, 117
    surrender of, 168–69
    war crimes and, 55–56
    war strategy and, 17, 20–21
    See also specific place names
Japan, Sea of, 22, 41, 122, 124, 126,
    148, 176

Japanese
    aircraft, 3, 4, 11, 25, 28, 39, 41, 47,
        91, 98, 133, 148, 149, 156
    Allied attitudes toward, 21, 22, 32,
        164, 175–76
    antisubmarine warfare, 3, 105, 116
    Army, 53, 102, 109, 136, 137, 138
    atrocities, 47, 53–56, 97, 167
    attack on Pearl Harbor, 11, 15, 17, 25
    aviators, 148, 153, 156, 158, 168
    civilians, 117, 161, 167, 168
    convoys, 71, 74, 116, 132
    fishing vessels, 30, 31, 34, 35, 36, 37,
        39, 66, 77, 149
    Guadalcanal and, 44, 69
    hospital ships, 47, 164
    Navy, 18, 37, 70, 78, 82, 137, 150,
        158, 168
    prisoners, 17, 37, 45, 58, 138, 145,
        146–58
    shipbuilding, 71, 75
    shipping, 2, 5, 8, 69, 73, 75, 82, 94,
        96, 109, 116, 122, 124, 160
    submarine service, 17–20, 29,
        42–43, 53, 118, 162
    survivors, 45, 48, 57, 59, 67, 132,
        136, 145, 147, 150, 151
Java, 19, 91
Javanese, 140–41, 142
Java Sea, 5, 36, 59, 79, 93, 104, 113,
    116, 121, 126, 164
Jean Nicolet (U.S. merchant ship), 56
Jemaja Island, Anambas Islands, 120
Jinkins, William Thomas Lloyd, 102–4
John A. Johnson (U.S. merchant ship),
    20, 55
Joint Army-Navy Assessment
    Committee (JANAC), 2
junks, 2, 48, 69, 110
    American attacks on, 106, 107, 108,
        109, 113, 114, 122, 126, 135, 143,
        177, 179
    British attacks on, 95, 96, 97, 99,
        100, 180
    construction of, 95–96, 109

junks (*continued*)
    crews of, 96, 106, 107, 108, 109,
        113–14, 126, 135, 177
    Dutch attacks on, 91, 181
Junyo Maru (Japanese transport), 162

Ka, Mishuitunni, 156
kamikaze attacks, 168
Kannon Maru No. 5 (Japanese vessel), 77
Karafuto, Japan, 125, 127
Karimata Strait, 36
Katoomba (Australian passenger ship),
    20
Kennedy, Marvin G., 42–43
Kershaw, Alex, 175
Kimball, Franklin S., 110, 111
Kimmel, Manning, 173
Kimmel, Thomas, 173
Kinei Maru (Japanese ship), 77
Kinfroe, Sam, 110
King, Ernest, 166
King, Tom, 104
Kinsella, William T., 107, 121, 135,
        139–40, 151, 173
Kiska, Aleutian Islands, 18
Kitazano, H., 58
Klakring, Thomas Burton, 36, 83, 85, 174
Kojima, Masayoshi, 158
Korea, 49, 105, 115, 117, 122, 124, 139,
    171
    Japan and, 136–37
Koreans, 96, 102, 105, 106, 124
    Allied attitudes toward, 136–39
    as prisoners, 137–38, 149
Kouta, Takero, 53
Kraken (U.S. submarine), 121
Kranzbuehler, Otto, 52
Kretschmer, Otto, 131
Kroesen, F. J., 91
Kubota, I., 58
Kudo, Kaneo, 55
Kurile Islands, 76, 118
Kusaka, Lieutenant Commander, 56
Kwantung (British merchant ship), 19
Kyushu, Japan, 30, 78, 120, 139, 158, 165

Laconia (British liner), 15
Laconia Order, 52
Lagarto (U.S. submarine), 87
Lahaina (U.S. liner), 19
Lamprey (U.S. submarine), 110, 121
La Perouse Strait, 41, 122, 125, 126
Lawrence, William, 174
Lemay, Curtis, 161, 166, 169
Lemp, Fritz-Julius, 13
Lewellen, Bafford Edward, 69
Leyte Gulf, 82, 168
Liberty ships, 20, 55, 71
lifeguarding, 83, 128, 133–34, 158
Lipscomb, F. W., 95
Lisbon Maru (Japanese transport), 162
Lizardfish (U.S. submarine), 110, 114,
    126
Lockwood, Charles, 63, 87, 115, 133,
    141, 146–47, 169, 173
    attacks on small craft and, 29, 31, 72
    Awa Maru and, 163
    code breakers and, 70
    deck guns and, 3, 7
    Mush Morton and, 44, 45, 48, 123
    Operation Barney and, 122–24
London Protocol (1936), 12, 14, 53
Loomis, Sam, Jr., 173
Loughlin, Charles, 163, 170
Lowe, Keith, 170
Lundquist (torpedoman), 125
Lusitania (liner), 12, 13
Lüth, Wolfgang, 3
Luzon, Philippines, 75, 82, 89, 116, 150,
    162

MacArthur, Douglas, 44, 82
Macassar, Indonesia, 100
MacMillan, Duncan Calvin, 43
Madura, East Java, 140
Maidstone (British depot ship), 92
Makassar Strait, 93, 95, 134
Makin Island, Gilbert Islands, 118
Malaya, 90, 94–97, 109, 113, 138
Malays, 79, 96, 99, 136, 144, 145, 156
Mallard (U.S. ship), 86

Manchuria, 115, 122, 138
Mansell, Paul, 76
Manunda (Australian hospital ship), 47
Marcey, Lincoln, 84
Marcus Island, 63
Mare Island Navy Yard, California, 6, 7, 22, 25, 27, 32, 44, 85, 146
Mariana Islands, 58, 82, 117, 161
Marines, 69, 83
 prisoners and, 154–58
 submarine landing of, 118–19
 training by, 104, 176, 177
Mars, Alistair, 59, 96, 97, 98–99, 164
Marshall Islands, 25, 69, 134
Matsumura, Kanji, 20
Mauer, Jason, 158
Maxson, Willis E., 133–34
McCain, John S., Jr., 173
McGrath, Thomas Patrick, 25
McGregor, Donald, 27
McKinney, Gene, 133
McKnight, George, 110
Mediterranean Sea, 3, 50, 63, 92, 93
Mendenhall, Corwin, 66, 115, 164
merchant seamen, 131, 166, 167
Mergui Archipelago, 99
Merrill, Wayne R., 39
Midway Island, 51, 64, 83, 104, 118, 152, 153, 155, 158, 177
Miers, Anthony Cecil Capel, 50–51, 57, 63, 84, 89, 93
Mikuma (Japanese cruiser), 152
Mindoro, Philippines, 77
Mitsuma, Seiza, 148, 152, 157
Miyashiyo Maru (Japanese vessel), 66
Mizuho (Japanese seaplane tender), 6
Molucca Sea, 81
Monontaka, Sadao, 56
Montebello (tanker), 19
Montevideo Maru (Japanese transport), 162
Moon, Calvin, 2
Moore, John A., 86
Morton, Dudley Walker, 44, 45–48, 50–51, 57, 122, 123, 146, 160, 176

Nakagawa, Hajime, 54–55, 56–57
Naku Maru (Japanese trawler), 142
Namiki, Takashi, 83
Nanko Maru (Japanese trawler), 39, 149
Nansing Maru No. 16 (Japanese trawler), 142
Narbada (Australian steamer), 19
Narwhal (U.S. submarine), 11
Nauman, Harley Kent, 4
Nautilus (U.S. submarine), 118, 119
Nethercott, Ian, 94
New Britain, New Guinea, 26, 46, 48
Newcastle, Australia, 20, 26, 118
New Ireland, New Guinea, 36
Nimitz, Chester, 11, 15, 52, 132, 166
Nimitz, Chester, Jr., 147, 173
Nitu Maru (Japanese freighter), 48
Noreen Mary (British trawler), 35
North Carolina (U.S. battleship), 18
Norway, 12, 14
Nuremberg war crimes trials, 35, 52–53, 132, 147

O-19 (Dutch submarine), 101, 134
O-21 (Dutch submarine), 101
Oahu, Hawaii, 17
Ofuna, Japan, 165–66
Oi, Atsushi, 71
O'Kane, Richard, 5, 46, 47, 134, 156, 175
Okhotsk, Sea of, 112, 120, 125, 150
Okinawa, Japan, 31, 75, 112, 119, 168
Okuno, Siso, 153
O'Neil, Guy E., 77
Operation Barney, 122–23
Operation Galvanic, 118
Operation Python, 103
Operation Starvation, 117
Orestes (merchant ship), 20
Ota, Eigoro, 58
Otani, Kiyonori, 54
Owens, Clifford J., 103

Paddle (U.S. submarine), 162
Padfield, Peter, 159
Paine, Roger, 173

Paine, Tom, 159
Palau, 57, 59, 83, 149
Pampanito (U.S. submarine), 132, 167, 171
Panay, Philippines, 78, 133
Pangkor, Malaya, 94
Parche (U.S. submarine), 6, 34, 83, 151, 171
Pargo (U.S. submarine), 104
Parks, Lewis, 25, 26, 27, 33, 83, 96, 163, 171
Peabody, Endicott "Chubb," 105
Pearl Harbor, 29, 30, 44, 48, 51, 59, 63, 67, 70, 86, 89, 119, 128, 136, 152, 155, 157, 176
    American reactions to attack on, 11, 15, 21–22, 25, 32, 47, 160
    attack on, 6, 11, 16
    Japanese submarines and, 17–19
Peleus (Greek freighter), 51–52, 159
Penang, Malaya, 54
Pennsylvania (U.S. battleship), 21
Peter Silvester (U.S. merchant ship), 20
Philippines, 16, 74, 77, 80, 81, 82, 91, 93, 113, 116, 133, 134, 141, 167
    See also specific islands
Philippine Sea, battle of the, 58
pickets, 34, 37, 38, 73, 75, 77, 79, 81, 83, 85, 87, 179
Pierce, George E., 125, 164
Pintado (U.S. submarine), 36, 81, 115, 174
Piper (U.S. submarine), 87, 119
Piranha (U.S. submarine), 119
Pleatman, Ralph F., 27, 28
Plunger (U.S. submarine), 25, 134
Pogy (U.S. submarine), 38
Point Blair, Andaman Islands, 100
Pollack (U.S. submarine), 2, 25, 29, 30, 69
Pomelaa, Indonesia, 99
Pomfret (U.S. submarine), 87
Pompano (U.S. submarine), 5, 25, 27, 33, 38, 39, 83, 96, 101, 120, 153, 154, 163, 164
Pompon (U.S. submarine), 159

Port Moresby, New Guinea, 54
Post, William, 142
Potsdam Declaration, 55
Pownall, Charles, 133
Pratas Island, 119
Prien, Gunther, 13
prisoners of war, 15, 46, 132, 146, 161
    Allied, 132, 161, 162, 163, 165–66
    See also Japanese: prisoners
Puffer (U.S. submarine), 7, 81, 107, 119, 126, 127, 142, 164, 170

Queenfish (U.S. submarine), 133, 163, 170

Rabaul, New Guinea, 36, 47
Rainer, Gordon B., 174
Ramage, Lawson P., 6, 21, 34, 73, 83, 123, 151, 175
Rangoon, Burma, 99
Raton (U.S. submarine), 142
Ray (U.S. submarine), 107, 110, 121–22, 135, 139–40, 151
Raymond, Reginald Marbury, 63–64
Razorback (U.S. submarine), 2, 163, 171
Red Cross, 15, 145, 163, 164, 166
Redfin (U.S. submarine), 38–39, 104, 149
Redfish (U.S. submarine), 21
Requin (U.S. submarine), 120
Rice, Robert Henry, 29
Richard Hoovey (U.S. merchant ship), 56
Riley, Tom, 23
RO-31 (Japanese submarine), 18
Rogers, A. P. V., 177
Ronquil (U.S. submarine), 84
Roosevelt, Franklin D., 44
Roscoe, Theodore, 42
Ruiz, C. Kenneth, 2
Russell, Dale, 22, 124, 136, 165, 171, 172
Russia, 41, 125

S-37 (U.S. submarine), 21
Sado (Japanese frigate), 57

Safari (British submarine), 35
Sailfish (U.S. submarine), 166
Saipan, Mariana Islands, 22, 38, 74, 83,
    112, 123, 161, 168
Salmon (U.S. submarine), 4
Samar, Philippines, 89
sampans, 2, 34, 180
    American attacks on, 29–31, 38,
    63–64, 65, 66–67, 74, 75, 76, 78,
    110, 179
    definition of, 65
    pickets and, 37, 38
San Bernadino Strait, Philippines, 89
San Francisco, 27, 51, 55
Sanji, Kitojima, 155
Saratoga (U.S. carrier), 18
Sasebo, Japan, 78
Saufley (U.S. destroyer), 43
S-boats, 7, 93
Scanland, Francis, Jr., 120
Schade, Arnold F., 143, 144
schooners, 2, 50, 63, 65, 67–69, 71, 72,
    95, 99, 100, 114, 143, 180
Schratz, Paul, 31, 63, 64, 158, 173, 175,
    177
Schumer, John, 140
Scorpion (U.S. submarine), 63–65, 173
Scotia (Norwegian tanker), 54
Sculpin (U.S. submarine), 1, 4, 51, 57,
    66, 164, 166, 174
SD radar, 6
Seahorse (U.S. submarine), 27, 28, 59,
    115, 116, 120, 123, 148, 152, 157,
    170, 174
Seal (U.S. submarine), 85
Sealion (U.S. submarine), 6, 132, 133
Sea Owl (U.S. submarine), 87, 119
Searaven (U.S. submarine), 133, 174
sea trucks, 77, 114, 120, 121, 127, 180
Seawolf (U.S. submarine), 6
See, Tom, 110
Segundo (U.S. submarine), 80, 108, 137,
    170–71
Seiler, Quentin, 21
Seko, A., 58

Selby, Frank G., 32
Selene (British submarine), 108
Sencenbaugh, Donald, 142
Sennet (U.S. submarine), 119
Services Reconnaissance Department,
    103
Severn (British submarine), 92
Shadwell, Lancelot, 98
Shakespeare (British submarine), 98
Sharp, Don, 22
Shelby, Edward E., 76
Shibetoro, Kurile Islands, 118, 172
Shigeyoushi, Inoue, 17
Shinyo Maru (Japanese transport), 162
Sieglaff, Barney, 22, 122
Silversides (U.S. submarine), 32, 37
Singapore, 46, 73, 81, 83, 93, 115, 120,
    140
    Japanese and, 37, 97, 109, 138
    shipping to and from, 96, 113, 126,
    132, 144, 163
Singora, Siam, 113
Sirdar (British submarine), 95
SJ radar, 6
Skate (U.S. submarine), 125, 133
Smith, Chester Carl, 110
Smith, John Ronald, 21, 85
Snook (U.S. submarine), 33, 66, 81, 85,
    162
Soewito, Wasio, 141
Solomon Islands, 18, 69
South China Sea, 36, 73, 74, 108, 116,
    119, 120, 126
Southwest Pacific, map of, 26
Soya Strait. *See* La Perouse Strait
Spadefish (U.S. submarine), 7, 8, 23,
    102, 123, 125, 140, 154, 156, 176
Spence, H. W., 105
Spiteful (British submarine), 95
Spot (U.S. submarine), 109
Spruance, Edward, 173
Spruance, Raymond, 87
Stark, Harold, 11, 16
Statesman (British submarine), 95, 96,
    100

Steelhead (U.S. submarine), 83
Sterlet (U.S. submarine), 31, 87
Sterling, Forest, 43, 47, 156
Stoic (British submarine), 95
Storm (British submarine), 93, 95, 99,
    100, 145
Straits of Malacca, 90, 92, 94–95, 96,
    100, 119, 143
Strow, Albert, 147, 155
Sturdy (British submarine), 95, 97, 98
Sturgeon (U.S. submarine), 162
submarines
    American, 2, 3, 5–6, 18, 19, 57, 83,
        101, 103, 104, 119, 121, 134, 162,
        167
    attack statistics of, 3, 18, 30, 65, 73,
        74, 82, 91, 114–15, 162, 179–81
    British, 35, 77, 89, 90, 92–96, 100,
        119, 145, 156, 180–81
    commanders of, 3, 5, 19, 54, 70, 89,
        97, 131, 169, 173, 177
    Dutch, 90–92, 115, 181
    I-class, 17, 20, 162
    Japanese, 17–20, 53, 118
    losses of, 82, 91
    numbers of, 83, 115
    tactics of, 3, 5–6, 52, 84, 101, 115,
        121
    See also S-boats; U-boats
Subic Bay, Philippines, 93, 108, 114,
    115, 145
Sugamo prison, 57
Sulu Archipelago, 81
Sumatra, 90, 95, 138
Summers, Paul Edward, 132
Sunfish (U.S. submarine), 76–77, 81–82,
    151
Surabaya, Java, 7, 90, 91, 142
Surf (British submarine), 92, 94
Sutlej (British ship), 54
Suzuya Maru (Japanese ship), 36
Sydney, Australia, 20, 26, 35, 40, 54, 118

Tactician (British submarine), 92
Taiei Maru (Japanese steamer), 57–59,
    153

Taiho (Japanese carrier), 58–59
Taikai Maru (Japanese vessel), 84
Tairai Maru (Japanese freighter), 156
Takao, Formosa, 83, 165
Tally Ho (British submarine), 92
Tambelan Island, 120
Tambor (U.S. submarine), 7, 84, 88,
    101–2, 151–52, 154–55, 157
Tamura, Yakichi, 58
Tang (U.S. submarine), 5, 22, 119, 134,
    156, 165–66, 175
tankers, 5, 19, 71, 73
Tantalus (British submarine), 156
Tantivy (British submarine), 95, 96
Taurus (British submarine), 92, 100
Tautog (U.S. submarine), 11, 22, 122,
    141
Telaga Islands, 38, 149
Templar (British submarine), 92
Tench (U.S. submarine), 122
Tenshin Maru (Japanese ship), 154
Tenshin Maru No. 3 (Chinese junk), 102
Thomas, Willis Manning, 33
Thompson, William, 68
Threadfin (U.S. submarine), 157
Thresher (U.S. submarine), 5, 21, 31,
    37, 43
Thule (British submarine), 59, 96, 97,
    98–99, 143
Tigrone (U.S. submarine), 134
Till, Geoffrey, 2
Time magazine, 44, 47, 136
Tinian, Mariana Islands, 117, 161
Tinosa (U.S. submarine), 31
Tirante (U.S. submarine), 105–6, 137,
    149
Tjisalak (Dutch steamer), 56
Toi Misaki, Japan, 30
Tojo, Hideki, 155
Tokyo, 18, 63, 112
    bombing of, 37, 87, 146, 160, 161,
        166, 168
Tolle, William, 110
Tongariro (merchant ship), 20
Tonkin Gulf, 108, 126, 154
Toon, Frank, 113

Torbay (British submarine), 50, 63, 89
torpedoes, 3, 22, 25, 35, 49, 58, 84, 95,
    98, 100, 114, 115, 122, 127, 132,
    161–64
  Cutie, 87
  electric, 70–71
  faults of, 4–5, 139
  Japanese, 19, 20
  magnetic exploders and, 17, 44, 70
  Mark XIV, 17
  numbers of fired, 2, 74
Tradewind (British submarine), 162
Transbalt (Russian freighter), 125
trawlers, 2, 25, 27, 29, 30–31, 33,
    34–35, 37, 39, 74, 89, 138, 139,
    180–81
Treader (U.S. submarine), 177
Treaty of London (1930), 12
Trengganu, Malaya, 113, 141
Trepang (U.S. submarine), 87
Trespasser (British submarine), 92
Trident (British submarine), 92
Triebel, Charles O., 33, 66
Trigger (U.S. submarine), 22, 163, 164
Trimmer, Bill, 21
Trincomalee, Ceylon, 92, 98, 100
Trout (U.S. submarine), 152
Truant (British submarine), 90, 92
Truculent (British submarine), 95
Truk, Caroline Islands, 53, 166
Truro (British steamer), 13
Trusty (British submarine), 90, 92
Trutta (U.S. submarine), 135
Tsushima Strait, 122, 123
Tulagi, Solomon Islands, 133
Tunny (U.S. submarine), 115–16, 125,
    148–49, 164
Tyree, Alexander K., 123, 124

U-17 (German submarine), 12
U-30 (German submarine), 13
U-36 (German submarine), 13
U-47 (German submarine), 13
U-99 (German submarine), 131
U-156 (German submarine), 15
U-181 (German submarine), 3, 16

U-247 (German submarine), 35
U-506 (German submarine), 15
U-507 (German submarine), 15
U-551 (German submarine), 35
U-852 (German submarine), 51, 52
U-boats, 3, 6, 14–15, 21, 29, 34, 35,
    51–52
Ulithi, Caroline Islands, 26, 87, 119
Underwood, Gordon, 123
U.S. Naval Academy, 27, 41, 42, 63, 80,
    113, 173
U.S. Navy, 16, 28, 41, 77, 96
  Bureau of Ordnance, 7, 77
  Bureau of Personnel, 81, 150
Utah (U.S. battleship), 32

Veder, David, 48
Velle, Rudolph William, 77, 78
Victoria Cross, 51, 89
Visenda (British trawler), 35
Voge, Richard, 6, 70, 87, 116
Vozniak, Carl, 23

Waddy, Rowan, 104
Wahoo (U.S. submarine), 41–49, 122,
    123, 146, 147, 156, 175
Wake Island, 102, 133
war crimes, 52, 56, 59, 132, 167
Ward, Norvell G., 36, 116, 133
Warder, Frederick, 6
Washington Naval Conference (1922),
    12, 35
Wasp (U.S. carrier), 18
Weneker, Paul H., 168
Westbrook, Edwin M., 110
Wilkins, Charles, 148
Withers, Thomas, Jr., 5, 30
Wolfe (British depot ship), 92
World War I, 3, 6, 12, 13, 17, 29, 34,
    101, 166, 173
World War II, 2, 3, 13, 67, 76, 167, 168
  civilians and, 8, 58, 59, 117, 133,
    159, 160, 164, 165, 166–68, 177
Worthington, Robert Kemble, 139
Wright, William Harry, 36
Wylie, William, 63–64

Yaku Shima, 112, 120
Yamagumo (Japanese destroyer), 4, 166
Yamamoto, Isoruku, 18
Yangtze River, 81, 96
Yap, Caroline Islands, 57, 59
Yellow Sea, 36, 48, 81, 112, 121, 137, 139, 140, 154, 177

Young, Edward, 93, 95, 97, 99, 145
Young, William, 46

Zamboanga, 26, 141
Zwaardvisch (Dutch submarine), 91